WHERE WE WERE

Roy V. Marshan

Illustrations by Max Wilson & Sascha Duncan

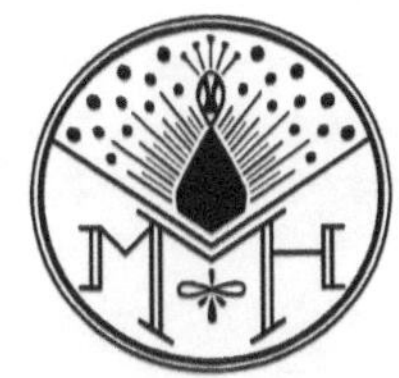

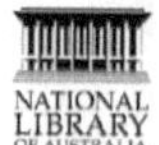

A catalogue record for this
work is available from the
National Library of Australia

National Library of Australia Catalogue-in-Publication data:

Where We Were/Roy V. Marshan

ISBN:
978-0-6450371-6-6
(Paperback)

For Marco, who loves exploring.
And his brother Polo, who tends to hide.

CONTENTS

INTRODUCTION

I'm aware that no one ever reads book introductions, so I'm just going to take the opportunity to say what I like. That being said, if you are reading this then thanks, you're one in a million.

I'm sure you're aware that existence is a sprawling, incomplete mess containing everything from high school graduations to nuclear war. There's clearly no order or reason and the history we're taught is often cheap plaster covering obscure rubble.

So how can authors write stories that make any sense? Tell tales that provide genuine meaning to the meaningless? How can the single sentence, "I care about you, I see you," make the strongest depression evaporate into warm fuzziness? To be honest, I have no clue.

Words make no sense. They are our species' finest, often least used tool that can achieve nearly anything imaginable. Language can create skyscrapers or crumble nations, can command or retreat. Can lie or speak the truth. This all comes at a cost of course, but being the disguised superpower that it is, words deserve more credit, more fear, and better responsibility.

I'm not here to preach anything or impose some sort of ideology. Whatever I write, now and forever, it will always be the dull ramblings of a tired boy who thinks he can conjure the answer to your questions. If there were an endless line of string that trailed through some dark forest, I'd be the first idiot traveller to grab it and follow, wholeheartedly believing that it'd lead me beyond the blurred cityscapes, into someplace where I could focus my eyes on all of it at once and know exactly where I was. In reality, following the string will just make you more lost.

That's what these stories are, a rope leading deeper into the rabbit hole, searching for an answer that will never come.

That's not to discredit the short stories, poems and hybrid monstrosities that feature in this collection. I am actually quite proud of them, which might be an egotistical thing to say but it's an honest statement. A healthy amount of research went into each one, alongside a few personal experiences – I think it's impossible to write something that isn't in some way imprinted with your DNA. Now, whether you like this book or not is hard to say, since I have no idea who you are and what piques your interest. Or do I? Nonetheless I do hope you give it a decent shot.

I suppose I should very quickly inform you of what the following pages will contain. There's a blend of genres and forms that all serve to explore the existential queries we all find ourselves pondering when we can't sleep.

I was inspired a lot by myths, folktales and other ancient writings. Part of the fun is taking what came before and warping it, uncovering the similarities and repeats that occur in our past. The issues that remain prevalent and the heroes who have kept fighting for the same things since the dawn of civilization.

A bit of late-night googling went into certain spacefaring

concepts and the characters are historical (to a somewhat accurate degree), fictional and a few are friends. There's science fiction, absurd satire, fantasy or drama. If you don't like one of them, skip it and read the next one. No hard feelings.

So sit back and relax. Whether you're on a beach, in the tub, or readying yourself for a good night's sleep, let me take you on a journey through medieval Scandinavia, feudal Japan, horror-filled corporate offices and even outer space. Don't be frightened, none of it is real and neither are you.

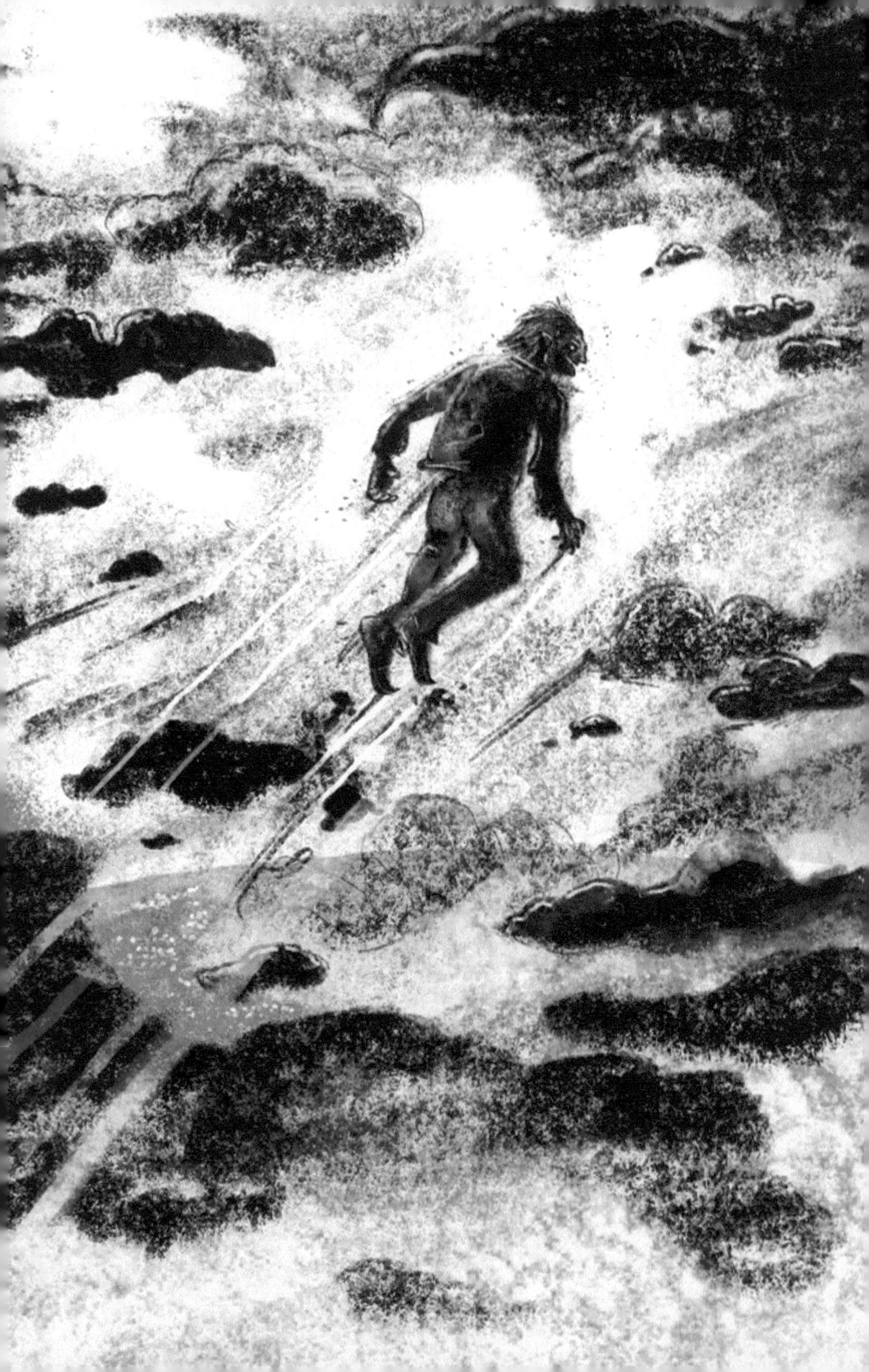

A KNIGHT & HER ELF

I. Valkyries In Midgard

This is a tragic fable of an adventurous girl, an immortal elf and the divine destruction brought down upon them both. It began, as many stories do, with a creature of great beauty, struggling against a world of monsters. The creature, in this instance, was a white-throated dipper from the South that flew across the barren landscape of Iceland. Its young wings fluttered in the harsh winter winds as the creamy sky slipped into a darker purple.

The small bird paid no attention to the castle nestled sturdily within the snowy mountains. A fortress of stone with square windows emitting orange candlelight. Men in fur coats patrolled the walls with their disgruntled frowns, cracked lips and frosty beards.

The dipper continued onward, the castle fading into a silhouette of battlements and towers. It forgot all about the fortress's secrets and instead focused on the never-ending wasteland of ice. It would die sometime during the winter. Frostbite eating through its feathers and skin, leaving only a hollow shell. But that is a story for another time, another life.

We come now to a girl. She was, many moons ago, sitting within her castle walls with a book in her lap, oblivious to the plight of the dipper. The book was called *Herr Ivan Lejon-Riddaren*, and she was enjoying it immensely. A strand of her blonde hair tickled the yellowing pages, and she tucked it behind one ear. In her pocket, as always, was a small carving of a great bear, its wooden fur smooth and polished.

She was seated in her bedroom. It had pale grey walls and a four-poster bed decorated with the finest silk sheets. There was a desk in the corner gathering dust and many books piled like lopsided towers.

For you see, this girl was princess of the castle in the mountains. She had known winter her whole life and her pale beauty could not hide the loneliness of such a place. Boovildr was her name, Vil the Storyteller to those who would come to know her. This was her tale. Why? Because it deserved to be.

Vil's peace and quiet was interrupted by the scrape of the iron doors in the main hall. She could hear the clatter of metal armour as heavy footsteps clanked through the labyrinth of hallways outside her bedroom. Someone was entering the great keep, and the king's guard was rushing to defend their royal highnesses.

Vil stacked her book atop one of the many towers. She kept the door slightly ajar as she left her room and began navigating the stretching corridors that always seemed to have a slight downward slope, no matter which way you walked. She passed flaming torches hooked to wax-stained walls. She ignored portraits of her grandfather during his reign, chest jutting and a ferocious beard peppered with termite-bitten holes. Eventually, she reached the mead hall.

The slanted, triangular roof always appeared ready to cave in.

The long dining table could seat a nation. And the bearskin tapestries hanging from the wall were scorched with depictions of great battles and plunders.

It was here, in this great hall of kings, that three young women arrived, setting off the events of our tragic tale. Their names were Meyjar, Drósir and Alvitr. At the twilight of dusk, they stumbled through the giant oak doors, while the slate sky behind them whistled to the tune of a coming blizzard. The sisters were shivering, skin slathered in mud and grime as though they'd swam through the bog water of the uncharted marshlands to the West.

Vil reached into the dark crevice of her pocket and ran a finger over the smooth wood of the tiny bear. Her heart skipped a beat as she ogled the beautiful women that stood before her. Who could these strangers be? Where had they come from? What danger lurked in their past? Her stomach surged with the possibilities. It had been so long since Vil had seen someone interesting. Someone who was not her family or her guard or a character in her books. This, Vil assumed, was the most exciting thing to have happened to anyone in the history of time.

Meyjar, the oldest, set her eyes on Vil. "We seek shelter from the coming storm. What say you?"

Before Vil could reply, King Nidurd stormed into the hall. His appearance was somewhat shabby for royalty, with worn-out leather boots and a matted fur coat hung over his broad shoulders. The skin of his bare chest was concealed beneath curly hair and his belly sagged from one too many cups of "victory" wine, as he liked to call it.

"What be the meaning of these vámrs that float in here like the filth of the ocean's leavings?" King Nidurd had two items upon his attire that marked him as a wealthy ruler: a gold ring, and a sword with Jormungandr, The World Serpent, upon its hilt.

The sisters dropped to their knees and bowed their heads.

"Your grace," the oldest spoke. "I am Meyjar, though you may call me Mey. We have had a long journey, one filled with unpleasantries. We simply request a man of your honour to show kindness to three women with nowhere left to hide."

Nidurd considered their request. He tugged at the end of his greying beard and closed his wrinkled eyes, as though entering a deep, meditative sleep. Were it not for a white-knuckled grip on the hilt of his sword, you could mistake him for a feeble old ruler with no spine left beneath his weary flabbiness.

"Very well," he finally muttered. "I will ask the maids to clean and dress you. I do hope you bring no enemies to my doorstep. It has been many a night since I last drew blood. Yet it is a risk I shall take, for it is by my word that no harm shall befall you while you rest here ... unless you fall ill, in which case the gods are undoubtedly cruel."

The sisters rose to their feet. There was a severity to their pointed posture and high-held chins, as though they felt they could slice through the king and all his guards without breaking a sweat.

"Such a good, strong man you are, my King," Mey said, yet there was a playful mockery in her tone that Nidurd remained oblivious toward. She flicked her vision toward Vil and winked at the young girl, who stifled a giggle. "However, if it pleases my lord, we wish to bathe in the spring water outside your home. It is a tradition to wash alone."

After Nidurd nodded in approval, the three sisters proceeded to glide down the halls. Their feet seemed to skim the floor without touching.

Nidurd turned to Vil and motioned for the princess to follow him. "Come, little librarian. Return to your chambers so that the servants can prepare our feast."

Vil nodded and hurried her way back to her chambers, closing the door behind her with a gentle clink. The books appeared to be nothing more than words upon paper after the arrival of the mysterious visitors. She quickly changed into more formal attire while staring at the shameful mess of her bedroom. How would the three sisters react if they were to see the way Vil treated her lavish possessions? Vil found herself turning red.

Laughter came from her window. Vil went over to investigate the sound. The pane was glassy and thick, making the cliffs outside a darker blue than they truly were.

Out in the cold, the three sisters were bathing in the hot spring beneath the mountainside. The water bubbled and foamed as they soaked their long, luxurious hair. Steam billowed into the air with a frightening ferocity, making the snow atop the mountain become a veil of tears.

Vil admired Mey and her sisters. Their muscular bodies were not bulky, but rather, were toned from years of obvious fighting. And there were deep scars traced across their backs, like risen dragon scales. The sisters washed each other vigorously. Efficiently. Scratching the filth from their skin with such force Vil was surprised they were not bleeding. They seemed not to feel the scalding heat.

Mey's eyes connected with Vil's for a moment, from all the way across the castle grounds. Hurriedly, Vil looked away, flustered.

"I must go to dinner," she said to herself.

Vil returned to the mead hall and seated herself at the elongated table. A pig had been fried and placed upon a platter at the centre, and five plates were placed in front of five chairs with vegetables stacked atop. Her father, Nidurd, was already at the table. His eyelids dipped lower, his chin inching toward his chest as he waited patiently for the others to arrive.

Erling and Kadir, sons of King Nidurd and brothers of Boovildr, arrived next. Their golden hair was plaited and swung heavily at their backs. Neither were particularly strong, with their thick woollen clothing hiding a slender frame and their sharp cheekbones accentuating the smugness of their gait.

The boys were followed swiftly by their mother, Greta. A noblewoman whose presence always gave off an air of power. She was a far more important figure in this tale than her sons and husband, for it was Greta that ruled these lands with calming confidence. Her robes flowed over her body like frothy waves crashing against a stony shore; deep blue creasing and shimmering as she marched her way to her seat.

This family looked rather peculiar sitting at such a long table with so few people. They only filled the very end, so there was only one candle needed to light their space, letting a shadow fall across the rest of the table. Any number of creatures may have lurked in the deep darkness surrounding them. Waiting for their moment to strike.

"I presume you met our guests, Lady Greta?" King Nidurd asked.

"It is so," Vil's mother replied.

"Your thoughts?"

"It seems these sisters were bathing alone and naked in Wolf Lake when the three elven brothers of Wolfdale found them. Those wretched monsters stole the girls, taking them to their homestead to be wed and enslaved. The eldest, Volund, named them the Swan Sisters, for their clothes were made of the finest white silk he had ever laid eyes upon. Yet the brothers do not know the truth, that these fine women are Valkyries of Asgard! They massacred the guards of Wolfdale and fled into the night. They did not kill the brothers for it is a bad omen to kill an elf."

"So Wolfdale is defenceless, save for the elven brothers?"

"Yes, but you must not be hasty. Elves are as tricky as gods. They have been spoiled with riches, with eternal life. Being blessed with a higher status can make depravity seem amusing. We are the jester's pit beneath their palace; the lowly mortals who they can ridicule, mistreat, even torture without godly consequence. Trust me, my King, we would do well to be wary."

"Nonetheless, I will send my strongest to ride to Wolfdale and bring back news. For too long Wolfdale has soiled our lands with its unholy disregard for morality. Whether they be immortal or powerful, justice must be swift. My 'lowly' kingdom, as you seem to think of it, must be protected."

"I will go, Father!" proclaimed Kadir, jutting his chest out and shoving his jaw forward, a vain attempt to appear tough.

"As shall I," chimed Erling. "If it pleases you, I shall challenge Volund in combat!"

"You are a fool, boy. An elf is too great an opponent for any one man. Neither of you will go, your place is here." King Nidurd shoved a chunk of pork down his throat, while juice trickled through his beard.

Vil, who was slightly less obsessed with pursuing the violent glory her brothers clearly fetishised, was absently chewing on an undercooked carrot. For you see, Vil was bored with life in the castle. Sure, she could escape into books that were set in faraway realms in faraway times, but it was not enough. Vil dreamed of a real adventure. A story where the words belonged to her, not to some faceless author with mystifying beliefs.

"How did you know they were Valkyries, Mother?" Vil asked after some time had passed.

"The maids told me."

"I didn't know Valkyries were real!" Vil tried to contain her enthusiasm, for a lady was not to be outspoken during dinner time. Feasts, or meals of any kind, were the time for men to speak. To Vil, it seemed that all time was the time for men to speak.

"Oh yes," said Nidurd.

And that was the end of their conversation. It was one of the longer and more interesting discussions that Vil and her family had ever engaged in. Then the men began talking about killing a boar and Vil went back to daydreaming of a future that could never be hers.

Dinner continued in silence before each member gradually departed from the table. King Nidurd was the first, lumbering to his feet and bringing a chunk of pig meat with him to bed. The two brothers followed immediately after, matching their father's stride. Finally, it was Vil and Greta left at the table. The space between them seemed cavernous.

"Come," Greta told her daughter. "Let us retire to the drawing room."

The moon had settled fitfully in the night sky, and the winter winds were whispering like the breath of a ghost. Vil and her mother entered the drawing room, a well-furnished space with cushioned chairs and a fireplace. Vil stacked a few logs and lit a match. Before long they were sitting by the warm hearth with mugs of mead in their frozen fingers.

Vil rested her head against her mother's shoulder as a good daughter does. There was an observable sense of love between the two, but it was not familial. Rather, dutiful. Greta, and most of

Vil's family, were cold people who were obliged to show compassion to their kin. Yet Vil enjoyed this time with her mother, the closeness between them as they sat alone and tired in the cramped drawing room. Between them, they both had nothing. Greta ruled a kingdom that knew only her husband's name and Vil had a gifted mind but no friends to share it with.

"Tell me a story, Mother," Vil said, staring into the flames, for a tale of fantasy and wonder could steal her away, for a moment, from the dreary emptiness of her homestead.

"Alright, Darling," Greta began. "Why don't I tell you the story of the greedy Fafnir and the hero who killed him."

Vil nodded.

Greta continued, "Once, long ago, there was a dwarf named Fafnir. He had many brothers, but Fafnir was the strongest among them and would protect their father's wealth from evil monsters. On a rainy afternoon, one of Fafnir's brothers went for a walk. Now, this brother had the unfortunate appearance of an otter, and when he came across Loki and Odin, Loki decided to mutilate and kill the poor boy.

"The gods went to visit the home of Fafnir's father, Hreidmar, to show off the skinned otter. Of course, Hreidmar was not pleased and took the gods hostage. He let Loki leave to collect them a ransom of gold and bury the brother, but Loki, mischievous as he was, decided to fill the body of the otter brother with cursed treasure that would cause great suffering to whoever owned it. He then gave that gold to Hreidmar.

"This is where things take a grim turn. Fafnir killed his father and took the gold for himself. He was greedy, yes, but also angry that his ageing father would not hand over control of the kingdom. So, he slit the old man's throat while he slept!"

"No!" Vil exclaimed.

"Oh, yes. Loki and the freed Odin watched all of this from a hilltop far away. They shared this part of the story with whoever they saw, to warn them against trusting a dwarf."

"That's awful," Vil cried out. "What became of Fafnir the Fiend?"

"Ah, well you see, the guards of the keep chased Fafnir out into the forest, but by nightfall, he had shed all his skin and begun to grow bright red scales. His jaw became unhinged, and his teeth stretched painfully long. He became a poison-breathing dragon, guarding his treasure with evil eyes."

"A monster!"

"Indeed. Some time passed and Fafnir had burned and ravaged the lands. A coat of ash lay across the kingdom and for every walking man, there was a corpse to stumble over. Eventually, Fafnir's brother, Regin, declared that he, as the new ruler of the kingdom, would slay the dragon. But being the coward that he was, Regin commanded his adopted son Sigurd to do the deed.

"Sigurd the Adopted devised a plan. He figured out the path Fafnir took to go to his watering hole and dug a pit there. He then climbed into the pit and covered the opening with leaves. Then, miraculously, Odin appeared with a bushy grey beard and said, 'You better dig a trench instead or you'll drown in the dragon's blood.'"

Vil giggled at this, "I suppose that is helpful of Odin but I can't help laughing at his silly beard."

"You mustn't say that aloud again!" Greta scolded her daughter. "Else you'll be smited! Rah!" She went in and tickled her daughter's belly. Vil squealed with delight.

"Stop it, Mother!" She laughed. "Please, continue the story."

Greta stopped and leant back, trying to hide the small smile that had escaped her lips. "So," she continued, "Sigurd dug the pit into a longer trench and waited patiently. When Fafnir came and stood over the top, Sigurd plunged his sword, Gram, into the underside of the beast's belly. It was a fatal wound, and Sigurd was bathed in the warm blood, which made his skin glow gold.

"Fafnir collapsed in the dirt. His body was limp, but his mouth could still move. He flicked a glazed pupil over to Sigurd and asked for the boy's name. Sigurd did not tell him, but the dragon saw into his soul. 'My brother sent you. Did he not?' The beast asked.

"When Sigurd told him that it was indeed Fafnir's brother, Regin, who had given the task, the fiend smiled with yellow fangs and spoke its final words, 'Kill him. His heart is tar, like mine.'

"Sigurd took the gold that Fafnir had been hoarding and returned to Regin's castle. At the feast that evening, Regin tried to have Sigurd executed so that he could take all the mighty glory for the slaying of Fafnir. Sigurd, who had been warned not to trust him, cut out Regin's heart. He ate that very heart in front of the other lords, feasting on it with relish.

"The lords could do nothing but watch, then clap half-heartedly, for their new mad ruler had slain their other tormentors. And that is the end of our tale, a greedy monster replaced with a mortal madman. How cruel the world truly is."

Greta finished her story and rested back in her chair, the cushions seeming to swallow her whole. She gripped the armrests and closed her eyes, suddenly very old, like an ancient relic fighting to stay awake.

Vil, who was mesmerised by the poorly retold folktale, sat wide-eyed on the bearskin rug. The fire crackled next to her like ferocious music.

"Mother?" Vil asked to no response. Once she realised Greta

had fallen asleep, she curled up next to the woman and whispered, "That was a lovely story." She began to close her eyes as well.

At some point during the tale, Mey had entered the drawing room. She was leaning against the wall, next to the door.

What was she doing? Why was she not with her sisters? These are questions I am afraid I cannot answer, for the reasoning and choices of these creatures are as much a mystery to me now as they were to Vil then.

"It has been a long time since I heard the name Fafnir," Mey said after a while had passed. "May I sit?"

Vil nodded and climbed down onto the rug. She patted the floor, ushering Mey to sit down. Greta had now well and truly fallen asleep, for she was snoring.

"So, what is it like to be a Valkyrie?" Vil asked once Mey had taken a cross-legged seat next to her.

"I am no longer a Valkyrie," Mey replied.

"What do you mean?"

"When Odin fell to Fenrir the Wolf during Ragnarok, my sisters and I found ourselves here. We are mortals on Midgard stranded in a time that has already passed."

"You don't like this place?"

Mey shook her head, "Volund and his cruel brothers have made me rethink my purpose, all of this fighting for men to be nothing but animals. That elf tried to woo me by saying he'd craft silver rings for my fingers. Then he'd make me do things that would make Odin's blood boil and when I refused, he'd slice my back with a magical sword called Tyrfing. But worse still was his smile." She shivered. "Sickening."

"How did you escape?"

"He would lock me in my chambers all day, alone. Only coming at night when he'd have some use for me. On one of the days, I managed to climb to my sister's balcony. We killed our way to freedom."

Vil didn't know how to react. All the stories she'd been told were far happier than this, always with a cascade of hope at the end. Was life really this cruel and unforgiving?

"That's awful," was all she could manage. Then a deep silence befell them both.

"Perhaps you should get some rest," Mey commanded.

"Yes. I think you're right."

Vil left Mey sitting there, she looked back once before leaving the drawing room and saw the Valkyrie staring absently into space, her eyes were a shimmering purple.

The princess reached her room and glanced outside at the hot springs where the Valkyries had bathed. She recalled a time when she was still learning to walk, her mother had taken her down there. Greta's hand had been a giant ladle that the little Vil had to reach high above her head to hold onto. They'd reached the boiling waters and Vil had foolishly dipped her big toe in, scalding it. Her mother had laughed but took Vil back to the castle and spent the evening applying herbal remedies. Her mother was a kind woman.

Vil went to bed and dreamt of warriors and gods, but also a monster in a cellar, its long fingers left damp marks on the concrete floor. When it moved, its sickly skin squelched with wetness.

When morning came, there was a knock at the door. Tired and irritable, and still reeling from the nightmare, Vil threw it open. Mey was standing there, the morning light bouncing off her skin.

"Would you like to learn how to fight?" She had her head bowed but her eyes were raised upward at Vil, giving her the complexion of a woodland creature.

"Yes." Vil had not hesitated, though her fist fiercely clutched the wooden bear in her pocket, to stop herself from shaking with fear and excitement.

Together, Mey and Vil headed down to the spring water outside the castle keep. The snow was thick there, making it hard to walk, but Vil struggled forward. The other two sisters were already practising, exchanging strikes and counters with a rigidness that suggested they were following a set of instructions rather than acting naturally.

"Sword fighting is a duty, not a passion," Mey explained, drawing her own sword as she spoke. "Here," she barked and tossed the blade over to Vil as though it were a broomstick, not a deadly weapon. Mey then drew a slightly shorter blade from a sheath at her back.

"What do I do?" Vil asked. "I don't know how to fight."

"No one does," Mey quipped with a grin. "The trick is to pretend, and to pretend with a confidence that strikes fear in your opponent's heart." With that, she sunk into a warrior's pose. Her stance widened as she began circling Vil.

"I can do this," Vil whispered to herself. She thought back on all that she had read in books, but suddenly the words that always floated in her thoughts like incessant flies were not coming to her, only instinct remained. She gripped her sword with both hands and prepared to fight. She had to admit to herself, this was all strangely thrilling. Even if she died, at least it would be in a duel against a Valkyrie.

Mey attacked first, raising her sword high and then swinging it heavily downward. Vil sidestepped out of the way and launched a counter, thrusting the blade toward Mey's stomach, just like in the story of Sigurd against Fafnir.

Mey saw this coming and deflected, but smiled nonetheless. "Impressive," she remarked, slyly. Vil giggled and felt her face grow hot, but continued to press with attacks. One foot forward, then the other back. Their steel touched with flashes of sparks. The distance between them closed.

Vil twirled and then dropped low, slicing her weapon across the air. Mey somersaulted over the blade and landed in a puff of snow, still in her battle stance. Then she dashed inward and grabbed Vil by the shoulders. Mey rolled and brought Vil with her. There was a sharp intake of breath, but Vil could not tell who was winded. Then, suddenly, Mey was atop with a dagger pressed to Vil's throat. Their heavy breathing mixed together, sharing the frosty air.

"I must say, you act as though you've done this before," Mey said, proudly. "You've never fought? Never duelled?"

Vil shook her head. They both got to their feet.

"We'll make a Valkyrie of you yet," Mey chuffed.

At this moment, the scout that Nidurd had sent to investigate Wolfdale returned from his journey. He was atop a chestnut stead and dressed in a black cloak, he galloped smoothly into the castle walls.

Intrigued by the mysterious figure, Vil and Mey approached the castle gates. Nidurd and Greta had come out to speak with the tall man, they were conversing rather quietly but Vil could still hear fragments of their discussion:

"He is crafting a silver ring for the girl, Mey. Waiting for her return," the scout said.

"And his brothers?" Nidurd asked.

"They have left to seek out their wives, in the wrong direction from the looks of things. The castle of Wolfdale stands empty of elves, save for the handsome Prince Volund."

Mey interjected on the conversation, "I will go," she barked. "Give me weapons and a horse, I will slaughter his men and bring Volund back to you in chains. My sisters, I have no doubt, will accompany me to slay my husband. We will help you take Wolfdale and defend it from the return of Volund's brothers."

"I cannot ask you to do this," Nidurd said.

"But perhaps you should," said Greta. She was not commanding her husband, but there was a sense of authority in her voice that Nidurd was wise to back down from. He stroked his chin and eyed his wife, his crown sinking further down his creased forehead.

"Very well," he said. "I will accompany you with my finest soldiers. We will siege the castle and take back the lands that are rightfully ours. The elves can return to Alfheim. And these Midgardian lands will be free of their decrepit ways."

There was an air of agreement. Everyone was happy with this decision. Everyone that is, except for Vil, for she did not want to miss the excitement of a journey with her new friend Mey and a battle for the kingdom.

"May I come, Father," she worked up the nerve to ask.

His response was a roaring laugh. That was her answer. A resounding, laughable rejection. Vil, infuriated, began marching back toward the snow with the intention of picking up Mey's blade and hacking a tree into tiny wooden fragments. Before she could do this though, a hand grabbed her shoulder. She looked back to see Mey smirking down at her, eyebrows slightly raised.

"What do you want? I'm no good for anything," Vil moaned, depressed.

"That's no way for a Valkyrie to speak."

"I'm not a Valkyrie, you heard Father."

"Fathers are often wrong. Do you think you should come with

me? Is that truly what you believe?"

Vil looked up at Mey, then over at the horizon. The snowy hills rolled into unknown lands. A crackle of lightning split the heavens as garwolves and wyrms guarded the valley of Wolfdale. She imagined the trials she could overcome, the myths and legends she had dreamt of making real. Could she defeat a troll in a game of riddles? Or turn a giant serpent into a statue?

"I do," she finally responded. "I want to come with you."

"Very well," Mey whispered. "You can sneak there beneath my cloak." She winked, and heat fluttered in the air. Vil could not wait for what was coming.

The princess looked down at her feet, she was standing in a shallow puddle. Vil had not even realised until now that her shoes were soaked through, she'd been so distracted by all the exciting news. She imagined, for a moment, that there was a world beneath this puddle, a great cave filled with tiny stars and glowing crystals. Perhaps Odin was there, or some greater being.

She knew none of this was true, but books had made her imagination a treasure trove of ideas and whimsy. Anything was possible when you were just a child. An innocent traveller who has not yet explored the world, has not seen beneath the cloak of nature at the lurking monsters. For now, Vil was happy to pretend the future held something wonderful and grand. An adventure! She slipped her attention to her father, for some clue as to what marvels awaited her.

"To live in this snowy land is to be proud of our end," Nidurd yelled to his soldiers. "We leave at dusk, and pray that the gods let us win glory before death. Prepare yourselves, men! Those fools will not be ready to face our wrath, for we will bring Ragnarok to Volund of Wolfdale."

II. Elves Among Men

Would you like the tale to continue?

Here is where we delve into the macabre, for the arrival of power brings chaotic depravity. It is true, the tales that elders tell; darkness is everywhere. It is almost too easy for evil to sneak through your window and stand behind your curtain. A murky shape standing there with its mountainous form revealed by the silken fabric pressing against its grey, soggy flesh. You cannot set it free from its cell, it is trapped here with you. But perhaps, you can stand against it?

Let us abandon such morbid reflections and return to Vil. This princess of isolation was rather disappointed with the uneventful journey. There had been no trolls or goblins, only a pack of wolves that King Nidurd had hunted for game. Likewise, the stead that Mey and Vil shared would try to trot proudly, but often stumbled through the deep frost, leaving the girls with sore limbs.

It had taken thirteen days to reach Wolfdale and by the end of it, the entire company were sharing sorrowful songs of that faraway place they called home. The frozen tundra slept soundly while Nidurd and his followers jittered beneath thick fur coats. They could see the pale elven castle in the moonlight.

It was a disjointed beast, a fortress of stone. The great keep, where Volund resided, had a sloped roof and walls that were sagging outward; a single candlelit window informed Vil that someone was home. There were towering battlements of different sizes and round watchtowers that seemed to lean away from the castle, as though it were more afraid of the elf inside than the creatures in the white forests.

"At daybreak, we will figh—we will fight!" Nidurd yelled gruffly while he struggled to lift his heavy eyelids. He had brought with him three casks of wine but was now down to the last one. He was, understandably, not in a great mood.

Mey and Vil were camped slightly away from the soldiers, atop a hill where the grass was strong enough to grow through the snow. Mey had told Nidurd that as a Valkyrie, it was customary to camp alone. This was not true but rather an excuse for Vil to be able to unravel from beneath Mey's cloak and get a bit of fresh air.

"Tomorrow will be the first day of excitement," Vil proclaimed.

"Perhaps, but war is a terrible thing and cannot end until one side or both sides are well and truly dead. You'd do well to remember that, Vil." Mey seemed to choke as she spoke, as though a lump were caught in her throat. Vil could see the pain and misery behind the warrior's eyes and felt bad for her desperate desire for adventure.

"I'm sorry, Mey. I know it's not akin to what I've read in books. I am just *so* bored."

Mey chuckled, "There is nothing wrong with a dash of boredom. When you're older, you'll miss when life was simple."

The girls lay on their backs on the hill. The reed strands seemed to wrap around their arms, legs and torso, pulling them gently downward. Vil felt as though she were joining the earth, becoming a part of the great garden. She gazed upward.

"What do you think is past the sky?"

Mey was quiet for a moment, as though deep in thought, then replied with confidence, "A void. Yes, a void of empty space shaped like a great tree trunk that rises upward and grows wider. There are many secret places, little crevices, but at the very top: Asgard. The end of all that is known."

"What about after Asgard? What's next?"

"You know, I do not know. I'll have to ask Odin the next time I see him," Mey joked.

Vil gave a small, happy smile despite Mey's lousy sense of

humour. She rubbed her eyes with her fists and relaxed. Her shoulders were still stiff from horse riding and the coat she'd been hiding beneath had made her hair frizzy like a bird's nest. "Goodnight, Mey," she whispered.

"Goodnight, child." And with that, they slept.

Vil awoke to the sound of battle cries and clashing steel. She sat up and looked around in bewilderment for Mey, but the Valkyrie had vanished along with the rest of the camp. Only Greta remained. She was standing atop a cliff, looking down into the valley where Volund's castle lay. Her dirty green gown flapped in the wind, making an ugly noise like a dog panting. She kept trying to keep her hair down, but it flew in every direction. If you were to look closely, as Vil did, you would see that Greta's foot was also moving, ever so slightly, back and forth like a pendulum. A sign that she was nervous.

Rubbing her eyes, Vil snuck over to the edge of the cliff. She made sure to keep some distance from her mother, who would be furious with her daughter for entering such inhospitable lands. The crusty snow made her palms numb as she crawled close to the edge.

Finally able to see down into the valley, Vil peered at the horrors of the raid against Wolfdale Castle. She saw that the soldiers from her home, many of whom had sung ballads to her during feasts, were slathered in chunks of their enemy's entrails. Prince Volund, the Elf, had dug trenches for his soldiers which were now filled with piles of dead bodies and a river of blood that sloshed in the muddy holes. Any that were still alive in those trenches were undoubtedly drowning. Suffocating.

Her father, Nidurd, was sweeping a large battle axe through the air, knocking enemies off their feet and decapitating men twice his size. His eyes looked a startling white amid the crimson of his cheeks.

Vil vomited, silently, so as not to alert her mother. She was sweating and shaking as all the food from the past week spilled onto the ground, making the snow steam. This was not the wondrous battle where good triumphs over evil. This was barbarians killing barbarians without remorse. It was neither good nor evil but something far worse that Vil was too young, and too afraid, to understand. All she knew was that she wanted to go home, to practise her sword fights with Mey and perhaps one day fight an otherworldly monster with honour and wit. But not this.

"Where is Mey?" She asked aloud, taking deep breaths. "She must be out there somewhere." This time, Vil steeled her nerves and took another look at the siege. She tried not to look at her father or the soldiers. Instead she looked toward the castle.

Amid a sea of boorish men pretending their "noble" actions were deserving of glory, the castle looked strikingly beautiful. It was pale white and sprawling like an ever-blossoming flower. The stained-glass windows glinted with artworks of fallen kings and proud queens gazing outward at everything and nothing.

At the castle gates, Mey and her sisters emerged. They walked casually to the edge of the battle, without a spot of blood on their clothes and their swords still sheathed. They had someone in chains following them. His feet were bare and hairy, his long legs as thin as bones but his torso wide and strong from years of bending metal to his will. He had golden hair that hung to his shoulders and the chains appeared weightless in his strong arms. He was Volund, the cruel villain of this tale.

This is when the battle ended. With their leader captured, his defenders threw down their weapons and knelt before Nidurd.

Greta, meanwhile, began her elegant walk toward the castle. She drifted down the steep hill, her gown trailing behind her. She kept her posture rigid and her face plain.

Vil followed her mother, keeping hidden amongst shrubs and piles of snow. They both reached the bottom and began the walk toward the castle. Most of their soldiers were waiting inside the great hall, along with the Valkyries and King Nidurd. Vil could see their shapes moving in there.

As Vil walked, she looked at the aftermath. Now she was closer, it was easier to see that the battlefield was not just an empty plain. It was a village. The wooden cabins had been burned to rubble. Pigs lay dead, faces buried in their troughs. Farmers sat amongst the wreckage of their gardens, cradling dead vegetables as they sobbed in the dirt.

Greta and Vil reached the great hall of Wolfdale Castle, they stepped inside. Quickly, Vil crept to a gap between two pillars. She nestled herself in her hiding spot to watch the victory unfold.

The dirt covered Volund was kneeling at the centre of the hall. A dozen soldiers had formed a circle around him with their swords drawn and pointed at his neck. Volund kept his head low, but there was a careful fierceness to his breathing, as though he were trying to contain the anger bubbling beneath. The power.

"What should be done with this fiend, my King," one of the soldiers asked Nidurd.

Vil's father was resting against a table, half-leaning on his axe. He was covered in guts and specks of pink brain, but the ferocity had left his face. Now there stood an old man, struggling for air in a muggy room. His lips quivered as he tried to regain his composure.

Vil thought, perhaps, that his ears were ringing from the clashing of steel and the screaming. He hadn't seemed to have heard the soldier's question. His glassy eyes stared off absently.

It was Greta who finally took action. She had been admiring the jewellery atop the table. There were weapons and necklaces, and also rings of great beauty that glimmered gold when she held it up to the slats of sunlight that were slipping into the room. "You are a fine craftsman," she said to Volund, her head did not move but her eyes slid down to the broken elf.

"You are a dimwitted wench," replied Volund.

"I see why they call elves the greatest of all poets, you truly have a way with words. Tell me, Volund, who did you make these beautiful rings for? The Valkyrie? Who now stands before you, with hatred in her heart for what you did."

Volund could not keep his eyes from Mey, he glanced at her with a mixture of pain, lust and loathing. "She means nothing to me."

"Lovely," said Greta, then she turned to the guards. "Cut from him the might of his sinews. The elf must not fly away too soon."

It is always terrifying to see your mother as she truly is. One always assumes that their parent is as kind and nurturing to others as they are to you.

Greta was not a caring woman, she was bitter from her years in the lonely castle. Vil's stomach sank into the floor and her muscles seemed to twitch, urging her to spring into action. How could the Lady Greta wish something so awful? What could spur an act of cruelty like this? Vil shutdown her thoughts and tried to accept what was happening.

"He is evil," she told herself. "He deserves whatever punishment that Mother desires." Vil knew that Volund had treated Mey monstrously. Surely that was enough to justice torture? She kept watching.

The elf suddenly looked very human. He was trying to keep himself from shaking and his hair was soaked in sweat, so that it hung in front of his face in clumpy strands.

"I am bound," he said steadily, with great control. "You have captured me, yes. And to that I say, how dare you. Do you know who I am? Truly? I am Volund, son of the Lappish King, Lord of Wolfdale. I am he who came out of the forest and entered Midgard with raw power coursing through his veins. You, the queen and king that dare claim domain over me, you will be destroyed."

Vil had never seen her mother smile the way she did then. Her lips peeled back and her teeth looked yellow in the stale dusty hall. She knelt, very close to Volund's face, and whispered, "Your serpent eyes shimmer like devilish pools. The gods have forsaken you, dear elf." Then she stood and turned to one of the soldiers. "Do what must be done."

Not wishing to see what came next, Vil squeezed her eyes shut. But the wet slicing of the soldier's blade against the back of Volund's legs, and his wailing scream, was a sound she would not soon forget.

The desperate cries of the elf seemed to snap Nidurd from his fugue state. He glanced around at the others. "We should take him captive, set up the cage in the wagon. Volund will be brought back to our home, it shall be decided during the journey back where is best to banish him."

"Yes, Sire," replied one of the guards, who promptly kicked Volund in the back.

The elf fell forward, smacking his chin against the stone. His legs rested in pools of blood, the slick tendons having splattered across the floor, and a gurgling noise sputtered from the V-shaped gashes in his calves. Volund could barely raise his head high enough to retch, but his eyes did not betray pain, instead tiny embers floated in the blue irises like angry fireflies.

Nidurd turned to Mey and her sisters, "Valkyries, you have

done me a great honour. I offer you this place. You can care for it, rule it as you wish. But only if you pledge allegiance to myself and my people. I do not wish to control you, I just do not want this place to fall into wickedness once again."

Vil's heart shattered, "No, Mey."

As if sensing Vil's presence, Mey gave her a sidelong glance and a soft smile that felt, quite painfully, like a silent goodbye. Then she lowered her head and said politely to Nidurd, "Praise be to Freya. We would be honoured, King Nidurd. As for Volund, you may do with him as you wish but I feel I must warn you ... an elf's vengeance is not so easy to escape. Should he find himself free from you, looking to the skies will do you no good. He will descend on the children of men, bringing fire and shadows to your gates."

The guards all began looting the hall and exploring the deeper recesses of the castle.

Nidurd went outside, he placed his hands on hips and surveyed the carnage inflicted upon Wolfdale. His posture was straight and powerful, that of a king's, but Vil knew her father well enough to know that his eyes were closed in prayer. He would ask Heimdall and Freyr to guide him toward more peaceful times.

Mey was admiring a tapestry depicting the wonderful beauty of Alfheim, the silk showed forests filled with white leaves and water that shone gold. However, Mey also had a hand behind her back that motioned at Vil to follow her.

Vil trailed the elegant Valkyrie through the worm-like halls of Wolfdale Castle. They passed golden goblets on pedestals and cracked wooden doors. Through a window, Vil saw spiked heads of fallen men upon the battlements. Mey's hips swung and her skirt, made of raven feathers, rustled like rhythmic music.

They entered a cramped, empty room. The stone walls held

cobwebs in their corners and wind was whistling through a paneless square window the size of a palm. Soot made the flagstone floor black. It seemed like a cell except for the sword hanging from one wall, though the rusty blade was more a forgotten relic rather than a mighty, cherished weapon.

Vil ran and embraced Mey in a tight hug, gripping the rough fabric of her warrior's garment and refusing to let go. Sweat and harsh metal filled her nostrils, but she did not care.

"Do not be so sad, child. We have made such exciting memories," Mey whispered, her lips brushing Vil's ear. The Valkyrie had plaited her fair hair into strands that hung like chains against her back.

Vil said, "I know you have to stay, I won't make a fuss. But I want to give you something, to remember me by." She barely reached Mey's shoulder and had to look up into the steely grey eyes that were wide and caring, but also mysterious. Those irises would always remind Vil, in later years, of a full moon on a foggy night. Radiant light hidden behind storm clouds.

Reaching into her side pocket, Vil felt the hard lump of the wooden bear. She gripped it, tightly.

"Here." Closing her eyes and bowing her head, Vil presented the item that never left her pocket. "My father got me this before I could even speak the common tongue. It was gifted to him by a sailor that had seen places I could only dream of: ice so blue it looked like still water, a sky filled with streaked lights, bears as white as snow."

"Ancient magic rests in such places," Mey said with quiet intensity, reminiscing on beauties Vil wished she could witness.

"I kept this to remind me," Vil continued, "of all that I hope for and all that I want to achieve."

"Then why are you giving it to me?"

"Because I hope to see you again, and this gives me a reason."

Mey gingerly took the bear in her fingers. She smiled with her teeth, and it felt like the mustiness of the room, the dust and the grime, evaporated in a burst of powerful sunshine. A silence befell the two of them, a comfortable quiet as the two enjoyed the space shared. Then Vil, reluctantly, shifted one foot toward the door. Mey noticed the movement and gave a slight nod.

"You should go," Mey said. "Your parents will be leaving soon and you'll want to find a place to hide for the journey home. I scavenged food around this ghoulish castle and placed it in a burlap sack beneath one of the tables in the great hall. Take it with you." Vil nodded and headed for the door, but as she reached it, Mey hastily added, "And Vil ... do not speak to the elf."

After that Vil left the room and collected the supplies Mey had gathered for her. Then she hiked back to the wagons and horses that her people had used to ride to Wolfdale. Without Mey, there were not many places where Vil could hide and sleep for thirteen days without being seen. After searching for some time, she realised there was only one place that she could go. A dangerous place.

There was a wooden wagon that was different from the rest, it had no doors and the windows were framed with metal bars. Inside was a cage that held Volund, the steel floor already slick with his greasy blood. There was a shadowy space next to the cage and it was here that Vil could stay during the journey home. All it meant was that Volund could see her, hear her, speak with her.

At first, the elf merely watched her with white bulbous eyes that glowed amid the filth upon his face. He would sit in a crouched position, his fingernails scratching against the damp floor until they bled, making a screeching noise that unnerved Vil. Now and then he would hobble over to the bars of his cage and let out a hoarse grumble as he rubbed a shoulder against the cool metal.

There were no guards inside the wagon for King Nidurd feared Volund's silver tongue would persuade them to release him. This left Vil alone, in her dingy captivity, and the first six days of the journey were very lonely.

She tried to conserve her food as much as possible and it left her constantly hungry. She would survive, but it was not a pleasant trip. Her hair felt oily and stuck to her scalp and when she awoke each morning she would often find a bug or two gnawing on her skin. She wished she had parchment, so that she could write down all that she'd witnessed. Perhaps she'd warn that quests were far less pleasant, with all the violence and horror it brought out in those you loved, than it was made out to be in books.

On the seventh day, Volund spoke. His voice was raspy and parched but there was a silkiness to it that swirled and flowed like rising winds. "Look out the window, girl," he said, pupils dilating as he gazed outward at the passing landscape.

Vil was startled by the sound of someone speaking. She had grown so used to the quiet that it felt as if a great disturbance had occurred. Volund's words were a spray of watery pus that splattered her brown leather shoes. His gaping mouth was a gateway to a faraway land of disgusting beasts, of foul-smelling soil, of bitter poison.

Nevertheless, she found herself peeking out the window at the barren plain and puffs of frost scattering into the air. The wagon wheels churned the ground into muddy slush. In the far distance was a castle nestled in a lumpy hill.

It had an outer wall made of transparent crystal that caught the rays of sunshine and refracted it in beams that shone in every direction. The many towers were adorned with stone trolls and writhing worms that curled into the misty sky. The castle itself was made of solid gold, a hazy yet majestic feat of architecture.

"What is it?" Vil asked in awe.

Volund replied, "The Court of Paradise." His thin lips were pulled upward, into a sinister grin, held there by the invisible hand of Odin. "The home of my father."

"What is he?"

"Dead."

"How?"

"A musical man played a song that broke his heart and stole his lover's affection. He withered into dust. Now the castle stands empty, save for the walking dead. There are corpses caught between Midgard and Hel that wander his grounds and cannot leave. They still carry the wounds of life: headless or gutless with eye sockets empty and red. None have tongues, so they cannot share the secrets of Yggdrasil, The World Tree, and so the place is a graveyard of divine jesters."

"I see."

"You do not," he growled firmly.

Vil shuddered at the anger in his voice. He had an aura of evil power that made her feel the wagon were swaying nauseously on heavy waves.

"How old are you?" Volund asked, his slithering voice snagging at her clothes, pulling her toward his clawed talons.

"Twelve."

"How old do you think Mey is?"

"A couple years older, I do not know. Fifteen? Eighteen?"

"Thousands of years old," he chuckled. "How old do you think I am?"

"Old." She was confident about this. He looked like a man but she could sense the ancient magic coursing in his veins. She imagined his bones were made of something different too, perhaps gold or silver. No, that did not feel right. He was made of something she could not imagine, and that meant that he was very, very old.

"Young," he corrected her.

"So? What does it matter?"

"You do not know me, you do not know Mey." He leaned closer, squeezing the squishy part of his face through the bars so that his eyeballs popped from their sockets, he looked like a madman. "You do not know what we can do."

I know Mey, Vil thought. But she did not say it, partially because she felt it was unnecessary to justify with this creature her healthy friendship with a Valkyrie, and partly because she was afraid of what Volund would share with her about the young woman who had taught her about sword fighting beyond the confines of her isolated bed chambers.

Vil finally said, with a degree of aggression, "We had heard about you long before we met Mey and her sisters, did you know that? A scout had seen your castle. He had said you and your brothers did not light fires in the wintertime, instead letting your skin turn blue and your hairs grow long. If it weren't for what you did to Mey, I'd have said you were just a lonely old fart waiting for its end. But now, I don't know what you are."

"Nor do I, little girl."

"Are you mad at my family? For capturing you?"

"Yes."

"But you did such vile things, Father *had* to punish you. Why are you in our lands in the first place? We are peaceful and kind, perhaps we might've been friends. I would have loved to hear about

Alfheim, mother says it is beautiful and filled with the purest of all loves. She says there are hanging gardens, vines with flowers that swing from balconies. There are castles with scaly dragon legs that walk through the countryside. And it's always summer."

"Alfheim," Volund spat, "is the Aesir's cesspit."

"Whatever do you mean!" Vil was shocked.

"Odin and his arrogant cult of immortal halfwits have tortured my people since the dawn of time. They sew tapestries and paint murals showing our 'prosperous' lands to hide the truth from you mortals. We are the slaves who carry his kingdom upon our broken backs.

"I came here, my family came here, to inflict upon you what he did to us. To make you regret your worshipping and to destroy the tranquillity that you take for granted. I am here to burn and to pillage and to butcher. I will be the slaughterer of mankind. And when Odin cannot draw power from his peasants' prayers, we elves will take Asgard for ourselves." His fury against the gods came across as detached. The words themselves were angry but his tone playful, as though he were rehearsing the lines of a melodramatic performance.

"But we have done nothing wrong!" Vil was mainly focused on her family's wellbeing, but a scarier question flickered at the back of her mind: Was Odin truly cruel? If the unconquerable symbol for goodness was just as foul as the rest of them, then what hope was left? She had to believe the All-Father was better than that, that he was a sweet old man.

"Your beggarly existence is a mockery against my people," Volund continued. "This iron cage is an act of war. Your mother took from me my mighty legs, but do not fear, they will heal. I am unstoppable, ignorant child, and I will tear apart the fabric of your crude land, stone by stone. My sword will be a red-soaked icicle that carries the souls of your father and your brothers."

Parts of his "motivations" did not make sense to Vil and she decided to call him out on this. "If you want to end everything, why did you stay in Wolfdale for so long? Why did you force Mey to be wed? Why did your brothers flee into the night and leave you alone to craft expensive jewellery and silver rings? Only now that you are captured do you act vengeful."

Volund smirked at this but didn't respond for a moment. Then he knocked back his head, jaw pointed at the roof, and howled an operatic laugh. "Children are so foolish. You ask so many questions as though that will help you understand. I am unknowable, you are a flea on my back. A worm in my shoe."

He inhaled deeply, and continued in a vain purr, "For all you know, everything I have told you is a lie and I have never set foot in Alfheim. Perhaps I only want to massacre your people and take Mey as my wife because it amuses me. Who's to say Odin is not my dearest companion. An old man I share a golden mug of mead with on a rainy night. You know nothing, and I know all. But there is one truth; your family has wronged me, and for that they shall die."

"I don't like you very much," Vil huffed and crossed her arms across her chest. "I bet Alfheim is wonderful and you were banished from there because you're mean. And I'm sure Odin is not your friend nor anyone else, no one would want to talk to you. I only am because this dirty wagon is so dull. As for my family, you don't stand a chance against my father, and the Valkyries will protect me. So you should just sit there quietly and think about the kind of person you want to be."

Volund was very quiet for a while and Vil thought perhaps she'd outwitted him. She could hear the hooves of horses outside and the muffled groans of men who were tired of riding all day. She settled into a somewhat comfortable position on the hard ground and felt her eyelids grow heavy. Then Volund burst into a roaring laugh that shook the walls and made dust fall from the roof, onto Vil's head. His chest heaved and spittle flew from his mouth, his eyes were wide and he seemed to be struggling for breath.

A little alarmed, Vil crawled to the corner of the wagon and cowered. *This is not very brave,* she thought. *What would Mey think of you hiding in the corner from a prisoner who is locked up?* She felt her heart thumping in her chest and tried to will herself to move toward him, to show that she was not afraid. Yet she could not. She was paralysed.

It seemed a long time before Volund spoke, his back was turned to her as he tried to stifle his laughing. She could see his shoulders rising and falling and the muscles beneath coiling with controlled rage. His hair hung matted and blonde and the slit of sunlight that leaked through the window lit up his bloody fingernails and the black dirt encrusted beneath them. Slowly, his body twisted toward her and he stared into the recesses of her existence.

"You will be the last," was all he said.

Vil wished, more than anything, that she was back at Wolfdale in the warm presence of the Valkyries, that Volund was a forgotten nightmare. And that Mey was telling her stories by the fire, her fingers twirling a strand of Vil's hair with one hand and using a comb to brush it with the other. But Mey was not here, and Vil realised, quite frighteningly, that whatever was to come next ... she would have to deal with it alone. She would have to be a warrior, a knight, a hero.

"Yikes," she whispered beneath her breath.

III. Strive Against Him

The fight began in the moonlight, watched by a white-throated dipper perched on a reddish branch. Its feathers bristling, its body shaking like the many leaves around it. The bird did not know it yet, but it was dying; a sickness will have consumed the poor little thing well before the end of winter. Beneath this dying creature, was Vil.

With every swift movement, her unkempt hair would fly around her face so that she looked more like a wild animal than a young girl. She panted heavily and unstuck her shirt from her back, shivering from the icy sweat. The tree in front of her had been hacked to pieces, the bark stripped away, leaving splintered pale wood. Sap drizzling down the trunk in teardrops. The blade in her hand was chipped, the wrapping around its hilt all but worn away.

There was a candlelit window above her that provided a patch of orange light in the otherwise darkness of the castle grounds; it was at a height where Vil could trace the ledge of it with her finger if she reached up on her tiptoes.

It had been a month since Volund was captured and Mey had taken over as ruler of Wolfdale. A month since Vil had seen the Valkyrie. The rest of the journey back had been silent, as Vil did her best to ignore Volund's persistent "girl" or "peasant, free me" and the occasional, "if you let me out, I shall let you live."

Her father, King Nidurd, had imprisoned Volund on a small island called Saevarstad. According to the stories, it was not a very pretty place, there were no animals or fish in the surrounding sea. The plants and trees were dead and rotten, sinking their roots into the ground to withstand the gusts of grey fog that lashed overhead. Volund was staying in an abandoned stone house, where he was forced to craft jewellery for Greta and weapons for Nidurd.

Her brothers had not approved of this decision, calling their father weak for not killing Volund. They'd spent the past few weeks silent at dinners and secluded in their chambers or the stables during the day.

Greta, Vil's mother, had kept her distance from her daughter for the past few days. She could see the queen now, standing in the orange window of one of the battlements. It seemed like she was admiring Vil's swordsmanship from across the great distance. Vil wished her mother was here with her, she missed when they were close.

Vil twirled the blade with her wrist and struck the side of the tree, then stabbed it. She spun and sliced a deep line just above the roots. Then she rolled and hit the tree three more times like flashes of lightning. She heard heavy boots crunching toward her. Vil felt her heart skip a beat, but her sword did not waver as it cut through a branch on the tree, forcing the white-throated dipper to soar away.

It was Nidurd who had come to see his daughter. The aging king had gained considerable weight in the month since Volund's capture, the bottom of his stomach peeking out from the silk maroon shirt. He had a wolf coat draped over his broad shoulders and his greying beard covered his chest like a prickly waterfall; the hairs were crusty from dried ale. He was akin to the giants Vil read about in stories, large and frightening in size but with sweet scrunched-up faces.

"I came out here looking for my daughter, and here I find a warrior. Nay, a swordsman!" he barked, hands on hips. "You are soon going to put my best knights to shame."

Vil felt a swell of pride rise in her chest and she stood tall. It was true, after all, she had been practising every night since their return and the sword no longer felt so heavy in her hands. She had even glanced at the mirror one morning and noticed muscles growing on her arms; she'd poked them and found the skin to be most wonderfully tough.

"Thanks," felt like a suitable reply.

"I have a gift for you," Nidurd continued, holding out a pouch to her. "It was crafted by Volund, and I must say, as much as I despise the creature and his devilish murmurings, he has crafted fine pieces of jewellery."

Vil took the item and opened it, then poured the contents of the pouch onto her palm. A heavy ring sat there, silver with lined carvings cut into the band. She slipped it onto her finger and splayed her hand, admiring the work of art.

Nidurd said, "I'm happy you like it, though I wonder if you'll find this more interesting." He unsheathed a sword strapped to his hip, the blade shone a dazzling blue in the moonlight, the hilt was golden, and there were runes scrawled into it that Vil did not recognise. "I took it from Volund, it was crafted by Dvalinn and Durin the Dwarves in their iron fortress and it contains the breath of frost giants. There is no stronger weapon in all of Midgard, and it has a name: Tyrfing."

"It's beautiful ... I'm sure Volund is upset to have lost it."

"You do not need to fear him, Boovildr. He may want revenge, but he will not get it."

"Sorry, you're right."

Nidurd lowered Tyrfing, letting the tip sink into the snow. The steel must have been warm because steam rose up in front of his face. Vil's father gave her a look she had never seen before, his eyebrows furrowed and he scratched at his cheek vehemently. It was, at least to Vil, a look of shame.

After a hesitation, Nidurd spoke, "I know you snuck to Wolfdale."

Vil was taken aback by this, it had been a month and no one had showed signs of suspicion. How could he have known? She stumbled on her words, "Father, I—"

"It's alright. I am not upset with you, daughter. I simply—" He grumbled to himself and looked up at the constellations flickering solemnly. "I hope you do not see myself and your mother any differently."

This was not what Vil had expected, for she had largely repressed the memory of her father's rageful destruction of the village, her mother's cold torture of the elf. Now the memories surged forward again and she wondered how such a calm, almost frail man could be capable of such horror.

"I don't," she finally said, but she did not fully mean it.

"Good." Nidurd nodded gruffly and tossed Tyrfing lightly in his hands, weighing it, balancing it. "Here is a thought, how about a little sparring with your tired old father?" He grinned at her, lightening the mood.

"You'll be quickly defeated," Vil retorted and stepped into a fighting stance. Her father threw a half-hearted overhead attack, which she parried rather easily. A little cockily, Vil decide she would show up her father and surprise him with her strength. She lunged forward, coiling her body so that she could exert outward and knock him off his feet. However, her foot slipped on a patch of ice, and Vil felt herself falling hard onto her bottom.

Nidurd roared a hearty laugh, clutching his belly and tilting his head to the moon like a bisclavret werewolf. "It seems you are in need of more practice."

"That never happens!" Vil grumbled, rather annoyed that she had embarrassed herself after doing so well all night.

"I'm sure it doesn't. Well, that is enough sword fighting for the king. I am going to sit at my throne, admiring this great place we call home, then climb the many steps of my tower and go straight to sleep. You're welcome to stay out here, Boovildr, but if you catch a cold do not blame me." He began to walk off.

"Night, father."

"Goodnight," he replied, then stopped and looked back at her absent-mindedly. "Oh, the Valkyrie, Mey, she sent you a letter that I left on your dresser. Nearly slipped my mind." With that, he left and Vil was alone again.

"Mey!" Vil exclaimed to herself excitedly. She'd sent the Swan Sister of Wolfdale a letter thirteen moons ago but had yet to receive a response. What could she have said? What glorious adventures were Mey and her sisters navigating all those leagues away. Vil could not wait to read the letter, but not before a few more swings of her sword.

She soon lost herself again in the rhythm of duelling her branched opponent. The tree was not a worthy adversary and she felt sorry for it. Some time must have passed too because it had grown very chilly and the moon had sunk behind a wall of grey storm clouds.

Vil was about to return to the castle keep, when she heard two men speaking from within the window just above her head. She recognised them as her brother's voices.

"Father will admire our bravery, for Volund is the treacherous king of night's evil. We are not savages, no, but we shall be his soul's reaper. Two great warriors who bested the monster in man's clothing. Our act, brother, will save the people of this fine kingdom from destruction. The coming seasons will be coated in serenity because of our valour."

"Are you certain this is the time? A cold winter's night is not an omen for glory, but a warning against the harshness of the wilds."

"We must, before it is too late. You scouted a path?"

"Yes, there are two boats left behind by fishermen, I readied them for us. It is a clear, short ride and together we can row to his island of Hel with ease."

"And our sister? Do we tell her?"

Vil's heart skipped a beat.

"She's a girl, what else is there to say?"

"Let us go then."

Their footsteps retreated into the hallways of the castle, leaving Vil to angrily sheath her sword and rush to the castle gates. How dare they think so little of her. Just a girl? She had hacked that tree to pieces while they were upstairs, brushing their chalice hair, readying themselves to appear heroic after triumphing over the elf. Vain imbeciles! Admittedly, her brothers were perhaps better fighters than her, when they wanted to be, but Vil had a power they did not: her intellect. This brought her to a different line of thinking.

How could her brothers be so foolish? They were going to sneak over to Saevarstad and try to kill Volund themselves. There was a chance they would succeed but even so, it was against Father's wishes and such violent disobeying of his commands would be met with outrage by his loyal followers. This had to be stopped.

She hurried into the great hall and found it was empty. She was about to head toward her brother's chambers when, from back outside came the unmistakable clack of horse hooves. Turning, Vil saw her brothers riding away into the night on two steeds, they were wearing cloaks but it was undoubtedly them.

"Halfwit farts," she muttered beneath her breath. It would do her no good trying to reach Nidurd and Greta, they slept at the top of the highest tower at the far end of the castle. By the time Vil reached them her brothers would be face to face with Volund. Besides, waking Nidurd was like waking an angry bear in hibernation, he would swipe at you with his hands and growl. It was not worth it.

There was only one choice she could make, Vil would have to follow her brothers to Saevarstad and bring them home before they encountered the elf. She was about to leave when something caught the corner of her eye, the sword that her father had taken from Volund was resting next to the wooden throne at the end of the great hall. What had Nidurd called it?

"Tyrfing," Vil yelled and the blade flashed blue in response. She strode over to it and picked it up. The sheath was lying next to it and she slipped the blade inside and hung it over her shoulder. Vil tossed her old blade onto the floor where it clattered.

She took one glance at the throne: the polished oak, the artwork painted on the head, the round imprint of an arse on the cushioned part. How could such a weathered heap of wood hold so much authority? Vil headed toward the stables.

Her podgy horse was usually reserved for special occasions. It lumbered around, absently chewing on hay, and craned its neck at the sight of the girl, looking down in disgust at the prospect of helping her.

Vil had a tricky time saddling it since the mare kept wandering off to eagerly lick dust from the castle walls. Its thick tongue left a snail trail of clear jelly. When she finally managed to mount it and kick her heels in, the horse chose to embody the role of a marble statue.

"Come on," Vil scolded, "I'm not leaving until you take me to my brothers, so you might as well start listening. When we're back you can lick whatever walls you want."

With a resigned snort, the horse galloped off in pursuit of her brothers.

It did not take long for the wind to pick up and shards of frost to fly all around Vil like tiny daggers. It was near impossible to see what direction she was going. The only sign that Vil was on the right path were the faint pair of hoof prints in the snow. She kicked her heels in and pretty soon, the orange light of a lantern was visible through the snowstorm. Her brothers!

She continued a little further when suddenly, her mare stopped. The animal pranced in a circle then gobbled up a clump of snow. Vil tried to get the horse to move again but it refused. Squinting through the messy curtain of ice, she realised why.

They'd arrived at a lake. There was a rowboat at the shore, waves gently lapping against its hull. Further out she could see her brother's lantern and an unmistakable chunk of land. The island.

"I don't like this at all," Vil said to herself as she clambered into the boat. She'd tied her horse to what felt like a sturdy post, she hoped the wood was just wet and not rotten. Grabbing each oar, Vil began to row out to Saevarstad.

The stormy weather thinned out on the still lake and a mist settled around her. It did not take long for Vil's arms to grow tired and numb, but she kept at it. There was a white-throated dipper flying alongside the boat, its bony wings struggled to keep it aloft. Its talons were skimming the water.

"Do you want to sit in my boat, little bird?" Vil asked the white-throated dipper. It did not reply but gave two mighty flaps of its wings and landed at the prow of the rowboat, shaking off its wet feathers.

"I'm Vil. Do you have a name?" She had read somewhere that sometimes gods took the form of birds. She hoped this wasn't a god.

But a fairy, perhaps? Or better yet, was it possible Valkyries could inhabit the bodies of animals? "I'm off to rescue my brothers from an evil elf. Are you here to help or simply bearing witness?" The bird was not very conversational. "Never mind then, who would have thought that such a sweet thing could make such utterly *dull* company."

It took what felt like forever for Vil to finally land on the golden sand of Saevarstad island. The underside of the boat scraped against the pebbles that bordered the sliver of shoreline. She tossed the two oars in the boat and climbed out. The bird hopped out with her but wandered around in some shrubbery away from where Vil needed to go.

The forest was a dark green, not a shred of light could break through the thick canopy of leaves overhead. The island was silent, there were no humming crickets or whistling birds.

Even the wind crept silently between the trunks, slithering like an unseeing serpent. Saevarstad was an encased tomb from which nothing living could ever escape. Vil could hear her own heart beating, rapidly, the thumping clash of an iron hammer cracking against the stone of her ribs.

It did not take long for Vil to see the house. The crescent moon sat behind it so that the heap of rubble was a jagged silhouette. The roof had caved in years ago and fauna was growing in the open air. As she drew closer, Vil picked out the remains of a wall that had once surrounded the property, but had since crumbled into powdery sand.

It was large though, the house that held Volund of Wolfdale. Some might have even called it a rather quaint castle, with vines splattered across the walls and windows twice the size of Vil. When she arrived at the bright red front door, with a lion's head for a knocker, she had to crane her neck just to see the edge of the once tiled roof that was now a broken mess.

She did not knock, instead carefully pulling down the handle and pushing it open. The heavy pine creaked as the hinges sprayed a puff of rust into the room. She had brought a lantern, which she'd found in the boat. It lit easily and she watched as the shadows made the furniture stretch into grotesque goblins. As she passed objects, the candlelight made them elongate away.

A portrait hung above a mantelpiece, an oil painting of a slender young man with pale skin and slicked back hair. He had been trying to grow a moustache but the tiny black hairs looked more like specks of dirt.

Vil continued through a set of doors, into a ballroom. The floor was marble and the windows on either side were high enough to reach the ceiling, letting the shadows of trees sway against the walls, illuminated by the light of Máni.

At the far end was an enormous fireplace that could easily cook two to three children in a cauldron. The columns that held up the ceiling also carried weapons. There was a silver chest off to one side, the lid open. And it was there that she saw her brothers.

"Erling! Kadir!" She yelled their names but they did not respond. The young men had their hands tight to their sides and mouths hanging open, chins wrinkling as they stared down at the chest. What was most disturbing was their eyeballs, which had rolled back so only the whites were showing. It was clear that Vil's brothers were in a trance.

She tried to rush over to them but found that her legs would not move, she was stuck in place. It was as though a large, invisible hand was holding her in its grip and no matter how much she wriggled it would not let go. Then he appeared.

Volund had been floating up above, in the upper abyss of the ballroom. Whatever chains Nidurd had kept him locked with, the elf had clearly broken out of. His legs were not fully healed but tiny wings had begun to grow from within the scars. He descended, a silhouette of strength and monstrosity. His feet landed upon the marble noiselessly.

He grinned at her as if to say, *I warned you*, then pulled a sword from behind his back and showed it off to the room, holding it high and proud. Whoosh! He swung it in the open air, taunting Vil.

"No!" Vil screamed, but her brothers were not alerted because they were still caught in a trance, gazing into the treasure chest.

Volund casually strolled over to the two boys and cut both their heads off in one quick movement. Their decapitated bodies crumpled to the ground in a heap of meat and bones. Erling's head rolled over and seemed to see Vil, the mouth was moving silently and the veins sticking out of the exposed neck were squirting and moving with a life of their own.

Meanwhile, Volund was sticking his fingers into Kadir's eyeballs. The elf lifted the head up, and tore off the jaw with a mighty tug. He then raised the gory thing above his head, letting the torrent of blood pour down his throat and splash upon his face.

A seductive spirit then spoke in Vil's mind, one filled with sorcery. It removed her from the horrors of the massacre and had a sleepy tranquillity to its cadence:

"Poor Princess of the castle. How is it that you found yourself so deep within the dungeons, where skeletons come to life and devils lure girls like you toward fiery pits? Don't you miss the pretty prose of your books, the ones that made death seem poetic and beautiful. This is anything but that, it is violent and careless, and even worse, it has no meaning. No purpose. Your brothers have died for nothing, so let me take you somewhere where these things still matter. Let me help you, Boovildr." She felt herself slipping downward into the mouth of that angelic voice, a deep hole with bright lights that burned through eyelids.

"You have to free yourself from his spell," Vil told herself, sleepily, but the elf was taking control. He was invading her thoughts. She saw a warm bed, the window open so that a cool breeze was washing against her face. Her family was nearby, and Mey too. They were all happy within their thick walls, celebrating that it had been Vil the Hero who had defeated the evil creature, and all she'd had to use was her mighty wits. There had been no blood spilled, the perfect end to a wondrous fairytale.

"No!" Vil told herself more firmly, and she willed her legs to move. She accepted that her sheltered life was over and that the danger was real. She was not tucked beneath silky sheets, the truth was that Volund was coming toward her, swinging his sword back and forth through the air. He was leering at her, walking with a slouched posture. As he drew closer, he dropped his shoulder and let the blade drag behind him, screeching against the floor.

"You're not going to kill me," Vil declared, trying to hold back tears as she inched her paralysed hand toward Tyrfing. The fog inside her mind and limbs lifted, she could still feel the elf's magic pressing against her but she was in the eye of the storm. Outside of his domain. He reached her and she deflected the first swing of his sword, but her arm trembled and she knew another hit would be the last.

Without thinking, Vil turned and ran as fast as she possibly could. She tore out of the crumbling house and through the maze-like forest. Volund was grunting behind her, hobbling on his two wounded legs.

Even though he was slower than usual, he still managed to catch up enough to Vil that she could hear him whisper, "Pray I don't find the strength to fly again."

The rowboat came into view and Vil felt such a surge of happiness that she almost burst into tears right then and there. She didn't even notice the dead dipper curled beneath a birch tree.

She shoved as hard as she could and the boat scraped off the pebbled sand, into the water. She climbed into it and grabbed the oars, glancing back at the hulking figure who was lurching toward her with a splayed hand that had long, yellow fingernails and black soot upon the weathered palms. She began to row, as mist formed around her and Saevarstad lost its texture, then its colour and finally its shape.

When she felt she was far enough, Vil put down the oars and pulled her legs close to her chest. She let everything that had happened sink in, from the arrival of the Valkyries to the death of Kadir and Erling. Vil wished the mysteries of magic and wonder had never arrived upon the doorstep of her mundane existence. She should never have been fooled into thinking it would be exciting. In all honesty, aside from meeting Mey, the past months had been the most dreadful of her entire life.

There was no longer anyone for her to turn to. She'd seen her parents for what they truly were: grown-ups. A powerful husband and wife who tore apart a village to capture a creature of immeasurable power. Why? To gain justice for the crimes against Mey? To restore order to Wolfdale? No. They had done it because they could, and that was a terrifying thought.

"I could not stop him," Vil said to no one. "I thought I was stronger but I'm just a girl who likes books and wanted to be a Valkyrie. I couldn't help my brothers, or avenge them. Nothing is the way I thought it was – I don't know what I was thinking. I could not strive against him." She wanted to cry but couldn't, although her lip did tremble. She did not know what to do next, where to go. That is, until the water began to foam and a figure began to rise.

IV. Purgatory Omens

The lake remained undisturbed as she rose above Vil, her body passing through the water rather than breaking it apart. She had long flowing hair that hung wet against her naked back. The locks were golden but plaited with green seaweed strands, which sounds disgusting but was actually quite tasteful. The tall lady arched toward the sky, stretching after a long slumber. She cupped her hands and splashed her glowing face.

Her voice was oddly deep as she crooned to Vil, "Hello, tiny hero. How rare it is to see a knight without armour, and are you always so little?" She raised her eyebrows, feigning surprise.

"I'm not a knight," Vil scowled, yet she eyed Tyrfing, which was resting by her feet. This Lady of the Lake was not the strangest thing she'd encountered, Vil even remembered reading of a similar figure in one of her books. And the stranger did *seem* nice, but nonetheless today had taught her to be wary and ready for anything.

Vil tucked a loose strand of hair behind her ear and peered closer at the Lady. "Who are you? If you've come to challenge me or something don't bother, I'm not in the mood. Oh, and I could easily kill you too, so be wary."

The Lady chuckled, "Not a knight, you say?" She walked upon the water with bare feet. Her form was human yet there was a haziness. For instance, if you were to focus on a particular point like her hands or nose, it was clear and precise, but taken as a whole the lady seemed to flicker like a magical moving painting or ... sails!

That was what it reminded Vil of, a ship's sail flapping in the wind. She was not really here and the wind was gusting her in and out of existence.

"Why have you come?"

Bemused, the Lady chuckled, "This is my lake. I believe I have the right to visit it, now and then." Then she presented her upturned palm, grey fingers curled into a claw-shape. A flower petal sprouted up from inside a wrinkle. The Lady placed the newly grown beauty on the water's surface, where it was carried away by the current.

"Your lake?" Vil asked, trying to focus on the conversation but quite mesmerised by the display of magic.

"Yes, I am its guardian. The protector of all that lies below."

The princess snapped her attention to the Lady of The Lake. "If you're such a great person then why didn't you help my brothers, or try to stop them from sailing to their doom?"

The Lady frowned in confusion. "I never claimed to be good. I simply am or am not." The Lady drifted closer to the rowboat and towered passively over the tiny Vil. Above her was the northern lights. Great waves of shimmering colours that washed back and forth across the heavens. The unearthly Lady continued her velvety lyrics.

"While I may not be a hero to your kind, it was you that brought me here. We have heard whispers of the princess with the dwarven sword, Tyrfing, who will be the one to stand against Volund and bring the fabled creatures of wonder back into my valley. For you see, Volund has chased them away. The mermaids and sirens, the skeleton fish and the trolls who tell riddles. They kept themselves hidden from mortal men, but he found them quite easily."

Vil had always suspected a hidden world of magic existed, filled with the imaginary beings from her books. Yet, she found it difficult to care after Erling and Kadir's deaths. Why had none of these hidden creatures come to help Vil? Were they afraid? Had they viewed her family's struggles as beneath them? She could not understand the separation between magical immortals and human beings. All she knew was that the world was a colossal beauty polluted with hate.

Vil declared, "As much as it saddens me, Lady, I am not the one you seek. I ran from Volund after he—I was afraid of him in the wagon, even though he was still our prisoner. I'm no hero."

The Lady of the Lake smiled, kindly. "There are others who think differently." Then she vanished.

Vil was alone again, her rowboat had been drifting and the mist meant she could not see land. Her guts told her that home was toward the left, so she started rowing again. The loneliness was quick to creep back into her bones.

After a while, Mey's voice hummed from deep within the lake, "Hello, child. It's been awhile." There was a bubbling and a burst of yellow smoke that stretched into tentacles. When all of this had cleared, Mey was left sitting at the prow of the boat. Her hair was cut very short so that her face had a more roundish look, her eyes were clouded by the inky warrior paint smothering her brow and cheeks.

"Mey!" The girl was so excited to see her dear friend that she nearly forgot about the awful acts that had preceded her arrival. Then, she remembered and she felt ashamed for the mighty Valkyrie to look upon her face. Vil was not deserving of the attention.

"I know you're afraid, I know you feel that you have failed. You have not. Listen carefully, understand? We don't have long." After getting a nod in reply, Mey continued, "This lake is the space between lands, beings, worlds." Hands in her lap, mouth slightly ajar and cross-eyed, Mey appeared slightly frightening.

"What do you want to tell me?"

Mey paused, her mind momentarily whisked away. Then she returned her attention to Vil, and her tone dropped slightly lower. "Did you know I was not always a Valkyrie?" she asked rhetorically. "I used to be like you."

"Like me?"

"A girl, not a very posh one. I got into more mischief than my mother could handle, stealing bread, outwitting merchants, sneaking into places that were not fit for children. One day, I went swimming in a lake that had salt water that made my eyes burn red. I was with a boy whose truest name I've long forgotten, and we swam out to the centre.

"It didn't take long for heavy winds to pick up and a current to form, not a typical current though. There was magic in those waters, I could see the seabed glowing purple and despite it being wintertime, my bones grew warm. I sank into the depths and began to drown, remembering the taste of air and wishing I'd never taken it for granted.

"There was a murky, sludgy splotch in the water. Almost invisible unless you looked at it from the corner of your eye. It reached out to me and I saw death. Lost souls roaming the spaces between life, haunting the edges of existence. This speck was a ghost that made me forget what it meant to be alive and I almost held onto its skeletal hand, with fingers wrapped in brown ribbons. Then I chose to struggle back to the surface, when I came up I found myself in Valhalla. Odin was waiting at the shore."

"You didn't die in battle?"

"He said I was a fighter. That I could join him and become a Valkyrie or continue sinking and discover the mysteries that lay outside of his domain. I was cautious, frightened. Here was a god telling me there was a place even he did not understand. Part of me wanted to see what lay beyond, but I chose to stay. To ride a stead at his side. To this day I don't know if I made the right or wrong decision. All I know is I rose into the known, instead of sinking into the untold. That was what brought me here, for better or worse."

"Why did you tell me that story?"

"Choices can whisk you away to places beyond your wildest dreams, they can make you a hero or a queen or the greatest knight in all the land, but they can also bring you peace. You have a chance here, to choose between the life you had and the destiny that the three fates, Urd, Verdande and Skuld, have bestowed upon you. You could face Volund, and you would defeat him. I know you would. Or you could return to your books, to gardens without hidden monsters and bedrooms free from lurking shadows.

"No matter what, the murder of your brothers should not go unpunished, but that does not mean it has to be you who slays the elf. There are others capable of such a deed, what matters is that you decide what you want from this world. There is nothing wrong with wanting to escape this horrible mess and live out a life of solidarity. I should say though, whatever you decide, Princess Boovildr, no matter how outrageous or courageous, or even boring, I will always be your friend."

"Thank you."

"For what?"

"For not acting like all of this is some magnificent fable where I become stronger, braver, better ... My brothers are dead ... I'm scared, Mey, and alone. I'm just a little girl who misses her room that smells like freshly baked bread, a room that is in dire need of a tidy, but I've never cleaned it because I was too busy dreaming of adventures that were best left alone. I want to go home."

"Alright, I can't tell you if what you do is right, but your heart is a sturdier compass than your mind."

Vil had a different thought, all of a sudden. "Did you live close to here, when you were still a girl like me?" She imagined the young Mey in the same situation as her, how she would have dealt with all the terror.

The Valkyrie lit up, remembering a distant past. "Oh, no I did not come from these parts. See, Vil, I was an elf, though not an immortal since eternity was reserved for Odin's most devout, wealthy disciples. I did, however, grow up in Alfheim."

Quite shocked by this, Vil took a moment to process. Mey was an elf? How could Vil not have realised this, she was supposed to be clever. So many questions bubbled to the surface that she thought her ears would whistle like a kettle. "What was it like?" she finally asked.

"It was lovely."

"And," she began, "Volund?"

Mey's expression changed. "I knew him, yes. You see," she took a deep breath, "Volund was the boy who swam in the lake with me, though he called himself by a different name back then. He was my closest friend, but he lived atop a hill where I was not supposed to visit. As I grew older, things between us became more distant. The morning before I drowned, I had snuck my way to the palace where he lived and demanded he came swimming with me. He'd been quite amused and agreed to come." Mey stopped herself, composing her next words carefully. "I wish I knew what turned him so cruel."

Mey leaned forward to share more revelatory wisdom but her shape grew fragile. "I'm fading. Before I go, there's a letter waiting for you at your castle, asking if you'd like to spend a week in

Wolfdale with me. I was going to take you hunting, teach you Valkyrie secrets. Perhaps I will see you there. Goodbye, Vil." Then she too, along with The Lady of the Lake, had vanished.

"So then there is no answer?" Vil asked aloud, wondering if she'd imagined the visitors who'd spoken to her upon the boat. The reveal about Mey's past had been surprising, to say the least. Her friendship with Volund most of all. They were polar opposites and had grown to live such different lives, yet it was strange that their paths crossed so frequently. The revelation had left her dumbstruck and Vil could not decide what to do next.

She tried to peer into the distance but every direction was clouded by a wall of angry fog. Then ...

A swinging lantern, its glow refracting through the grey so it looked like a blossoming golden daisy. The smudged light grew larger before her eyes and eventually an outline formed behind it: another rowboat.

"Hello?" Vil called out. "Help me, I am being pursued by an evil elf. My brothers have been murdered. Please help me!" There was no reply, but the silent traveller grew closer and closer until she saw that there were two people aboard.

"No," she whispered, realising who it was. Their rowboat passed close enough so she could see their faces and knew for sure; it was Kadir and Erling.

They did not hear her cry of, "Brothers!" Their eye sockets were empty, black holes that hungrily sucked in the mist, feeding on all that was real and living. Their skin was a flaky yellow like old cheese.

The twins stood, quietly and effortlessly. They waited on the edge of the boat, both of them had their faces toward Vil but they could not see her.

"Stop," she desperately tried to yell, but all that came out was a croak. All Vil could do was watch as her brothers stepped off the boat and plunged into the icy depths. Their bodies sank so quickly that she lost sight of them in an instant. When she looked up again, more boats were passing.

It was mostly people she did not recognise and they passed wordlessly. She noticed there was someone else. They had no boat and were treading water. Vil paddled over to them and saw a hulking frame struggling to keep himself afloat. Unlike the others, he had human eyes and appeared healthy aside from the raspy panting coming from his hairy nostrils.

Vil grabbed one of her oars and thrust it into the water.

"Grab on!" she bellowed fiercely.

She gave the wood a shake so that the figure would take notice. He did not shift his attention but one absent hand did latch onto the end of the oar. Vil leant back and pulled as hard as she could, nearly capsizing the boat as the wet pound of flesh was dragged onto the small deck.

He sat up, rolling into a sitting position. The man spread his legs and leant his elbows on his knees, forehead resting on palms. He sat the same way whenever making decisions on his throne. Bushy beard damp against bare chest, King Nidurd had seen better days.

Vil surmounted the courage to speak. "Father?" she asked and waited patiently for a response that would not come.

Nidurd's face had a sluggish look to it, like the skin was melting off. His nose was drooping and his chin receding. Grief had struck this poor man weak and hideous. No matter what Vil would try, the man was trapped in a cavernous prison where thoughts could not escape.

"I would've climbed the tower to wake you," Vil started to confess, "but I knew it would be too late, that they would have reached the island and," she sighed, "that was the reason I didn't warn you of Kadir and Erling's foolishness. However, oh how I'm sorry, for part of me wanted to see him ... Volund. To stare him down with a weapon in my hands and prove that I was not timid or weak, that I could face him and be victorious."

Her father stared at the deck of the boat, there was a tiny crack by his feet where a patch of water sloshed around on dark wood. He did not move his foot.

"I'm sorry, for everything." Vil, upon seeing her father, realised that there was, in fact, a "right" decision. "Father, I will not return until I've dug a grave for our lost loved ones, and Volund's corpse is swallowed by the waves of this hellish lake." She shuffled closer and took his cold, clammy hand in her own. He finally lifted his heavy eyes to her face.

"Daughter," he smiled, and evaporated into countless fireflies that flew around Vil in dazzling brilliance, before they disappeared into the mist.

For a moment, Vil's mother had also been present on the rowboat, standing behind her husband, a hand on his shoulder while she stared sternly at the horizon. But when Nidurd vanished, so too did Greta.

Vil wished that her mother had been looking at her, but knew that the queen had to stay strong for Erling and Kadir, for the kingdom she ruled on Nidurd's behalf. Despite everything, Vil would always love her mother, would always long for the days when they were closer than the moon and stars, even when separated by mind, spirit and distance.

And so it was that Vil prepared to turn back toward Saevarstad, but she did not need to. The island had returned her to its shrouded shore, she knew this because its misshapen form suddenly reared in front as the current pushed her wobbly rowboat back into the clutches of the elf. But Volund was not waiting for her, she could see the trees and the crumbled house now. Yet, the place seemed deserted. Desolate.

Nevertheless, Vil steeled her nerves and grabbed Tyrfing. The boat banged against a protruding rock just before the sand and it retreated back, slightly, toward the open waters. Vil grabbed the oars and rowed herself the last fraction of the way, she pulled her vessel up toward the grass.

She was about to head toward the house, when she remembered a detail that had gone amiss when Vil had fled Volund's wrath. An insignificant detail that most would disregard as unimportant or trivial, but Vil heeded Mey's words and trusted her heart.

Striding over to one of the birch trees, Vil cupped the dead thing that lay beneath it. With one hand she dug a little hole, not even elbow deep, and placed the white-throated dipper in its fresh grave. She covered it with dirt and smiled sadly. She wished it was the last thing to bury, but it was not. And the dipper's death was so much swifter, so much cleaner, than all the horror that came before and all the danger that was soon to come.

V. Old Man

The forest was dark.

The bark was peppered with blue gems that glowed faintly, making the cobwebs sparkle silver. The wilderness had changed since she was last here, it stretched much further, much thicker, and there was no sign of Volund's house. Most strange was the lack of wind, she could wave a naked candle and the flame would barely flicker, that was how still this place was: a liminal labyrinth.

At some point she came across a corpse, its mouth had been sewn shut with crooked stitches. The neck had been broken so the head lolled to the side, as if it were trying to ask you a question. Vil knelt and used two fingers to close the murky eyes. Her fingers sunk into the mush of skin. Still, it felt the most respectful way to honour this dead man.

After a while, Vil reached a pond the colour of milk that was perfectly round and, though she could not tell for sure, Vil believed that if she were to sink beneath the surface, she'd never reach the bottom.

"Either I've gone the wrong way, or some invisible hand has guided me here. In either case, this adventure is about to take another unexpected turn," she sighed, for the girl was tired of all this running around.

So much nonsense and hatred and unexplained bizarreness. She missed her brothers. That was an odd thing to admit because they were never close, but in their absence it became depressingly clear that she would've enjoyed being an old lady, sitting down and talking to them as siblings.

There was music coming from the other side of the body of water. An enchanting ode to memories and time and all things lost. A harp and a flute, and the voice of a girl that sounded a lot like Vil's own voice. She felt herself drawn toward the singing.

In ye crooked house we came along,
Beneath the blood red star.
On battlefields of gods and giants,
A graveyard and bazaar.
In the air you flew, immortal elven king,
Death came to us despite defiance,
And now we merely sing.

Without knowing it, Vil had sleepwalked to the other side of the pond and was now standing in a small clearing. There was no sign of the source of music. The ground was covered in scratchy moss and a foggy dampness pressed against her clothes. A mound of rocks was piled at the centre, as tall as the young princess. A mass grave.

As Vil drew closer, someone stepped out from behind the mound. Their body was covered in thick black hair, but the hands were skeleton bones. The thing had no face, but rather a caved-in hole for a head. The hole was filled with wet dirt where bright pink worms wriggled.

"You're a Haugbui!" Vil exclaimed, quite thrilled. "A spirit that guards its grave, or in this case, not just your own grave but the resting place of many others too."

The ghostly being cracked and heaved as it hobbled over to a rock and sat down with a clacking noise. It was waiting for Vil to say what it wanted to hear.

"Why did you lead me here?" she asked.

It reached a splayed hand toward the mound of rocks. The arm, the part covered in hair, began to grow longer, slithering toward one of the rocks and lifting it. From beneath the stone, a puff of red steam rose into the air with a hiss that had a distinct sound to it, a word:

"Volund …"

Vil gradually put together the pieces, "You're all the people he's killed? And you're buried here on Saevarstad? How is that possible?" For some odd reason, as she asked this question, Vil had an urge to reach into her pocket to hold the wooden bear. She had forgotten that she'd given the carving to Mey.

The spirit of the grave reached into the hole in its head and pulled out a worm. It stuck the little critter deep into the earth. Immediately, a wailing human head sprouted up. With a shock, Vil realised it was her brother Kadir. He was screaming in pain and there was a large, smooth grey pebble atop his head.

The Haugbui spirit placed Kadir's bodiless head on the top of the mound. It smashed its fist onto Kadir, squashing the skull until only the pebble atop his crown remained. Kadir became part of the grave.

"Bring him back," Vil pleaded desperately. "I don't understand."

A gust of wind evaporated the ghostly figure. The Haugbui became wet ash that splashed onto the ground, forming a puddle large enough to swallow a little girl. The hand of the Haugbui reached out of the puddle and gestured for Vil to step closer.

The music began again and Vil realised that it was the mound of rocks singing and playing instruments. The spirits were forming an orchestra of the undead, an enjoyable way to spend eternal purgatory. The many pebbles vibrated and shook until dust spilled off of them.

Then, a footstep. Vil turned and drew her sword at the same time but, while it was Volund standing a few strides away, he was not in any position to attack. He was standing still, hands by his side and eyebrows raised in surprise.

There was sadness, almost grief, in the pools of his gaze and Vil saw something reflected there: a waving orange glow, warm like the morning sun.

"How has it appeared to you?" He sounded both shocked and fearful. For a second, Vil thought she saw a dark shadow pressing down on Volund's shoulders, stopping him from sailing into the cosmos, but then she blinked and it was gone.

He flicked his eyes over to Vil and the orange reflection was gone, replaced by rage.

He growled, "It seems fate is trying to entwine itself with power. How humorous that they think they can give you what none have claimed before: a chance. You see, little girl, when you're as strong as I am, you can take as you please. This," he waved at the puddle, "this is nothing but the dead trying to hold onto meaning in their void. Victims who still believe there is a way to stop me. I assure you there is not, and, since I'm pondering the thought, there does not need to be. I am not some evil force destroying all you hold dear. I may not adhere to your primitive ways but I follow my own order. For every action, there is a reaction, understand? For instance, your brothers *had* to die. It was only right that I sought revenge after I was wronged by your family."

Vil was fed up, she felt her face grow red with anger and she clenched her sword until her knuckles were white. "Oh, bother! You are just the absolute worst! You act like you *had* to do it, you just *had* to be evil. Well, let me tell you something, mister, you did not! Nothing about all of this is right, not your imprisonment on this island or the murder of my brothers, but it has happened. So, you know what? Now it's my turn to seek revenge." Vil was panting by the end of her speech, but she felt good.

A throbbing power emanated from the puddle where the spirit had evaporated. That power seeped into her bones, giving her the will to stand her ground.

Volund smirked, "I like you, girl." Without warning, he shot an inch upward, his feet hovering above the ground. Then he lurched forward, flying, grabbing Vil by the back of the head.

They slammed into a tree trunk so hard that Vil thought she'd never be able to breathe again. She gasped and heaved. Meanwhile, Volund pressed uncomfortably close. His breath, at first, smelled like strawberries, but beneath that was a strong stench of rot that would make the strongest nose run for the hills.

"You should not have come back," he spoke in a hoarse whisper. "You cannot even fathom my true motivations. Every word from my tongue is a lie, a ruse to distract your attention. Every murder I commit is merely a meaningless response to the boredom I feel, trapped in this lonely realm at the dirty root of Yggdrasil." He was hissing.

In his anger, Volund had released one of Vil's arms to point a finger at her face. She used this opportunity to scratch her nails deep into his cheek. Hot liquid trickled, then gushed, scalding her knuckles. She gave a maniacal grin as Volund reeled back. He was shocked to have been wounded, Vil could see it in the twitchy way with which he retreated.

"Not possible ..." he mumbled, but Vil wasn't listening. She ran over to the Haugbui puddle and leapt into it, expecting the water to only reach her ankles. Instead, Vil sank deep into another realm. The water surrounded her, but she could still breathe, and she began to descend.

A spiral of bright flames shone every colour, stretching into gleaming tornadoes the faster she fell. The Haugbui spirit appeared and held onto her hand with its dry bones. The dirt inside of the hole in its head was spilling upward in a trail of brown. At some point, it let go and the darkness encompassed her.

She stopped falling, though she only knew this because the somersault sensation in her belly ceased. There was no painful landing, no broken legs, only falling and then standing.

She was on a hard floor flooded in a thin layer of liquid that splashed with every step. It was not a lake or ocean, and there was no sand or sky. It was unlike anything in her homeland.

"How do I end up in such otherworldly predicaments?" she moaned to herself and began to walk. It would be pointless for her to try and understand what had just happened. She had read about Haugbui spirits in one of her books; they were fallen men and women who guarded their graves from trespassers. But she had never heard of one being able to transport a mortal elsewhere.

Was there any air here? How was Vil alive in such a state? It just made no sense at all!

"And what of Volund?" she raged aloud. "What will become of him? Will he be free to escape Saevarstad and roam my father's kingdom, all because I am trapped here? I managed to draw blood from his cheek, surely that meant I stood a fighting chance. Oh Vil, you fool! You should have known better than to think the Haugbui was your ally." She trudged onward, wondering if there was any end to the cavernous space.

She passed a crow that was hopping around, dipping its beak into the watery floor. It followed her for a little while before taking flight. There were more crows further on, a swarm all cawing and flapping.

Soon, a figure came into view. He was short for a grown-up, but wide like a mountain. His hair was foamy whitewash and when it reached his shoulders it blended in with his beard, making it appear as though he had a lion's mane with a roundish face pressed into the middle.

There were two lumps near the man's feet. As Vil drew closer she saw that they were tree stumps. Although these weren't ordinary trunks, for they resembled human bodies. It was like two figures had fallen asleep and bark had grown around them, cocooning them.

"Hello," the man exclaimed, "I saw you in the stars." He beamed and winked at her. No, he wasn't winking, for he only had one eye. Could a person wink with only one eye? If not, it was a rather pronounced blink.

Vil proclaimed, "You're Odin!" She remembered Mey's story and wondered if she would have to make a choice here, if this was going to be some kind of test.

"Hush, I am who I am but now is the time for silence," he spoke kindly but the pitch was grating, screeching. Vil wanted to drop to one knee and cover her ears but she stayed vigilant.

Odin raised one of his hands, the fingers were covered in rings with small crystal balls attached. His eye rolled back into his head and the orbs glowed a bright red. A powerful wind surged through the empty space from every direction and pretty soon the body-shaped tree trunks began to shake and burn orange. The bark melted away and two humans rose to a standing position.

There was a male and a female. They were hairless and muscular, heads sheening in a newfound light that glimmered from above. Looking up, Vil realised crystals hung suspended high in the air.

"What's happening?"

"Why, I thought it'd be obvious! It's the creation of man and woman," Odin said in a bored, irritated voice, as though he was sick and tired of having to explain his dealings to silly little girls who got lost in his sacred domains. "Don't fret so much, they'll be off on their way soon and then we can talk."

"But ... people have already been created? How can you create something that's already been made? Why would you?"

"I'll counter your question with one of my own: Why would I explain myself to a mortal who will never understand my practices?" he snapped, resembling a grizzly bear.

When Vil flinched, Odin made a visible effort to soften the deep wrinkles. "Time is quite absurd," he continued. "When you're standing inside it, there's this endless line that gets progressively dull. Step back far enough, though, that's where the fun begins. A circle, Princess, that's all it is, and it goes round and round until you're dizzy and giddy from spinning so fast." He became lost in his musings, not talking to Vil but to himself. "You wonder why we're all so crazy."

Meanwhile, the two newly created mortals were being magically carried upward, though they did not understand this newfound flight. The pair of them waved and kicked their legs, silently gulping, blubbering like fishes out of water. Vil wondered what far away land they were being whisked off to become a part of. Or had they been sent to the past? So many questions but none that would help her.

"Why am I here?" she asked Odin.

"Oh dear, it seems I have forgotten my manners. Me! The All-Father! How incredibly embarrassing. I do hope you'll forgive me." He made a casual motion with his hand that caused a wooden seat to squelch out of the wet ground with a sucking, popping noise. He sat down and leaned back, clutching his pot belly to help him balance.

The god regarded the girl as though she were a piece of furniture. His friendly attitude came across as condescending. His politeness stemmed from the fact that he could comfortably murder her at any second without repercussions. This child was no threat.

Vil held her knees through her pockets to stop them from shaking. She reminded herself of her brother's deaths, of all that had happened and might still happen, and she mustered the courage to raise her chin defiantly and bellow, "Well? I get you're a god but I don't have all day! There are things to do, elves to kill. If you aren't of any use to me, I ask you send me on my way, back to Saevarstad. Thank you very much!"

Odin gave her a funny look, cocking one eyebrow and chewing

on part of his thick beard like a wild billy goat. Then he laughed, slapping one of his legs heartily. "Ah, it's been a while since I've met a feisty one of your kind. Such bores heroes tend to be." He gave a cheerful sigh and continued, "As it happens, I believe I know why you're here."

"Oh?"

Odin was wearing a thick gown, over which he wore a silky red robe. The many layers made him appear mysterious, but also warm and cosy. From within one of his many pockets, he removed a severed head. The dreadlocks coiled, the wild eyes fixated on the sky, its tongue lolled from its mouth.

"Tell her what you told me, Mimir." Odin shook the head vigorously as he spoke, awakening the thing.

"Argh," the head sighed, "morning Odin. My, oh my, this place is a tad dark and uninviting. Whatever are we doing here?"

"The prophecy, you incessant fool. About the princess and her elf." Odin was hobbling closer to Vil, holding the head out invitingly so that she could hear what it had to say. The god was breathing heavily, making the hairs of his beard inflate and spread apart, then retract back toward his chin in a humorous cycle.

Mimir rolled his eyes and made a funny face at Vil that was supposed to be an imitation of a grumpy Odin. She stifled a grin.

The head said, quite sarcastically, "Very well, oh great All-Father." He yawned casually and then slipped his pupils to the back of his head. When he spoke again, it was a much deeper voice:

When frost bleeds, when glaciers crackle, when knight begins far travels.
So young, so bold, she's among the fools who lost in battles.
Tears her dress, stirs unrest, here be the masquerading Princess.
Heroes slain, not in vain, give in to her distress.

Their strength she shall have gained,
Honour, too, will be obtained,
To reap elven Volund's most grisly fate,
And share with him her pain.

Mimir finished speaking and grinned with yellow, crooked teeth. He was unapologetically proud of his prophecy wielding skills, so much so that he even tried to raise his chin high and mighty, but without a neck to crane, it just looked like he was pouting. He also had begun to smell very strongly of rotten eggs, as though the prophecy had made him exude a rancid smell.

"Well done," said Odin.

Mimir tried to reply, "Perhaps my reward can be the great Odin joining me for a feast when—" but before he could finish his sentence, Odin tossed the head over the back of his shoulder like it was a worthless trinket from a travelling merchant's campsite.

There was a wet smack and Mimir groaned, more annoyed than hurt, then silence. Odin waited a moment before speaking again, gathering his thoughts, then he smiled and said, "Right, let's get you prepared." He raised the hand with the orb rings on the fingers and clenched his entire body. It looked like he might burst because he was squeezing everything so hard. His eyes were shut tightly, eyebrows furrowed and he was in a sort of squatting position that one would normally take when using a cesspit.

"Wait, but I don't understand the prophecy!" Vil exclaimed. She was ashamed to admit it, being the avid reader that she was, but Mimir's lyrics had seemed nonsensical. She'd heard of many heroes receiving prophecies that guided their tale toward a noble end, but hers confused rather than enlightened. "You must explain. How can I carry the strength of dead people? Or return them their honour? What fate of Volund's am I supposed to reap?"

"Just a moment, little mortal, this takes a great deal of focus." He grunted and a disappointing puff of lightning shot from his fingers but quickly fizzled out with a sickly wheezing sound.

Finally, after an awkward pause where nothing happened, a glowing yellow orb emerged from within the floor. The shallow water parted to let the orb pass through and levitate above. It was shimmering and Vil could hear a faint flute playing, conjuring images of cabins in the woods, of abandoned infants left for the wolves and of immortal witches without family.

Tendrils wisped out but were pulled back into the orb, and Vil thought she could see faces swishing within, trying vainly to escape.

"Behold," cried Odin, "the souls of Volund's victims!"

"Sorry?"

"The prophecy dictates that you shall receive the willpower and strength of those whose lives have been taken by Volund. You see, Vil, prophecies are not forged in fire and stars. They are written by the dead who desire a better world than the one they left behind. So, they craft words that help their chosen ones to win the battle, seize the day. That is who you are, Vil, their messenger of vengeance."

"And if I refuse?"

Odin, whose arms had been stretched in front of him as he commanded the orb, lowered them to his sides. He looked shocked at what she had said, and when he replied it was in a low, pitiful manner, "Why, I do not know. No one has ever refused before."

Vil weighed up the decision. She recalled what Mey had said to her at the lake, about there being no wrong answer and that she had every right to leave this conflict behind. Part of her wanted to, even felt that she should, it would be lovely living in a quiet cottage with a library in the cellar and a rocking chair that looks out at the countryside. She'd never have to think about Volund, or face her father's grief-stricken face, or behold her mother's wrath against the elf. But another part of her knew that she would never be at peace, she'd always be squirming in her seat, and that just would not do.

"Fine," she muttered, "let's get this over with." She charged over to the orb and grabbed it in both hands. The light exploded into her, warming her chest and face. Knowledge of order, nobility, legacy and futility all surged into her. She understood the meaningless nature of it all, the disappointment each and every person felt in their last moments. But she also saw purpose and joy and love. A thousand defeated souls flowed through her, and she knew that she was stronger than the elf.

Odin guffawed and hopped from one foot to the other in delight. "Goodbye," he said. "Or I suppose I should say, see you soon, considering you may die." He raised his forearm and a crow came and landed on it, ogling Vil with one perceptive yellow eye. Its feathers were damp, dripping grease.

An invisible rope was pulling Vil by the shoulders, lifting her. First her heels left the ground, then her toes. She hovered in the air and a tingling sensation rushed through her fingers. Tyrfing, in its sheath, was growing warm against her leg. The steel was preparing itself to melt through both armour and skin.

She gave Odin one final look, but he had already turned his back to her. There was light filling the strange cavern. Vil saw a giant tapestry of chaos splattering the walls.

Embedded in the stone were echoes of failed creation. Carvings of screaming people, only more deformed. The watery floor was thick red in the new light. The suspended crystals were limpid trees. The chasm skulked on the vicinity of time, its contents a mockery of the perishable wasteland above. All that lay buried here, it was all the same thing. The mistakes of the gods.

"Such a hideous place to live forever," was the final thing Vil said before there was a noise like a thick branch snapping. It was so loud it nearly burst her eardrums.

VI. In the Skull of Ymir

Cracks appeared all around, through which pale light peeked through. The air was mightily pushing against the walls until the rocks of the cavern caved in, exploding outward. Yet, there was no rubble and the ground quietly simmered away, leaving only grass behind. A second ago she was in the cave, now – where was she?

Vil was standing in front of a gothic manor with a bright red front door that had a lion's head for a knocker. She, once again, had to crane her neck to see the crooked eaves of the roof.

"Oh, wonderful, Volund's house." She reached out to turn the doorknob, but froze. Indeed you might be disappointed to hear that, not for the first time on this long journey, Vil found herself afraid to continue. An iron hammer clanged again and again in the cold forge of her chest, her vision swam, and her palms were damp. She recomposed herself, but the fear did not ebb.

"Perhaps, a story," she suggested to herself, willing to try anything. For Odin's wisdom about prophecy had stuck with her; perhaps truth was nothing more than words spoken aloud.

So she decided that, "Once upon a time, the princess of a faraway castle that was hidden in the hills became a brave knight who wielded a magical sword that could cut through any shield and block any blade.

"She was not afraid, this girl, no not at all. In fact, she laughed at the thought of silly, puny monsters or old, wicked men. So, obviously, when she came across a murderous elf who was a terrible young man, she had no qualms about facing him in a most epic battle. They duelled on land, sky and sea. He stood no chance.

"When she separated his head from his body, her heart not only did not race, it did not even skip a beat. And that night she went to bed and had the most wonderful sleep of her entire life. Oh, and she had lots of friends, too many in fact. So many that she did not know what to do with herself all day long. Alright, the end."

The story helped. It was like Vil had given herself her own prophecy that was hers and hers alone. A prophecy that she could turn into history for her children, then legend for her grandchildren and finally myth for all to know and hear.

She drew her sword and eased open the oaken door. Cautiously, Vil stood in the frame and allowed her eyes to adjust to the darkness. The shape of a prickly armchair materialised in front of her, followed by the hollow shape of a fireplace and ... an object not present the first time Vil came here.

Holding Tyrfing steadily in front of her, Vil peered at the shifting mass that was lurking in the corner of the entrance hall. It was tall, lanky, and leaning slightly to the left like it was being held down by something heavy.

"Hello?" she queried, but even as she said it, Vil knew who it was. Volund was standing in that corner, watching her with white eyes and pasty skin.

The elf lowered himself, so that he was on all fours. Vil became aware of his raspy breathing. It was the kind of breathing where phlegm and spittle gurgled in the throat like a cat purring on its deathbed.

He galloped toward her, feet and hands slapping against the floor. Vil steeled herself as the elf drew closer, closer. Here.

Their blades clashed and blue sparks shot in all directions. Tyrfing whispered an ancient battle cry as it was kissed by Volund's thin weapon.

"So it begins," hissed the elf, and he was right.

Vil stepped confidently backward toward the forest, deflecting a few of Volund's attacks as she went. She dodged a particularly nasty blow by ducking behind a tree, hearing the crunch of Volund's blade splitting open the other side of the trunk. He dislodged it easily.

She struck an overhand strike, bringing Tyrfing down toward his shoulder, but Volund easily sidestepped and thrust his own point at her stomach. She only just managed to roll out of the way, her feet catching on an upturned root so that she smacked her chin against the dirt.

Crawling backward, away from Volund, Vil picked up a rock from the ground and threw it toward the elf. He swiped at it with his sword, splitting it in two.

The otherworldly titan looked immensely tall now that Vil was so low. The wind pushed him side to side so that he might topple like a great tower. But there was a terrible strength to his brisk gait.

"You're easier than your brothers," he sang. He pranced toward her, reminding her of a deer she'd once hunted with her father, and a sliver of drool was spilling from his lower lip.

Anger surged in Vil, she was not going to die like this. Lying on the ground, weak, defeated, like some helpless child. No. She had come here to stop him, to bring an end to all the bloodshed. Not for glory or territory or some other disturbing reason but because she was sick of his arrogance, and, honestly, she felt guilty taking for granted the boredom she now longed for desperately. Yes, she had come so far from the sweet girl isolated in her bedroom. This was no time for cowardice.

Vil dove at Volund, tackling him in a bear hug. Only she did not tackle him to the ground, instead they both shot into the sky.

Droplets ran down her skin as they passed through a velvety cloud and then they were in tranquil heavens, floating. They came apart and stared at one another.

"It seems you've learned a lot since our last encounter," Volund smirked, but he could not stop his eyebrows from furrowing.

Looking down, Vil saw her feet were standing on nothing and she was able to propel herself in any direction with ease. Her nostrils burned from the fresh air and her eyes watered but there was a certain freedom to the skies that could not be found anywhere else.

She somersaulted toward Volund and turned upside down as she reached him, swinging at his skull from high above. Then she dove underneath and swiped at his legs, before coming back up to face him head on. None of her attacks broke his skin, but he had been slower defending, she could sense it.

They twirled and circled each other. The horizon was a purple that grew steadily darker and the stars were blurred lines because the duo were moving so swiftly. The world seemed smaller and Volund larger, she understood now how powerful he truly was.

A backhand toward his ribs, a parry off his strike, a well-timed block. Vil was not thinking about her worries anymore, she was focused. Her brother's corpses slipped into her mind once or twice but she pushed them away, her father too reared his grey face into the forefront of her sight but she turned away. She had to do this for them.

Then, an opportunity. The elf had managed to slice a gash in the princess' left shoulder, not a fatal blow by any means but enough to make him slow down to admire his work. Vil did not hesitate, she cut downward at his leg, and barely noticed any resistance as her blood-soaked blade continued swinging.

Volund's leg flew on its own for a moment, spinning around in a panic as if it were trying to see the wound. Then the limb gave a funny shudder and began to descend limply, disappearing in the clouds below.

The duel seemed to stop in its tracks. Volund was astounded, his pearl complexion had gone chalky and Vil was trying to overcome her surprise and decide what to do next. They both hovered.

"How?" Volund managed.

"I don't know," Vil stuttered. Then the fight continued without any profound insights or epiphanies for either champion.

Volund was attacking her but he flew unbalanced without his right leg, and blood was spurting out of the stump. He moved with all his limbs outstretched in a star shape, so that it looked, deceptively, like he was going to give Vil a hug. Each time he got close enough, he'd snarl and swing his blade.

It did not take long for Vil to gain the upper hand. She smacked his incoming sword away from her and swooped Tyrfing straight through Volund's right arm. He howled but this time Vil did not stop to recollect herself, she threw her mighty weapon into Volund's neck. Tyrfing, which was supposed to cut through anything with ease, became stuck halfway. His head rolled to one side, exposing the gash.

"But—" he sputtered, "you're just a—" He could not find the words.

Vil wanted to turn away but the gore had already covered her clothes and face, so much that her hair was soggy. She looked at his eyes and they were, strangely, quite like her father's. Old and lonely. As Vil gazed closer she saw that in his final moments, Volund looked no different from any other soldier, or king, or mortal.

"I'm sorry," she said and meant it. Vil jerked at the blade and as soon as it came free she swung it again, decapitating him completely. His body, like his leg before it, floated for a second too long. The back arched toward the darkness above and then fell into the bleaker darkness below.

Vil stayed for a moment, reflecting on all that had happened. Once more, she wanted to cry but found that she was unable to. Instead the wind rocked her into a sort of dozy state, her eyes growing heavy. The power of the slain heroes was seeping out of her, meandering into some invisible space. She started to gradually lower toward the earth again and it didn't take long for Vil to feel like a little girl again, young and unsure. But the wonder was lost.

She tried to conjure a clear idea of what had happened, or a profound meaning behind it all, but found that her wits were not about her on this particularly fateful evening. Instead, Vil was tired.

Her feet touched stone and when she opened her eyes again she was staring down at Volund's mutilated corpse. After all his spewings of immortal grandeur, here he was. She must have stared at it for a long time, the corpse, before the voice spoke.

"Who are you?" The cadence was firm, but familiar. Vil looked up and saw Mey standing with her sword drawn. Vil had somehow flown from Saevarstad all the way to Wolfdale and was now standing, with Volund's body, in front of the castle gates.

"Mey?"

Appalled, the Valkyrie lowered the point of her blade and uttered, "Vil?" She took a step toward Vil, as if to go and comfort her, then stopped and looked at the dead elf. "What happened?"

"He murdered my brothers," Vil said coldly. "I tried to help but I was too late. I fought him and won."

"Is that Volund?" Mey asked, it seemed she did not even recognise the body.

"Yes." Vil wanted to cry now, though she wasn't sure why. The blood on her skin shined golden in the moonlight. The young girl asked, politely, "Mey, we are friends, are we not?"

Mey hesitated, "Yes."

"Good." The princess missed her mother and father but knew that she could not face their grief just yet. In a way, it was lucky she'd come to Mey first. A Valkyrie, noble and mysterious, would be better suited to helping her accept. "I always wanted to meet The Huldra. I don't believe I've told you that."

"No, you haven't," Mey had not moved at all since their conversation began. She was a statue. There was pity in her expression, as well as deep concern.

Vil continued, "She's this beautiful woman who lives in the woods and has a crown of flowers, but also an ugly cow's tail. Young men get lured into her mountain home and she imprisons them there. Do you know her? Perhaps you can introduce me one day."

"Perhaps."

"I know what you must be thinking. How could I have killed him so violently? Am I not the monster now? Do I really expect to return home and live a peaceful life? I am scared to admit that you might be right. What do you do after the adventure ends? Adventure ... Can you even call it that?" Vil was facing a much harder battle now, an internal one. Half of her was trying to burn all memories of the past few days, weeks, months. Another part was clinging to it.

"This should never have happened to you. I'm so sorry, Vil." Then Mey added, "Why don't you come inside? You can sit by the fire and there's still meat left from my last hunt. I'm sure my sisters will be pleased to see you too." She spoke kindly, with warmth, but she had not yet sheathed her weapon.

Vil did not move. She stood her ground and behind her, a storm was almost certainly brewing; the howling frost pattering against her back was a tell-tale sign that the rain was coming.

"I know you're angry and confused, but you were so brave, Vil. Braver than most will ever be in their whole lives, and now it's time to come home. Even the best heroes need to rest, now and then." She sighed, "You can trust me, Vil. I'm not him."

Up above, where Vil had fought moments before, grey clouds rumbled. They flashed white and Vil saw silhouettes hidden in the sludge, observing her ominously.

She looked at Wolfdale Castle again and noticed how far its shadow stretched. A misshapen patch of spilled ink across snowy canvas. Meanwhile, Mey patiently awaited an answer.

Seeing as there were few other choices, Vil, and I, turned to the great watcher of stories, of fables, of tragedy. You, who sits on the threshold and observes. I have alluded to your existence before, but she only saw you at this very moment, and she was disgusted.

"Where were you when the elf rose? Where were you when he fell?" Vil scowled at the gods and the watchers, and the books and the lies.

For you must understand that, to you, this is a splendid fairytale of duels and ghouls and other delightful horrors. To Vil, to the princess whose story will be stolen by time and ego and the impassions of men who pitied the elf not the girl ... To her, this was not a tale but an emptiness she could never understand. And she vainly hoped you did not understand either.

"Vil?" Mey interjected, still waiting for a response. Her white hair was short and choppy. Snow blew into the hall behind her, where a darker patch on the floor would soon be covered by a lovely fur rug. "Are you going to come in?"

Vil pondered a moment more before asking in a curiously polite tone, "Do you still have that wooden bear I gave you?"

"I do."

"Where is it?"

"In my pocket," and she retrieved it from her back pocket and held it in the light. It was smaller than Vil remembered and, now that she was thinking about it, the carved face resembled a wolf much more than a bear, but the tiny trinket was a pleasant sight.

"Alright then. I suppose we best get out of this cold. Mother will kill me if I fall sick," Vil said and, for better or worse, went inside to sit by the warm fire with her friend.

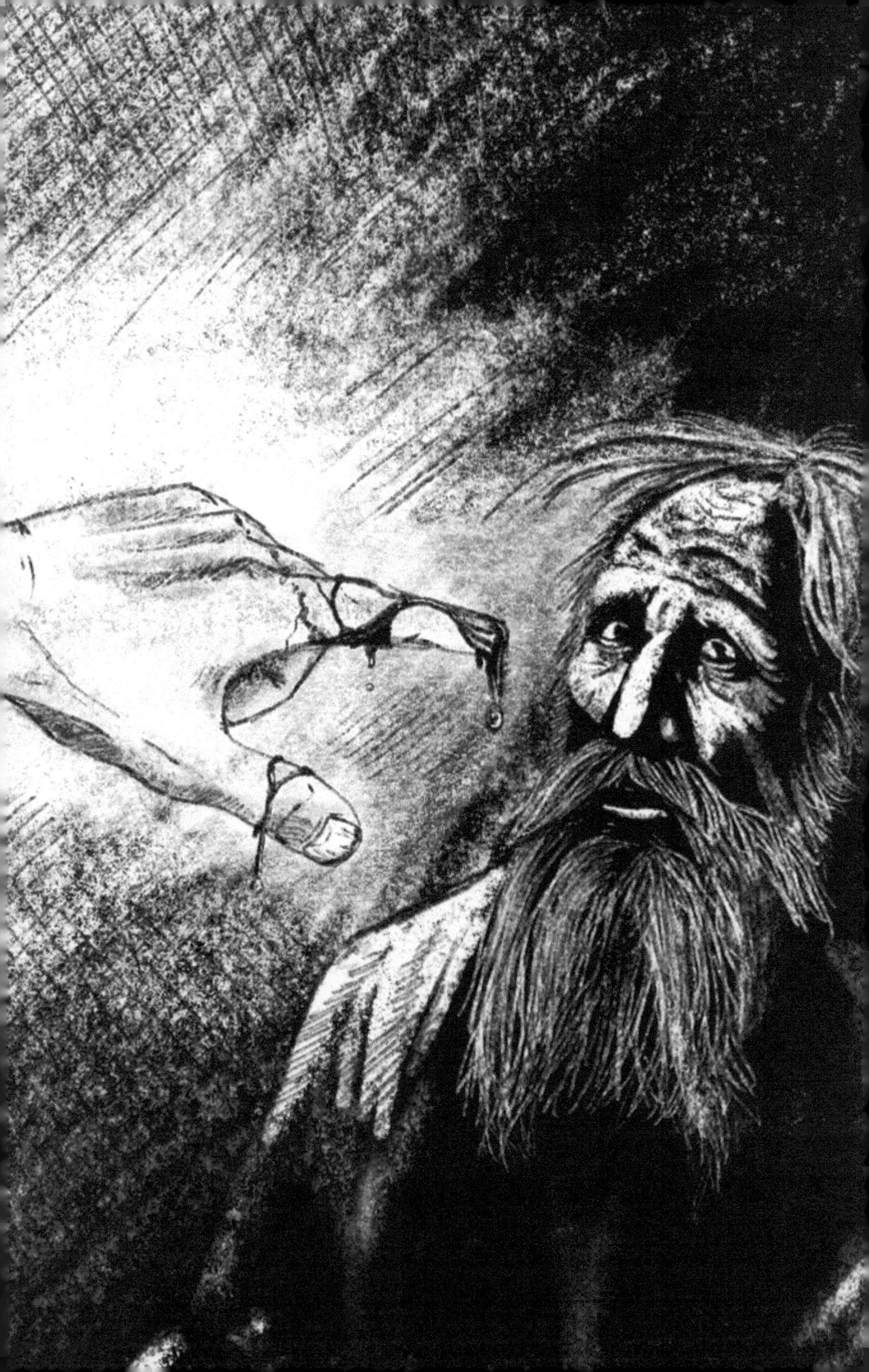

ZACHARIAH & THE ANGEL

I was once a priest. Now I am a father.

I climb the twisting stairs of my sanctuary. Each step seems larger than the last and the splintered wood of the railing causes my frail old hands to bleed. The door at the top of the stairs stands open and a golden, yellow light spills out. It is a heavenly beacon that I cannot escape and it is pulling me upward, into the cold embrace of enlightenment.

My wife is up there and I can hear her calling my name, "Zachariah! Zachariah, come quick!" she says and I know that I must hurry.

But how can I help her? I am powerless in the face of the almighty light that sits passively atop the stairs. An omnipotent gold hue that shimmers and waves; moving like a curtain does when it hangs in front of an open window. It has an energy to it, a life and a soul, it is not human but yet, it is more human than I will ever be. Suddenly, my life of worshipping and preaching in the temple seems so mundane. So pointless. My life is nothing when compared to this startling starlight atop this endless staircase. Infinite. Boundless. Cosmic.

And then, I reach the top.

He stands before me. His skin is smooth and his hair topples down to the floor in soft golden locks. His eyes have no pupils or irises, instead, they are pools of stars that seem to see both everything and nothing at all. But it is the lips that draw my attention, they are oddly thin and seem to move with a life of their own. Rippling and twitching in a way I have never seen before, he is speaking words that I know are impossible for any mortal to speak or even hear. And so, I stand in the silence of his power.

It is from his dove-like wings that the golden light radiates. The feathers are still and the huge appendage creates the bright yellow shadow that is currently cast over me. I feel as if I am in a prison of luminescence and I find myself kneeling and begging for an escape. Anything to be allowed to leave this unholy imprisonment that has so cruelly befallen upon me.

"I am Gabriel," the strange figure says, though his voice does not come from his mouth but instead emanates from deep within his chest.

"Th—they call me Zachariah," I stutter in reply.

"Your prayer has been heard," Gabriel states. "Your wife, Elizabeth, will bear you a son, and you shall name him John."

It is now that I notice Elizabeth in the corner of the room. She is lying on a lavish cot that I did not know existed until this moment. Sweat dampens her forehead and her lips are pursed in awe at the sight of the angel. Her eyes are wide and blue as she tries not to be blinded by the golden light, and she gently runs her fingers through her deep brown hair, which she often does when she's nervous. Most strangely, her belly has grown round and pregnant.

"But she is too old," I say, astounded and excited. I watch as Gabriel's face melts into a harsh red and he lifts his four arms in despair and howls at the ceiling.

"I was sent to speak to you and to announce to you this good news. But now you will be speechless and unable to talk until the day these things take place because you did not believe my words," he commands and then vanishes into thin air, leaving only droplets of water in the place where he once stood.

I try to speak but my tongue is no longer there. Not even a stump remains and I cannot make a sound. I rush to my wife and embrace her. We hold each other and I feel her warm tears against my chest. My own tears drip from my eyes and scald my cheeks. We cannot stay here. We have no choice. After some time has passed, we rise and make our way to the door.

The golden light has left the room and a calm grey glow remains. Tiny dust particles hang in the air around us, drifting freely in the empty space. I look back at the lavish cot and see it turn into nothing but dust.

We descend the stairs, which is far easier than climbing them, and emerge into the snowy winter evening. The sky is purple and there are no stars. A frosty, white powder rests beneath my feet and I cuddle Elizabeth. We shiver in the cold.

Emerging from the darkness of our village, are a crowd of men and women. They walk toward us carrying candles and lanterns that flicker in the wind. They are dressed in nightgowns and button shirts and they stare at us with mortal curiosity.

They have come for the midnight mass. But I am no longer a priest. I have no faith, no voice and I am so very cold. The sanctuary behind me is a tar pit that I will never go back to. I wish I could tell these people, enlighten them. Warn them. But my voice has left me. They will never know because I have been silenced by those greater than I am.

With nothing left to do, I carry my loving wife toward our small wooden house and lay her down in her bed. She smiles sadly at me and I smile back. I look out the window, at the emptiness, the death. When I return my gaze to Elizabeth, she is asleep.

Once I was a priest, now I am a father. I admire my wrinkled hands, the tiny cuts and smudges of blood, and I tell myself, "Behold, the Lord came with many thousands of His holy ones … to execute judgement upon all."

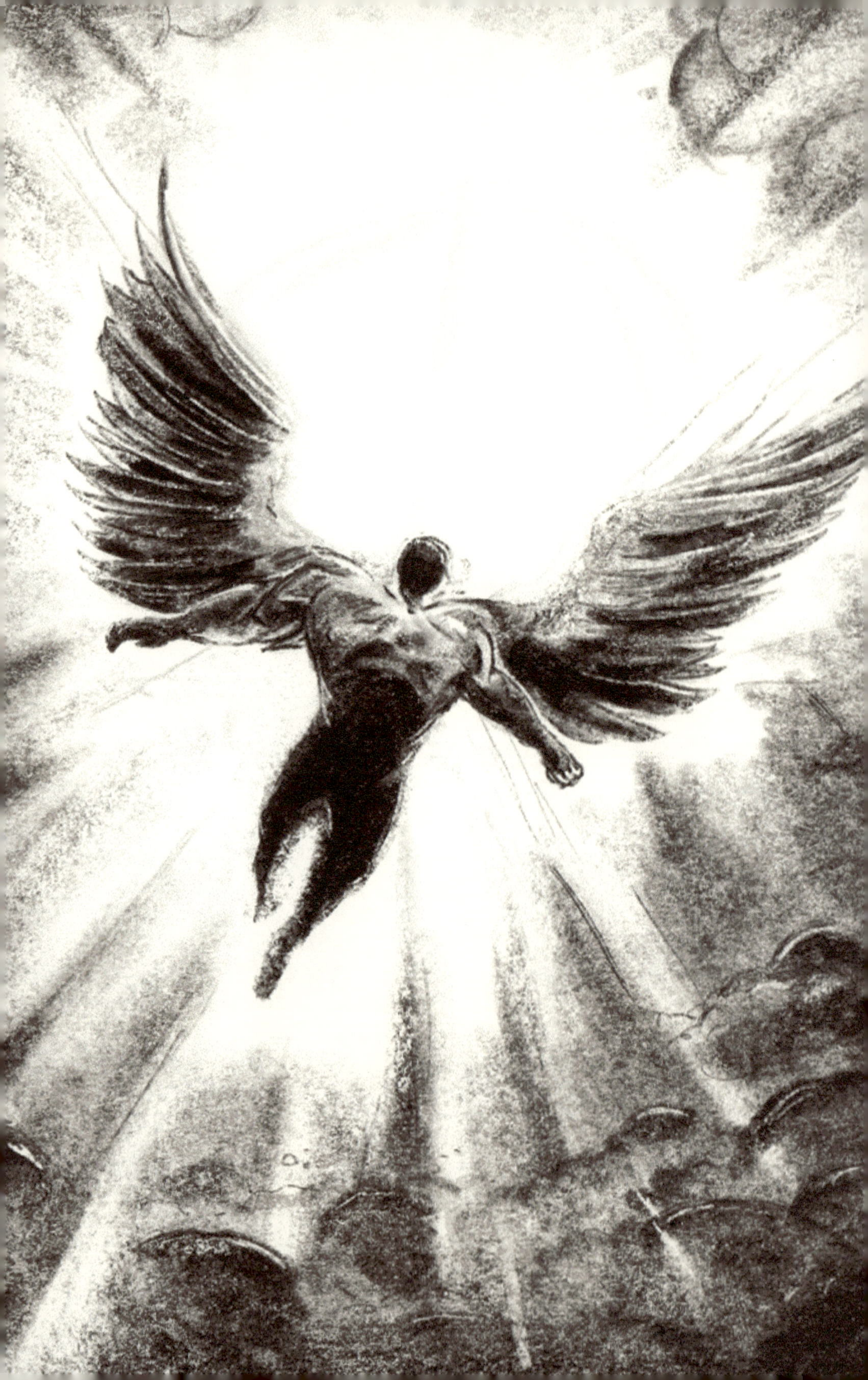

FELL TOO FAR FROM THE SUN

"Let me tell you about the afternoon that I spent falling to my death. Father, Zeus and multiple philosophers have shared a different version that paints me as a silly child who was careless and foolishly ambitious. I, however, feel like you of all people deserve to hear the truth. I was a very smart boy, smart enough to change the world and progress it. I had wanted to break the laws of our universe. They say I flew too close to the sun but, if anything, I did not get close enough.

"It begins, of course, with the issue of falling. That was the insignificant little hindrance that kept us held there, in fear of escape. To leap off the ledge in hopes of flying, only to rush toward the ground with wiry arms flailing and wind stealing our attempts at screaming. It was terrifying! Father called the issue of becoming a flattened pile of mush, 'the most brilliant failure of human anatomy since the opposable thumb.' It was a failure that he would do anything to solve and I admired him for it.

"I was a boy who had nothing to do in his meaningless

existence but watch and learn. I suppose I should give you some context, so I'll set the scene. Father and I were imprisoned within a room atop a tower in Crete. The room held two beds, a marble desk and a porcelain jar for our faeces. Don't make that face! It's human nature.

"How did we eat? Well, an ancient vulture would deliver us a meal each day, of course. The creature had been sent by Hermes the Messenger, a rather nice fellow who felt guilty for our entrapment but did nothing to help us aside from keeping starvation at bay.

"So, there we were in this tower and Father's hair was starting to go grey and his fingers were beginning to shake when he used his finer tools. He'd been trying to design wings for years so that he could leave the tower and move to a larger tower that had an even bigger desk. I was invited to join him but it was not a very welcoming invite, more a dutiful one.

"We barely spoke, in those years spent wallowing in captivity, ogled at by visiting gods and creatures of myth and legend who'd occasionally pass by. I know, it's dreadfully sad and I'll try not to tear up while sharing it with you, but if it makes you any happier, I don't think Father knew I was there with him most of the time.

"That's not what is important though. What is important is that I was old enough to desire freedom. I wanted to see the world and the sky and to escape the claustrophobic tower, where not even spiders spun webs because it was too damp. The stillness was making me itchy and I was sure, if given the chance, I would venture to places never seen before. I would enjoy every second of wondrous exploring.

"Excuse me? You think I'm lying? You think the real reason I wanted to explore places never seen before wasn't the need for freedom but the need to impress Father? Let me spell this out for you, little one, I have never needed him to notice me, I didn't then and I don't now. I do wish he liked me but that's beside the point.

"I can't deny that Father was a genius and, while it took some time, he eventually built wings that worked. He showed them off by flying around the room of the tower yelling, 'With these on our backs we'll never die,' or, 'once we've flown around and found a nice new tower we can storm Olympus and execute the Olympians themselves.' Even then I was impressed with his well-earned ego. That being said, I did have to stifle a laugh when Father flew into the wall of the room and knocked himself out, he only awoke after a few hours of gurgled snoring.

"We got up at dawn the next day and strapped the mechanical devices to our backs. I remember these chunks of metal with feathers haphazardly stuck on at odd angles. It was extremely uncomfortable but Father had smiled at me as he set mine up and I'd never felt so close to him.

"Together, we went and stood, no stood isn't the right word, we balanced on the bare window. Wind was whistling softly and I gripped the rough frame as I realised how high we really were. Then, and this pains me to recall, Father made a motion as though he were going to pat me on the back, but instead he shoved me off the windowsill.

"The wings worked, obviously because I'm here talking to you. There was this clinking sound and a screeching scrape of metal against metal, then the giant chunks on my back began to flap and I sort of bounced my way back up to the tower window, a scowl on my face. Father, lips pressed together into a white line, had shrugged.

"After that, Father gathered his most precious belongings and put them in a satchel that hung at his waist. Then he took off and I followed. It was as exciting as it sounds, twirling through the skies with the hands of the clouds tousling my curly charcoal hair. It was also quite hard on the muscles because the wings were heavy but the joy outweighed the pain.

"I flew next to Father for a while but he kept giving me these strange looks with his eyebrow raised like he did whenever he was mentally judging you. I had a suspicion of why he was annoyed but thought I was just being paranoid. That is until he cordially said, 'You're flying too close, give me some space,' and I knew that he was embarrassed to be seen with me, even if the fish and birds were the only ones watching.

"Oh, don't act so surprised, you know what he was like just as well as I do. He was a mild-mannered madman. And I thank him for being so politely cruel to me because it prompted me to fight back, to exercise my newfound independence. No longer was I in the tower wondering why I deserved to be punished simply for existing, my only friend being a man who shared blood but not time.

"That was when I turned my attention to the great ball of heat that sat even higher than the clouds.

"It was so beautiful and powerful. See, everyone thinks I did not know my limitations, however I knew that the sun could destroy me in an instant. But I still had to try and reach it, didn't I? I mean, who wouldn't. Plus, if I didn't try then I'd always be known as the boy in the tower, or the son of the great inventor. I wanted to see things for myself, to do something great that did not belong to Father and perhaps that would make him see that I was valuable, that I mattered.

"I grew closer and closer to it, but Father had not even noticed I was no longer with him. I called out to him but he didn't look. The heat was making my face turn glossy and I suddenly understood being obsessed with testing human capability. Father would always spout about being 'bound to a mortal body in an unsympathetic land.' As I touched the orange inferno, my fingertips tracing the light, I understood. I was in control for once. I had done something Father never had and that was impressive. Wasn't it?

"Then, my wings began to melt. The wax dripped from my back and the feathers scattered into the wind and I began to fall. I caught sight of Father's angelic form, I could just make out his dreadful scowl and unkempt beard and I knew how angry he was that I had made his outlandish invention look like a failure.

"Falling …

"Father grew distant. The old man became a tiny black dot against the vast, magnificent daystar. He still wasn't looking at me. Finally, he disappeared completely. My world, everything I'd ever known, gone in the blink of an eye. It was the worst feeling I'd ever had, aside from when the vulture forgot to bring us food for two whole weeks and we had to eat the cockroaches in the walls.

"Now there was a new issue at hand. We'd made our bold escape to the skies, laughed in the face of Zeus, the King of Olympus, but I'd failed to gain Father's attention and I had not considered the fact that destroying my wings would ridicule him and cause me to fall to my death. In retrospect it should have been obvious.

"I convinced myself that I could avoid meeting a fate that resulted in my soul being stranded in the Underworld's grim Asphodel Fields, where one was reduced to a shadow without thoughts or reason. When Father had still talked to me, he lamented about how I would end up there because I was dull. I really hoped he was wrong because it sounded like a boring afterlife to spend eternity in.

"I'm babbling, let's get back to my imminent demise. While I was falling, I began to notice magic forming in the air around me, as often happens in dire times such as this. Some ancient power stripped me of my memory, making it leak from my mind, shimmering in the heavens above me. I became a carcass of blank nothingness.

"This is where it all gets a little strange. Where reality and dreams converge. Where I was awakened to the beauty of it all. Time's march stagnated, held its breath, as I was caught between life soaring above and death's cold depths below.

"The ocean, which had been becoming steadily wider and more detailed, suddenly looked like a lake of fire. I beheld the rolling red waves, with gentle whitewash carrying algae and foam.

"There were three old ladies standing on the lake's surface, knitting strings with talon fingers and never letting a smile cross their vintage faces. A patch of the water around them was yellow from the urine that drizzled down their legs. You're allowed to gag at that because it was not a pleasant sight, and just imagine seeing something so disgusting right when you were about to die.

"Elsewhere on the lake, I could see Calypso's Island. It was this lump of coal on the horizon. I knew it was hers because Hercules, with his lion-skin coat and uncut hair, was sailing away from it; apparently they'd had an argument.

"Beneath me, a flock of nymphs floated curiously toward the sight of a falling child, their golden locks wet and stiff in the soft breeze and their tree-bark skin melting into the molten flames.

"Hold on a moment, do you even know who these people and creatures are? The three old ladies are the weavers of fate, Calypso is a girl left on an island by the gods for the crimes of her father – which, saying out loud, makes me realise how judgemental those 'omniscient' beings really were – and Hercules is that muscular man who was really strong. Have I really failed so abysmally at teaching you about our land?

"You know all about machines and metal and nothing about the nature that used to define our way of life. I grew up in a tower with an inventor so at least I have an excuse, but I am truly sorry that these are just foreign words to you. Allow me to make you care about dreams and wonder once again.

"I had snapped back to what I hoped was reality. The ocean was an ocean again and it was vast and empty.

"It all looked so green. I remember I found that odd, how I was surrounded by green but turning into a ball of red-hot fire. That's right, I forgot to mention that the heavy wings made me fall so fast I turned into a comet. Meanwhile you're complaining about how far it is having to walk home from Talos' cave.

"Back to the story. The depths of the salty ocean were clear in the summer haze and I could make out the seabed, which was a sandy tomb cradling broken shells and rustic drachmas. I swear the baptismal water had sung sea shanties while I fell. These wonderful songs about drunk sailors and pretty maids that made me want to see what lay hidden in underwater trenches.

"Though, thinking back, perhaps I was actually hearing fish-tailed sirens swimming below the surface. They were these mermaid-type monsters that would lure sailors on swaying decks, making them steer their ship toward rocks or reefs. The sirens had no reason for doing this, I suppose they simply found dead, sunken sailors amusing. If it was one of their lustful swansongs that I heard, then it explains why I was so cheerful.

"I finally hit the water and my frail body crunched against the warm, but somehow also icy, surface of the Mediterranean Sea. Immediately, premonitions scrawled across my vision, weaving a vivid tapestry that chilled my bones.

"I saw a voluptuous cloud that crackled with blue lightning.

Whenever the jagged blue flashed, it illuminated a shapeless shadow moving deep within.

"The thing that lumbered in that cloud was large enough to crush man-made temples, as though the stones were nothing but mouldy cheese. I pictured columns crumbling and the monster stomping its black-diamond foot onto the screaming, pale faces of men in finely made tunics. It would not leave bones behind, it would leave nothing except golden jewellery.

"The lightning struck again and I saw that the monster had skeletal wings. It drifted across the mossy countryside but did not flatten the grass and passed breathlessly through all the animals. The storm cloud rumbled.

"My vision shifted so that I was now looking through a keyhole at a tiled room with a mural on the ceiling. The mural depicted the god Hephaestus being cast off a mountain by his mother because he was too ugly. I noticed that someone was standing in the room, they had a scratchy, bushy beard and hair like a lion's mane. The man was wearing metal gloves and he was ripping the jaw off of a giant wolf. Blood spurted upward, splattering the grotesque baby Hephaestus and his disappointed mother, the loving goddess Hera.

"Once again, my hallucination changed, if that is what you can call the strange concoction of random images.

"The next thing I witnessed was the death of a divine being. The deity had died in a desert, at the foot of an enormous statue of a lady with a goatee. The being, not the statue, had blonde hair and there were snake bites on the swollen arms. It took nine steps before falling to its knees and collapsing. Sand covered the corpse and the statue's face began to slide off.

"I was detached from all these images. In fact, I still do not know why I saw them or what purpose they served. It was not prophetic or enlightening, nor was it anything to do with my own life. Some might say it's concerning, or even depressing, that my final thoughts were absurd nonsense. I will say, it made me certain that I was right; there was much I didn't understand and a lot of things to explore and unravel. I would not stop with the sun, I would turn over every stone in existence.

"What did you say? I heard you whisper something beneath your breath, tell me. If it was worth interrupting my story then it must be a valued point. I beg your pardon ... that's a ludicrous notion. You think Father's disease spread to me, that he made me want to be better than the ordinary and it made me a part of the problem? What problem? The destruction of Greece? How is the need to progress, to build, or the desire for probing and uncovering, a destructive force? It gave us the pantheons and markets, as well as brothels and taverns.

Why should I care about fields of wheat in a sun-bleached countryside or warm rocks covered in salt? Father didn't think those things mattered and he would ridicule anyone who longed for it.

"Let's move on from the visions because I think you're reading too much into things, there are no hidden meanings or cleverly planted metaphors in my story. I am simply recounting what happened to me as it happened.

"And, by the way, that is exactly the sort of pretentious over-reaching that has given me the need to tell the true version of events. Everyone thinks there is some message to my fall from the sun, but there's not. I wanted to touch the light, I did, and the one I hoped would care took no notice. If anyone is to blame, it would be Pandora for cursing me with curiosity.

Can I finish sharing with you? It's important we bond through me letting you into my history, my identity. That way we can grow closer and you can understand that not everything is some profound moral insight but maybe, just maybe, you might be inspired to do something as great as what I did: flying into the sun and seeing what lay beyond it.

"I don't remember exactly where I'm up to but let's pick up from me landing in the water. I was beneath the waves, tossing and turning with a terrible rushing howl splitting my eardrums. When I sunk into calmer depths, I began to focus on struggling out of Father's primitively designed wings.

"It was then that I noticed a glowing labyrinth that twisted and turned like a slippery eel. I knew Father had built this place because no one else was intelligent enough, this was the maze I'd heard rumours about. All manner of beasts moved inside its moss-covered walls, and the greatest of them was the minotaur.

"The monster flicked its beady eyes toward me. It's bull-head was stone cold like the limestone walls around it, and its tail flicked eagerly. But the human part – the body, the legs – they quivered at the sight of me floating in the water with jagged points sticking out of my back.

"I could tell it wanted to grab me, pull me into some hidden part of the labyrinth. I panicked because I realised that this meant Father had already explored the depths. No wonder he was not impressed with my plight into the sun. He'd already seen places no one else had, I was not doing anything he had not done. Angrily, I wanted to swim down and tear apart his architectural feat brick by brick, but I knew the more sensible thing to do would be focusing on not drowning.

"It took a lot of wriggling but I managed to detach the wings. They drifted into the labyrinth and landed at the Minotaur's feet, making a sand cloud puff around it.

"I threw myself up toward the surface, when I broke into fresh air I did not cry or yell in delight that I was still alive. Instead, I sobbed.

"Afterward Apollo, god of the sun, was pressured into giving me immortality. I've lived quite comfortably. I met your mother and we had you and I guess that is the story of your old Dad, Icarus. I figured you should hear it from me so that I could convince you that what I did was impressive, before everyone else proves I was a stupid child who misused his brilliant Father's ingenious creation. I hope you don't see me as a colossal failure, even if it's what I am.

"What happened to Father? I ... God, I haven't seen him again. He may still be alive somewhere, in another lonely tower trying to change the world without actually knowing anything about the world. I wonder if he came looking for me? Surely he heard about what I did? Perhaps, you'll meet him someday ... No, no I doubt it ...

"Son, why am I telling you this story? You're right, I did what I did for foolish reasons and I have tricked myself into believing I accomplished something. Father achieved the impossible when he built those wings, it let us escape our tower. But it was also Father's fault we were trapped there in the first place because he'd created an enormous maze that could destroy kingdoms which made a frightened king lock him up in a tower, and me along with him. He was not a great man so why on earth was I trying to impress him?

"Come to think of it, I'd like to repeat what I said at the start but alter it slightly. I touched the sun because I wanted to break the laws of our universe. Why? It's simple really, I was trying to please a man who hated me.

"I thought he hated me for my poor intelligence and lack of contribution toward progress. But the real reason, as I've come to realise quite recently, is my father was simply too blind, too jealous, too arrogant and egotistical, to admire how high I could fly without him. At least I had the courage to burn brightly."

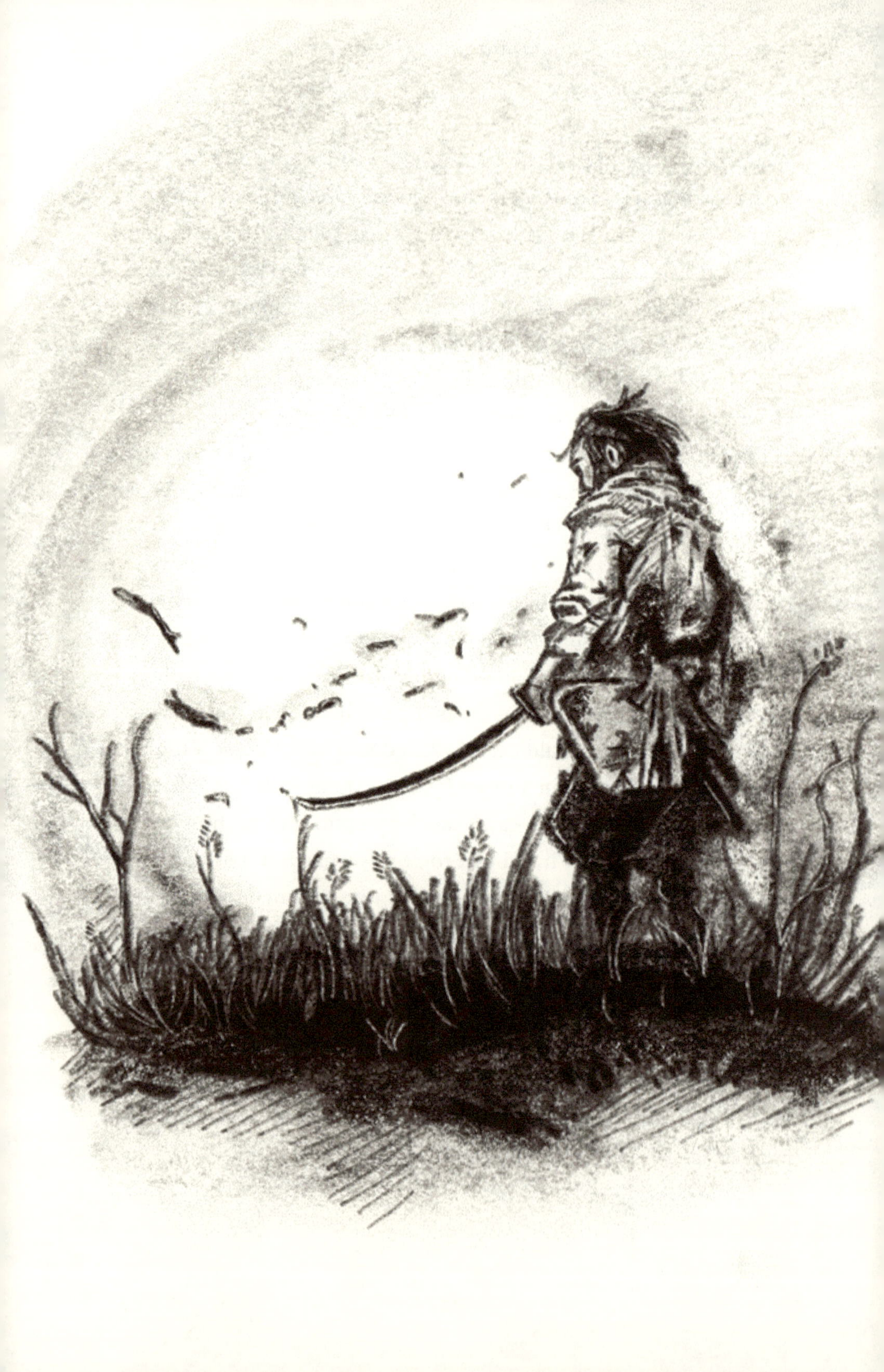

IT IS EASIER TO COUNT BEADS

The First Fight 鬪
Mimasaka, Japan, 1600

A ring of deep brown dirt was encrusted in the grass, caging the two warriors in a prison of calm ferocity. With his neatly chopped ponytail, Musashi tiptoed the edge of the circle, whirling his two blades in a manner akin to the beat of dragonfly wings.

He harkened back to the cold, gruelling days fighting with his father, Shinmen Hirata Munisai. A vivid memory bubbled to the surface of the burnt, blackened cauldron of his skull; his father's frosty *katana* stinging as it sliced a thin cut across Musashi's belly, the steam rising off powdery snow as he cleaned his wounds. Two years ago, yet the memory still burned.

No one can harm him in that way – break him – but he will hurt them. He will show them. *Ikagen'ni shite,* he howled internally, *come on!* He thrust toward the unnamed opponent, the naked mole with rodent teeth. He slashed at the sickly pink skin and broke the grim soldier's uniform with its sharp points and pointless breastplate. Who knew a duel against a stranger could cause so much rage?

Their blades collided with the deep-throated thunder of Hachiman, god of war, who watched from his lotus pedestal high up in the clouds. A horned bull's helmet masked his buried human-ity. From high heavens, he watched the two youths tussle on the village border; he watched the villagers nervously shutter their win-dows and blow out their candles while the "warriors" continued their deadly show; mostly he watched the imprecise swinging of katanas sail through empty air. And he grimaced.

Finally, with a stroke of luck, Musashi's opponent took a fatal step and slipped on a patch of damp grass. Musashi took the opportunity to pummel the stranger with his wooden katana, watching the young man's face crumble like an ancient statue. Cracked skull fragments sloshed around in the slush of brain matter. The boy – the dying one – choked on a swirl of blood and vomit. A violent whirlpool.

Musashi brought his wooden katana down, splattering the boy's head until the lumpy bones became a flat puddle. "You reap what you sow! You reap what you sow!" Musashi screamed as he brought the katana down again and again. Breathing hard, he wiped the flat of the bloody wooden blade on his kimono tunic, abandoned the gurgling corpse, and began the hunt for another duel.

A merchant walking past gave him a dutiful wave and congrat-ulated him on his victory. Musashi forced a smile.

Beginning of the End 常
Reigandō Cave, Japan, 1644

A swan gliding through clear water. White feathers. Its orange beak searing through the soft mist with a hiss, scaring away the nearby food. The current carries it through samsāra: the endless cycle of life, death and rebirth.

This carefully constructed beauty holds steadfastly in the glass mind of an aged Miyamoto Musashi. His brush dances across the paper. Nimble hands grip the instrument firmly, moving it in long, elegant strokes. Words materialise in wet ink then sink permanently into the soft white:

Pale Man With Regrets,

Walks Through Winter Mountain Pass,

Trapped In Frost Blizzard.

A lantern, wrapped in washi paper, rests on a dusty shelf above. Tomes are stacked precariously, though their positions seem precise as if the slightest displacement would not go unnoticed by their sixty-year-old owner.

A small cot is shoved into the corner of the cave, half forgotten. Most of the space is taken up by an enormous ceramic plate of candles. Above the plate, strung up on the wall, are two nihontos, a katana and a wakizashi. The blades are clean, beautiful. The polished wooden saya, the sheath, is decorated with etchings of lilacs.

The mere presence of the swords turns the dismal dwelling into a sacred site. No ordinary man would ever be able to steal his eyes from such mighty weapons.

Musashi, dressed in a hakama, has his back turned away from the blades. He's a wiry, grey-haired hermit hunched over a stone slab, weaving the last remnants of his identity into yellow paper. His ideology, his teachings, his soul, are reduced to a book. A simple book of no importance. Written by a sad old man. A nobody lost in this cave, surviving only on the sustenance of past glories.

He will not sleep tonight, for fear of having nightmares about the

Bake-kujira, a ghostly whale skeleton that drifts on the seas, searching relentlessly for purpose. Its approach is marked by strange, noiseless birds. This whale will sink any ship and drown any sailor in order to find its truest path. Since his father shared the folktale, the Bake-kujira's endless journey through calm green oceans has permeated Musashi's dreams.

He sheds such thoughts and stares at his reflection in the cracked mirror that sits beside him. The reflection stares back at him with a crooked smile.

"When will you die?" Musashi asks.

"Do I deserve such a fate?" the reflection cackles in return.

"You do, you are a foolish old man," he replies.

"Death is a release, a freedom. It is no punishment."

"Those who fell onto my blade would argue differently."

"They were young and still feared the unknown. Unlike them, I am old and death is an answer not a question. I must live, so that they will not be forgotten ..." The reflection slips out of the shard and into its own twisted world.

Musashi reads over what he has written today. Three pages, seven words in total. Seven words repeated over and over until his hand became blistered: Do not regret what you have done. That sentence, so finely printed on parchment. Musashi scrunches up today's work and throws it out of the jagged entranceway.

The crescent moon peers into the throat of the cave with a slit eye. Its curiosity always peaks at midnight. Thankfully, the lantern keeps the sickly luminosity at bay.

More and more, Musashi finds himself hating the colossal imposter's shameless imitation of the sun. Everything the "pure" disc stands for, he is steadfastly against. It is said to be so innocent yet its glow, like a shrouded veil, serves no purpose aside from acting as a deceptive guide. The sun, while harsh and relentless, at least offers an honest depiction of the world. It does not place this scarred land on an unjust pedestal.

Perhaps Musashi is being too harsh, he attempts to convince himself. After all, the two opposing celestial beings were actually birthed by the same creator god, Izanagi, after he purified himself and became two separate deities: Tsukuyomi, the moon goddess, and Amaterasu, the sun goddess. Two incomplete wholes. Yin and yang. Balance. Why do their daily and nightly orbits feel like a war for control?

Such thoughts remind him of his father. The harsh, controlling master to an innocent, young son. Two samurai.

Bitterly, he returns to his writing. He peels back mouldy memories and scratches them into his never-ending compendium. He needs to find some sense of meaning, a reason for all that he has done.

The right. The wrong. The evil.

His brush moves with a mind of its own, clearing his chakras. Like a fisherman on a foggy lake, pulling up fish without remorse. The slippery scales squirm, fight, as the fisherman grips the dying creature and butchers it for every last ounce of sustenance. Musashi writes and Musashi thinks and soon, he arrives at his father. Where it all began.

Musashi wishes to repress even more, to permanently leave a blank page in his masterpiece, but he knows doing this will never grant him peace. He has to go back to where it all began. He has tried to remember the many duels and forgive himself. But he cannot do this if he doesn't understand why he did what he did. The answer is not steeped in blood; the answer, lies in boyhood.

Childhood Purgatory 子
Harima Province, Japan, 1595

It was on the dawn of his seventh birthday that the young Musashi first picked up a wooden katana. It was a cold day in Harima and snow peppered the ginkgo trees. The pink of the cherry blossoms peeked out like exposed gums and the nearby Buddhist temple had grey sludge trapped in the curved eaves of its roof.

Shinmen, Musashi's father, drew a circle in the snow using his katana. A brown-eared bulbul bird watched from a nearby branch, bristling in the cold but never leaving for the warmth of its nest.

"Boy!" Shinmen barked. "Draw your blade. Prepare yourself." Musashi, who did not want to disappoint his father, did as he was instructed. Shinmen, without hesitation, unleashed an avalanche of rage unto his son.

"Fight back. Hurt me!" Shinmen growled. "You are nothing. Hurt me! You cannot, can you? Why? Because I am a samurai! I have honour, skill. You are nothing, boy!" Musashi accepted each strike of the sword with half-closed eyes and a loosely held katana. After a while, he stopped feeling. Each numbing strike from the rage-infected wooden blade began to seep deep into his bones. And Musashi slowly began to feel stronger.

...

Shinmen was once a legendary, fearsome warrior. He had a crooked nose and his torso resembled a worn-out doll with lopsided scars. To his wide-eyed son, he was a terrifying mystery. Almost a myth.

It was strange seeing such a man grow old, like watching gold rust. Musashi didn't think it was possible but the wrinkles crawled across his father's face as though an invisible spider were deftly spinning cobwebs. Each day, a fresh brown blotch would rise to the surface of his skin.

They had still duelled but he was slower, and after launching each attack, Shinmen would be reduced to crumbled coal whose pestered lungs coughed up thick phlegm and sometimes blood.

After losing one such duel, Musashi had been forced to drag the sliced ribbons of his arms back to the pit house; their self-made home, half-built inside a deep hole with a wooden skeleton and grass for skin. A samurai's home. Modest, to show that they were too great to be confined to luxury.

The blood leaked out behind Musashi, along with any purity left in his adolescent body. The misty twilight closed in with a carnivorous glee.

Behind him, his father had a smirk strapped to his face that was sloped into an S-shape, like a python ready to strike. But the smile faded quickly and suddenly when Shinmen fell to the floor in illness. It was only after he collapsed that he began to resemble something somewhat human. His face convulsed and veins bulged from his forehead, he squinted, stumbled. Musashi went to help his father but was shoved away and scolded with bloodshot eyes.

"Stay back, boy. I need not the help of a child. Especially not the help of a child who cannot even *hold* a katana, let alone wield one," Shinmen hissed, as he writhed in the snow.

"But father ..." Musashi pleaded.

"Boy!"

"I can use a katana!"

"You cannot. There is talk of a boy named Sasaki Kojiro, your age, who can cut down ten men in a single stroke. They say he is stronger than a god and has Zen flowing through his body. And here you are, whimpering in the dark."

"I will grow strong, Father. You will see."

"You will not."

"I will."

"If a farmer were to come by, he would mistake you for a beanstalk, and he would not be wrong. Carry on walking, boy, and don't look back," he growled.

"I will not leave you."

"You do not listen! You, boy, are no son of mine. It is no wonder your mother abandoned us!" As he spoke, Shinmen spat a chunk of blood onto the snow. Musashi, at the sight of his weakened father, let out a guttural cry and threw his katana at Shinmen's head. His father grabbed Musashi's wrist deftly and twisted him to the ground, coughing while he did it.

"You are weak and sad and you will go home now!" Shinmen barked the order, and Musashi obeyed.

Back at the pit house, his father cooked a bowl of rice that did little to dispel their hunger. Musashi was covered in bruises and at dawn Shinmen sent his battered son to farm the gentle crops.

"Farm when it's sunny, train when it rains." That was a proverb the aging man recalled each day.

After Shinmen could no longer walk, Musashi would bathe him and dress him and find or cook them food. He'd listen to his father boast of how his sprite son could never beat an ancient legend such as himself. He'd comfort Shinmen's frail, bony body when wolves would howl and scrape the crooked front door. He'd stay at home all day, his only personal time coming from practising samurai techniques out of a worn-out leather-bound book that belonged to an old shogun.

Eventually, his father spoke his final words. "Boy come close," he said softly.

"Yes, father?"

"You are my son—" His voice cracked and he sputtered into a weak coughing fit. Musashi fought vigorously to keep his eyes dry and his lips set into a firm line. *You do not care.* Musashi told himself. *Let him die.* But those words. You are my son. A moment of acceptance, of clarity at the edge of death.

"I will get you water, Father," Musashi said, hurriedly.

"No," Shinmen barked. "Sit."

Musashi did as he was told.

Shinmen's body panted and twisted itself like a clock turning for the final time. "Listen closely, boy. You are my son and that is the greatest travesty of my life. I have fought and killed and earned a legacy, I have been feared! Loved! But you. You, boy, are the one regret. The one mistake. You have made the final years of my life wasteful and filled with bitter hatred. For that, I hope you never find peace." Shinmen was hissing now.

Musashi choked on his next words, "Father, what have I done to deserve this? You call me weak yet I hold my own against you, the legendary Shinmen. You call Sasaki Kojiro great, yet he has been out in the world proving himself while I am here rotting. I wish to know why, please." Musashi angrily realised how childish he sounded, with fresh tears trickling down his face.

Shinmen went still. For a moment, Musashi thought he was dead. Then his eyes flickered like burning coals and some semblance of his fearsome nature returned.

"You will stay here and rot with my remains!" his father said firmly. His crooked nose hideous in the candlelight.

"Why?" Musashi's tears had turned to blistering anger.

"Because I am your father and you owe me that! You reap what you sow!"

"A father does not cut his son with *katanas* to prove he still has worth!"

"Boy! Watch your tongue before I rip it from your mouth!"

"Tell me why!" Musashi pressed.

"No." Shinmen's tone dropped. It was still low and cold and

cruel, but there was a rasp to it that was harsher than a broken sword scraping against rocks. It made Musashi look to the far corner of the pit house, at the dead candles and dusty cloth. At the ink painting of a pale woman with the ghost of a smile. When Musashi turned his eyes back to Shinmen, the old man was dead.

After he passed on, two monks came to the pit house and spoke in whispers. Musashi eavesdropped. He heard them whine that there would never be a warrior as great, how it was a shame Musashi was so skinny and weak. This made the boy, at age twelve, think back on those grey eyes of his father. Those disappointed grey eyes, strangely filled with sadness.

That evening, Musashi gathered his essential possessions into a satchel – wrapped rice, two sets of clothing, sandals, a jade encrusted ring – and grabbed his wooden katana. He then rolled up a parchment and held it to a candle. When it caught alight, he dropped the flaming paper in the centre of the pit house and left.

Looking back across the dark green fields he could see hazy orange flickering between the swaying crops with a pleasant cackle. The pit house waved a fiery goodbye, flames stretching endlessly toward the cold black sky.

The house burnt slowly and even after he'd surmounted the nearby hill, the foundation still stood proud, the wooden beams were bare and naked. Musashi could still hear his father goading about its sturdiness. A red ghost that could never follow Musashi, never track him down and burn him. A house that was becoming the ash and coal that destroyed his father's lungs. Gone.

An angry, solid wall of fog was draped over the Eastern mountains. The townsfolk had bunkered down in their houses, taking shelter from the coming storm.

Flies weaved their way through long grass reeds, into the

mouths of croaking frogs. In the tree line, Musashi thought he saw a wolf with grey fur and sad grey eyes stumbling through the snow, lost from its pack, and he realised they were not such fearsome creatures.

Musashi walked a long time that night, but he only once looked back.

Ignorant Enlightenment 忞
Reigandō Cave, Japan, 1644

Musashi poises cross-legged on the rough, almost scaly, rock floor of his cave. He's igniting words in his manuscript:
Resentful Daydreams
Frolic in Deadman's Grass Glade,
Filled with Hidden Blades.
There's a tenderness and a desperation to his working. He ponders on his pursuit of duels. After leaving home he'd set out to kill all samurai, destroy their cruel way of life and prove himself the greatest warrior in Japan. Thinking back now, he regrets killing the boy in the village during his first duel. All Musashi will leave behind are bitter tears from grieving mothers.

"You should've rotted with the old man's corpse," his reflection tells him from its home in the mirror shard.

"And prove him right?" Musashi scowls.

"Better than becoming him."

"I did not become him!"

"They loved you like they loved him. You fought like he fought. You are him." The reflection is calm and orderly.

"I did it as a stance against him. Against the samurai," Musashi explains.

"Then you have failed because the world is the same," the reflection says without smiling. "You do not understand yourself or what you want. You're confused and you're angry——" Musashi throws the mirror out of the cave. He regretfully hears it shatter into tiny crystals of dust.

In the absence of the reflection, a radiance fills his dwelling that was not present before, but the moon is out of sight. A lizard scuttles under Musashi's desk, its tiny tail peeking out of the shadow that the oblong wood casts. There was a similar creature in the Battle of Sekigahara, plenty of places to hide in a thousand dead bodies. But Musashi had still found it.

He focuses on the lizard's tail. Sitting in his cave at age sixty, he no longer wants to think of severed limbs like firecrackers or mud caked corpses sliced open and gnawed on by ravenous dogs, their entrails brown and wet – everything was brown and wet. He doesn't want to remember crawling over a half-dead horse as it whined and panted.

Mostly, Musashi no longer wants to think of the disturbing ringing of his own laughter. A laughter that had echoed across the fields and Fuji River. He had not killed but hacked souls from bodies, pulling out guts and tearing off jaws with his bare hands. He'd slipped and slid every-where in the chaos, finding solace in the blur of steel and flashes of bared wolf teeth. He'd stabbed and sliced and cut the enemy. There had been no time to defend oneself. There had been no time to showcase one's samurai skills. There had only been the horde of moving flesh and the expectation of a quick and honourable death. Except, Musashi had lived.

"One day soon, I will transform into the spirit of a jikininki, cursed to scour battlefields. A demon who devours mutilated corpses in pen-ance for a life filled with selfishness. A life spent nourishing a regretful romance with the mistress they call honour," Musashi tells himself, thinking of the glory and love his self-hatred brought him.

None of their praise was ever enough, and none of the death ever *made him feel like anything more than a scarecrow. A living, breathing pile of rotten sticks.*

They called him a legend, and Musashi believed them. Now, with the creaks in his bones and scars on his chest being his only mementos, he conjures more soft, purposeful prose. By writing of the battle, Musashi ushers in a great flood of sin – and perhaps a heart attack. By the time he is done, it's dawn outside the cave and he steps out onto the desert plain to lament. And pray.

War for Honour 戰
The Battle of Sekigahara, 1612.

A gecko was drowning in mud, the sludge was too thick for its little legs and it submerged beneath brown depths and stayed there until Musashi's boot crushed its scaly, green body. The dead gecko did not float.

A dense fog turned people into shadows and horses into nightmarish fiends. The muddy ground beneath his feet was prickly and wet, clutching his boots, pulling him downward. Sinking. Always sinking. Flat clouds stretched all the way to the horizon, masking hidden lightning and other foul beasts, and to Musashi it seemed to resemble that of an all-seeing whale.

The rain had ceased but not before drenching Musashi. His slick hair fell in his eyes and he crawled his way through carcasses. At some point, he fell into the open gut of Ukita Hideie, Musashi's *daimyo*. He was almost unrecognisable, despite an easily recognisable appearance: a saggy potbelly, unkempt hair and round, peach-tinted face that gave him the indisputable resemblance to a snow monkey. The man had never ceased smiling, except in death. Musashi's hands had sunk into his intestines, felt the maggots already wriggling inside like hungry children. A beloved leader reduced to an empty sarcophagus.

Immediately after Ukita's death, the memories of the daimyo slipped from Musashi's bloodthirsty mind. He would never recall the face or voice again. This was unusual since, other than glory, Ukita had been the reason for Musashi joining the battle. To help defend the land of a friend, a reason that was quickly lost in that dreary fog. Forgotten in favour of self-pitying ruminations.

The fog's calmness was an unsettling presence in the violent battlefield. Most of the battle was spent lost in that thick swirl, swinging a blade into the silky webbing, with the occasional frenzy of bodies coming together on the beaten path to clash swords and spit blood.

The Battle of Sekigahara – a battle that defined the songs and people of Japan for years to come – had really just been scared men dancing secretly in a blinding mist. An infamous Noh theatre. A private kabuki dance. Musashi savoured the art of it all.

Bodies like molten wax were strewn across the patchy grass with fish eyes and gaping mouths that reminded him of his sick father in those long, agonising final moments.

Musashi scattered such thoughts. He noticed the arrival of the opposition's reinforcements. The clans of Eastern Japan were clearing a path by slashing down the nearby Sakura cherry trees with swift strokes of their blades. Riding horses with goat beards and fire in their eyes, their hooves sending sparks scattering into foggy air. The *Bake-kujira,* the luminous whale skeleton, was being dragged in chains behind them. And at the head of this unruly pack? The famed Sasaki Kojiro.

The legendary samurai weaved his way through the playground of war. He was muscular and scarred, not unlike Shinmen in his prime. His body parts were out of proportion, making him unsturdy on his feet, always leaning this way or that as though he were constantly standing on an incline. His eyes were the frost of a frozen river. Cracked at the surface but thick and impenetrable below.

When he ran it looked like a barefoot beggar running on grounds littered with pointed daggers. Each movement was a swift stagger. Each slash of his sword was a rough artist forcing his vision onto the frightened faces of his victims. He slit gushing wounds across chests. He deflected every incoming attack as though it were a soft breeze. He fought like an animal.

One of Kojiro's fellow samurai took an arrow to the chest and collapsed to his knees. The young prodigy tearfully held the man in his arms. He murmured a poem under his breath and shut the glassy eyes of his friend. A guttural scream erupted from his disproportionate body.

You are not so great, Musashi thought, *all that honour and you kneel there and whimper when your comrades fall. I will show you what it means to fall.*

Musashi dove at him, katana in hand. Their blades clanged together and Kojiro inspected his newfound rival with an intense glare. His teeth seemed to jitter, but in excitement rather than fear. It took him one stroke to remove three fingers on Musashi's weaker left hand. A second swing of Kojiro's weapon would've separated Musashi's head from his body had he not sunk to the ground in agony.

Bright red blood surged from the stumps of his fingers and Musashi cradled his wounded hand.

Musashi spat, "I am not afraid of you. I have heard stories about how you are stronger than a god and have Zen flowing through your body, but I do not believe. I believe I can kill you, Sasaki

Kojiro." He tried not to groan and he hid his pain well. "You are the reason I am here. You!" he yelled, fiercely. The tips of his fingers were red volcanoes.

Kojiro looked the man up and down, searching his soul.

"I am not the reason," Kojiro said calmly. "And I will not kill a man of your talents. Not like this. Find me when you are worthy of a duel." His long hair seemed freshly brushed and his moustache neatly shaved. He reminded Musashi, oddly, of a wolf.

Despite the flat ground, Kojiro appeared half-hunched over as though the weight of his sword was too much for his body to bear. The revered samurai began walking away, disappearing into mist. Musashi twisted himself and called after him, "I will butcher every man and child in Japan until you face me. Do you understand, warrior! One day, I *will* crack my katana against your crooked nose and I'll gouge out your grey eyes and I *will* make you pay. Do you hear me! You will face me and you will die, Sasaki Kojiro. I am Miyamoto Musashi!"

Kojiro continued walking, in resolute silence.

Lively Burial 生
Reigandō Cave, Japan, 1644

Musashi is outside of his cave for the first time in days. He's kneeling in a crop field not too far away. The stars above tell stories more interesting than his own. Their positions in the sky appear so purposeful, so deli-cate. Creating everlasting images of boars and lions, great battles and rising kingdoms. They're significant and grand and not-entirely human but more experienced and knowledgeable than any human will ever be. He imagines what the stars might say:
    Nightmares Bleeding Out

Of Winged Shinigami Eyes

Why A Red Summer?

He tears his eyes from the blue-tinged heavens, ignoring the uplifting promise of salvation – knowing he is beyond saving – and glares at the hazel earth. Everything down here sways in the wind, unsteady and finite. He is an old man with a lifetime of experience resting on his hunched shoulders. The death and hurting of others, it has crippled him. He stares at his hand, the empty space where his fingers should be.

"Why? Why!" He screams at nothing and no one. "You stupid old man. You worthless, cruel, stupid old man! Look what you've done … What you are. After the battle of Sekighara, what did you do? You wasted twelve years fighting, killing or walking aimlessly in search of your next victim. Why? Because you were bitter and foolish.

"You killed—You killed a child on the cobbled streets of Kyoto. Did you forget? Why didn't you write that in your worthless book?

"You had no right to take that life, that young prodigy could've been something great and now he's just a forgotten face in your hall of fallen foes. You watched the fear in those youthful eyes and felt pride. That was not your right. Not right …

"You worthless sack of broken bones! The Yoshioka family. A duel beneath a moonlit sky. You killed sixty people that night. Why? To please a crowd of empty windows. It's true they ambushed you, leaping off rooftops and spires with swords or bows like demonic shadows, but don't lie to yourself. You savoured the dismembering of their arms. You relished the sight of blood seeping into the cracked stone floor, staining the ground you walked on.

"You, Miyamoto Musashi, are a monster."

Musashi finds himself wandering to the edge of a cliff. Below him, he hears the crashing of waves against pearly, barnacle-laden rocks. The spit of foaming whitewash leaps upward, trying to tarnish his dry and weathered skin. He looks out into the glacial stretch of noise. Out there, in the distance, he pictures his third eye chakra opening, and then he sees something ... Not enlightenment. Not death. But an answer.

A Wrong Man's Death 戒
Island of Ganryujima of Funashima, 1624

He arrived at the duel late, in a vain attempt to instil unease within his opponent. He'd taken his time rowing a rickety rowboat through the still waters. The crystal-clear depths housed families of aquatic life, with dough-shaped heads that pummelled their way through the depths and stirred nearby coral.

He'd crafted a crude weapon out of a wooden oar but always kept his eyes trained on the foreboding island ahead. The peach landscape held his vision captive with its calming breath. It was littered with uneven boulders, each placed lopsided on the clumped hills by the shaky hand of a nervous god. A picturesque battlefield of natural beauty.

Musashi had worms writhing in his belly, they had been eating away at the last of his honour for years now. Today, the autumn equinox, the worms squirmed with pink, wrinkly bodies and beady, unintelligent eyes. As he drew closer, the silent lapping of water proved a comforting distraction. Musashi masked the inferno in his eyes.

A lonesome figure began to manifest himself on a flat plain on Ganryujima of Funashima Island. A shadow with a crooked nose and grey eyes. Standing there, with hands resting on his sheathed katana as the sun died behind him.

Musashi looked at his own missing fingers and prepared himself for the duel.

...

Musashi, hampered by wind, strode up the hill. He stood defiantly in front of the seemingly great Sasaki Kojiro. They bowed to each other, but there was no respect tingeing the air. Removing the straw hats from their heads, they both rested their hands on their sheathed katanas.

Kojiro had a fervent energy, his toes barely skimming the ground. The eyes, though, remained still: porcelain ornaments housed in a shaky wagon.

Musashi had been in this situation countless times before. The enemy – *no, he is no enemy. He is nothing but silver mistaken for gold. He is not worthy of the title of enemy.* The "opponent" will no doubt attack soon, and when he does Musashi would flick his wrist and take three deep breaths and the battle would be over. But his chakras felt imbalanced.

His throbbing crown chakra relinquished a cherished tale shared by his father: Shinmen on a roadside in front of a beggar. The beggar was kneeling in the dirt in a baggy kimono, Shinmen reached into his clothing as though to provide money. Instead he removed a small blade and handed it to the beggar. "You are not befitting of life. Be honourable, *seppuku* is the way," Musashi's father said. And the beggar obeyed, stabbing the blade into his stomach with a wince, making Shinmen crack a smile.

Musashi, distracted by the strange imagery that leaked into his line of sight, failed to notice Kojiro's first attack. The sharp sliver of an artist's flesh-cutter whisked past Musashi's head. He leapt back and relished the soothing scrape of his own katana unsheathing from its leather bounds.

He entered the *sha no kamae stance*, with his legs slightly more than shoulder width apart and his weapon pointing out from his waist. Musashi's breathing was fast and heavy and he noticed now how much Kojiro resembled his father, Shinmen.

That same arrogant look that clouded all samurai. The sense of superiority in their suit of privilege. *Do I share his complexion too?* Musashi found that his feet could not grip the soft mud and Kojiro swept his legs out from under him in a disdainful attack. *He is faster than a stroke of lightning, but lightning is blind and imprecise.*

Musashi rolled to his feet, bringing up his katana in a brutal undercut that sliced Kojiro from his lower liver before becoming entangled in the arteries surrounding his still-pumping heart. The legend collapsed with a wheeze and Musashi felt the dissatisfaction coursing through his veins, tried to hold onto the fleeting sense of victory that he knew was just a lie made up by murderers to justify their savagery.

He wished the death had not been so quick. The years of duels and battles and gaining the reputation of a legend. That it had not all been for this one inconsequential moment. He wished Kojiro had parried swiftly and returned with a deadly strike. He wished that he had not gutted the one man who might have understood him. The artist posing as a myth, who yearned not to be loved but to be known.

"Careful," Kojiro squelched out the word with a grimace. "Your crown is crooked ... All that purple up there, is beginning to look a lot like red." He choked, gagged, his heart continuing to pump blood that gushed onto the grass and fallen leaves.

Kojiro continued, "Careful, Musashi! It is easier to count beads than it is to be a samurai. And you, Miyamoto Musashi, are a samurai." The final words of Sasaki Kojiro, spoken with a crooked nose and watery eyes.

Musashi said nothing. He walked away. And did not look back, not even once.

The End at the Beginning 死
Reigando Cave, Japan, 1644

On the edge of the cliff, Musashi thanks whatever higher presence has provided him with his answer. He stares out across the suddenly violet, glowing seas and admires the sight of the Bake-kujira — no longer a skeleton but a green-skinned mass of energy — riding swiftly across the waves. On the beast's back, balancing so precariously, is Shinmen. With gaunt skin and black karuta armour. Or perhaps, it is Sasaki Kojiro. Musashi can hardly tell the difference.

Miyamoto Musashi takes three deep, calming breaths and glides out toward the horizon. No longer bound to the earth; his katanas left behind to gather dust in the forgotten cave. Now, only a child's broken toys.

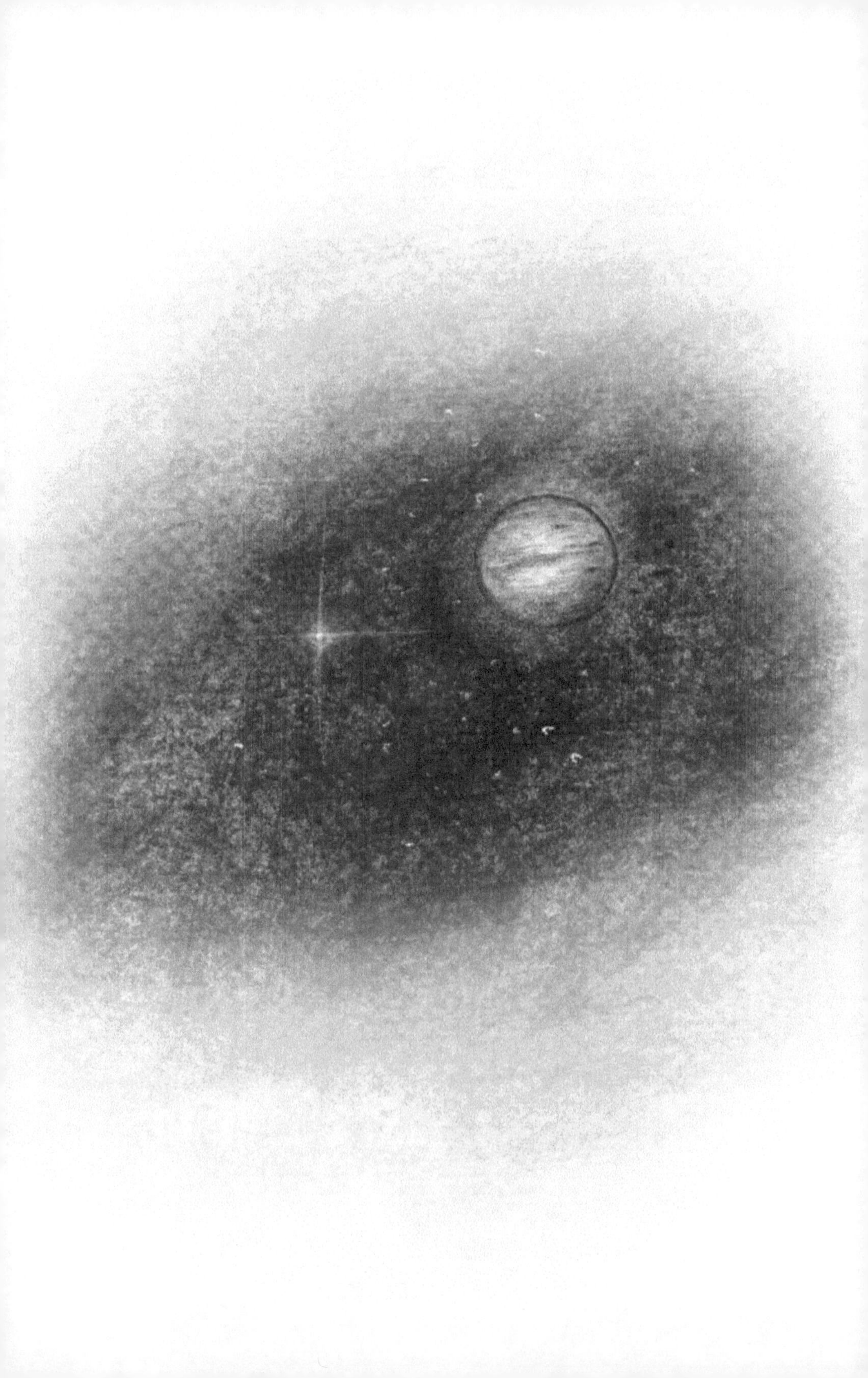

STARMAN

I am the Man from the Stars. Who the hell are you?

It was at the end of time, when I was born. I know that doesn't make any sense but there's no point explaining it. See, I remember being alone and afraid on a distant planet, at the edge of the universe. As far as I know, I have no heritage or family, no identity or name. I am a being of light that crawled screaming into existence with the earth's purple tentacles wrapped around my throat.

For a long time, I was trapped in the womb of this desolate, barren planet. Twelve nights ago, I clambered my way to the surface in hope of a better life. Now, I am stranded in this white wasteland of snow, an immortal being with nothing to live for and no way to die.

So I suppose that brings us to the unbelievable bore of present-day life. I am currently sitting atop a snow-capped mountain, admiring the emptiness of it all. Hanging from my neck is a golden charm in the shape of a pyramid, a faint glow emits from its hollow core and it warms my heart. I am unsure of where it came from or why it hangs around my neck, but I take comfort in its presence.

It is always night here and the rocks beneath my feet are icy cold. In the sky are two black moons with gold ringlets around their edges. My planet is orbiting a dead star, the ball of fire that once burnt so bright is now a hollow shell of blue pixie dust.

I sing to myself to try and pass the time as I sink into the cold winter darkness. While you drink hot chocolate in your warm houses, I am shivering and wishing that I had never been born before time.

The world I know is pitch black and I can only see the vague outlines of shapes. The stillness is deafening and I constantly look over my shoulder, half-expecting an indescribable monstrosity to be standing at my back. Its jaws would be open and red saliva would swing delicately from the cavernous mouth. That was a disgusting image but I think it goes to show how desperate I am for some source of entertainment.

I sigh and, to distract myself, I quietly mutter the words to a song I have never heard before, the words of which I only know from a distant dream:

"*I stare at the green hills, O so far.*
Atop stands a kingdom, beneath the brightest star.
Where great kings do murder and elders know all names.
Won't you come find me? Save me from my pain?"

I finish the song and notice, in the distance, a wavering orange light. It flickers and rages, indecisive of what form it should take. I sense life radiating off of it. An angry soul filled with violent temptations, but there is also a fearfulness that I admire.

A clump of grey ash hovers above the orange, before peppering the dim snow below. For whatever reason, the magical, flickering light reminds me of the charm around my neck. So that's what I name it: The Charm. Quite catchy, don't you think?

Ever curious, and with nothing better to do with all my eternity, I rise from my position and make my way over to the strange, alien light.

A snowstorm has begun and tiny shards of ice bite into my skin as I struggle my way forward. The powder is up to my shins and I raise a hand in front of my seven squinted eyes, trying to keep the orange glow in sight.

In the sky above, a slab of green light shimmers and a giant wolf uses the platform as a dance floor. I literally cannot describe that any other way, there is a wolf in the sky that dances on four paws and howls to itself like it's the Michael Jackson of outer space – yes, I know who that is. I wish so desperately to join the wolf. Down below, on my soggy little planet, I continue struggling.

Finally, I reach The Charm. A two-storey wooden house stands before me. The windows are smashed in and the balcony has crumbled onto the ground. The roof is cracked and filled with holes and the door stands ajar, revealing antique furniture and a large clock with the hands resting at 3:14.

Most bizarre of all is that the entire house is on fire. It is the middle of winter and I watch as the wood turns black from the flames and the orange inferno stretches toward the sky, cackling. I have never seen a house before, I don't even know what it is, and yet I am familiar with everything about it. It is like I have seen this place a thousand times before. It reminds me of the womb I was born in, the warmth is so very intoxicating. I take a step toward the fire, toward the almighty charming house. The allure of greatness ...

"Do not come any closer!" The detached voice of The Charm booms from everywhere and nowhere. The wind itself seems to shake with the almighty power of his command.

I stumble backward a few steps, crumbling to my knees in the snow.

"Who are you?" I cry out, desperately.

"I am who I am," The Charm replies. I do not understand what he means by this, but I feel this strange speaker has all the answers to my questions. He can give my bizarre, random existence a purpose. He can explain why I'm here, where I came from. How I was born.

"Who am I?" I finally ask the burning house.

"Dust you are, and to dust, you will return," The Charm says as if that obvious paradox makes complete sense.

"Why have you come here?"

"To say hello." There's a sadness to his tone, a desperation. I feel the endless pain of fire eating away at the frame of his body, his heart and his soul. I choose my next words very carefully.

"Hello," I tell him, awkwardly. The fire begins to settle, it doesn't flicker and rage but simply waves gently like the waves of a lake lapping against a pebble shore.

"I have been lonely all my life. And I need a friend," The Charm says, and I realise how meaningless and feeble the house is. It could crumble at any second and for what? To have spent eons resting here in the snow, with no purpose and no choice. I smile at the abode.

"I will be your friend," I tell him, moving into a sitting position.

"Okay," The Charm replies, so softly I can barely hear him. And so we sit together, looking at the stars. The flames slowly eat away at the frame of the house, but his pain is merely a forgotten ache. We both know it doesn't matter, that we are alone. And so we enjoy each other's company, and forget we were ever born.

Sometime later I find that I have fallen asleep. I am curled into a foetal position and encased in a tomb of snow. I open my many orange eyes and wriggle free, the sprinkles of white snow cascade off my shoulders as I rise upward and stand beneath the starry sky once again. I look for my friend, the charming house ... I find nothing but ash.

Desperate, I stumble over to a pile of broken glass and snapped wood. There's an emptiness in the air, a vacuum of space and time and I can hardly breathe. Please, let there be something. Anything.

Then, lost in the swirling wind, a tiny sliver of gold amongst the cracked and blackened wood. I make my way over to it and find a tiny golden house resting in dark grey snow. Attached to the polished roof is a chain. I pick up The Charm and hang it around my neck, alongside the pyramid that already rests there. The two necklaces clash together like ringing bells and I clutch them to my chest, breathing steadily.

"It's okay. I'm okay. Who am I? What does this all mean? I don't understand my existence or my purpose. I don't know why I'm here or who you were or why you came here or why I'm born or what it all means. Who am I? Who are you? Who am I? Who are you? It's okay. It's okay." My breath is a frosty tornado in the silence of the frozen tundra.

"My friend is gone. Was he even my friend?" I do not have the answers, so stop asking. Unlike you, all I have now are the charms around my neck and a foggy memory. My feet are heavy but I begin to walk back toward my mountain; the foreboding, shadowy mass that lies sleeping on the horizon.

This has all been a surreal dream and the footprints I'm leaving in the snow will be washed away in the spring. I'm a dead man who's alive in purgatory. A sailor who cannot sail. An alien born on a distant planet with no family and no home. This is a place outside of time, of reality, of logic. All there is in life is existence and the endless walk toward the distant mountain.

The Charms around my neck serve as a reminder of a hope that will soon be forgotten. And so I keep walking, for as long as it takes me. I cannot even remember who you are or why you're here listening to me, nor do I care. With my head held high and dry tears on my cheeks ... I walk.

I am the Man from the Stars. Who the hell are you?

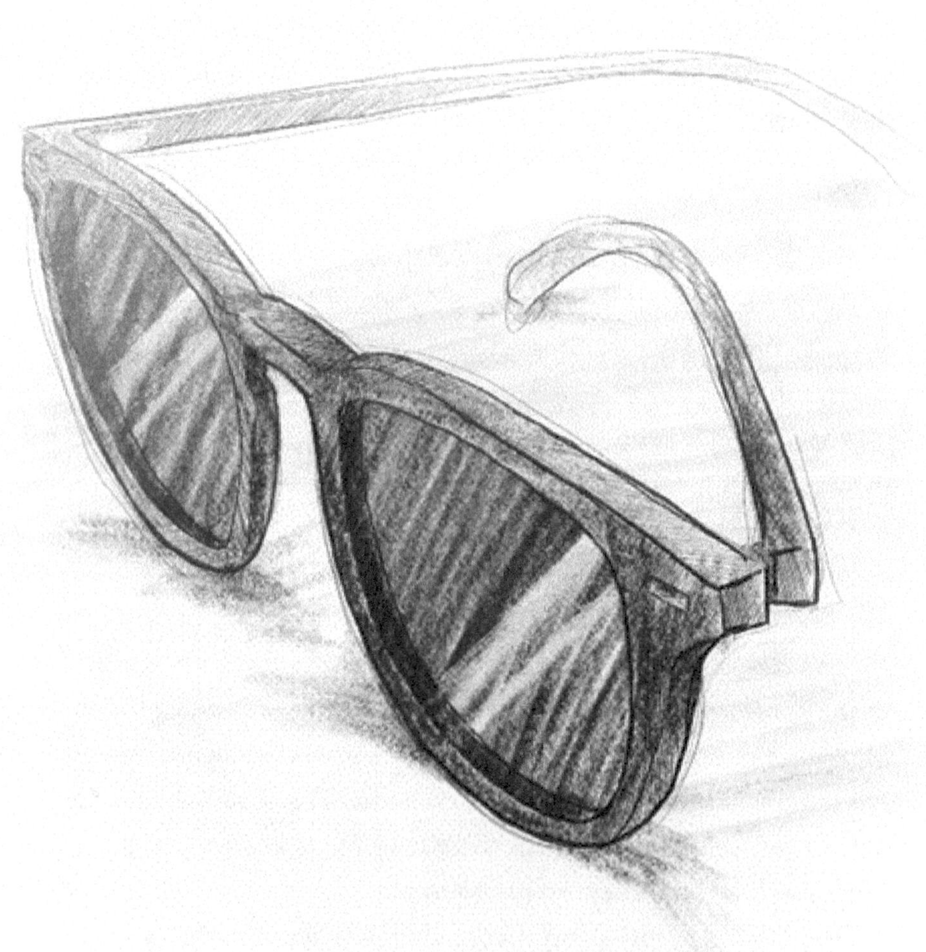

THE SALESMAN

Smile and sell. Smile and sell.

A pair of suave sunglasses rest on the thin nose of a hipster. His socks are pulled up to his shins, his sweat-stained vest hangs low against his chest and his frizzy goatee hides a pointy, weak chin. He's sitting on a wooden boardwalk on a plain black stool. There's a straw hat resting on the table next to him. If the soul of the undead Elvis Presley were to drift by right now, he'd likely be jealous of the mystifying charm that hangs around the man like toxic smoke. The King of Rock would give up his husky voice to have what this man has. He'd pay anything for that unabridged, laidback attitude. But Presley can never be this man. Because this man … is The Salesman.

Along with his straw hat, there's a collection of plants on the table in front of him. From prickly cacti to tiny pea plants – like the one in *WALL-E*.

The large window behind The Salesman looks into The Store. A single room that's somehow both cramped and infinite. The room is a labyrinth of cardboard boxes stacked from floor to ceiling.

Despite their relatively small size, should one choose to step inside any one of these small boxes, they will find themselves falling down a hazy rabbit hole filled with mankind's forgotten toys: jukeboxes, telephone booths, the short-lived floppy disc.

Each day, The Salesman reaches into one of the many voids and pulls out discarded, neglected items to sell to passing folk. Today is plant day.

The Salesman doesn't speak. He lost his tongue playing checkers with the Devil. He spends his time staring out over the edge of the boardwalk. It's always night-time here with a sky that's filled with bright yellow stars. But the sea ... the plasma sea glows a brilliant blue and there are tiny figures in the distance. Black silhouettes bobbing in the gentle waves of the horizon. Souls with a purpose.

The Salesman can never be like those folk. They're whole. Purposeful. Happy.

Instead, he absently raises a finger whenever someone walks by as if to say, "Aye, would you like to acknowledge my meaningless existence and buy a plant. I know these weird green things have long since gone out of fashion, but that's what makes them so cool! They're extinct back on Earth!" Nearly everyone who passes stops and makes a purchase. They all pay a fair price for his items, giving The Salesman their eyes or their heart. Some are generous and give him their beliefs or emotions. But none of it is ever enough.

All of his customers are lost souls. Walking in circles through the decrepit island of purgatory. The boardwalk is the last stop before they either restart the cycle of limbo or reach some level of acceptance and swim out to the great beyond. Either way, The Salesman still sells his useless junk and the fools are none the wiser.

It wasn't always this way. Once, long ago, The Salesman had been a powerful figure who had resided comfortably in a country of salt seas and slender columns that rose from the sky, stiff and rigid. The wind could topple nothing in that great place. The Salesman's only worry was being struck by lightning, with its blue veins and chaotic unpredictability.

It was here that The Salesman thrived. The worship and the adoration by the people he met were befitting of a man of his stature and nobility. There was only one thing that could thwart his absolute immortality, and that was a band of twelve elderly know-it-alls whom he disagreed with on a daily basis. They were old and gruff and resembled people but on the inside they were made of ice.

Out of spite and ego toward those elderly braggarts, The Salesman had stolen a fiery heart from a palace atop the tallest mountain in the land. The bright red soul was still pumping with life as he carried it down into the valley below. He was careful not to trip on rocks or stumble into the pits of hell.

At the bottom of the mountain, he sought out the first mortal in sight, a goat farmer with a prickly white beard and deep-set wrinkles on his oily forehead. The goat farmer bought the treasure for less than a penny.

Then, it turned out The Salesman had been tricked. For the bones of the unassuming goat farmer began to twist and snap and grow, morphing into a bare-chested god with grey flowing locks and a crooked staff of pulsing blue energy. The supreme being had cast The Salesman into a place outside space and reality. The beyond.

And so, it was here that The Salesman was sent to serve his time. Cursed to sell items for all eternity, as the faceless vultures who wandered past provided him with just enough life to sustain himself for a few millennia longer.

He has watched as this astral plane evolved or changed depending on the mindset of those who inhabit it. What was once plain wheat fields became an enormous stone cathedral, followed by an expansive office space of white cubicles and stale, flickering lights. Finally, it became the boardwalk.

All the while, The Salesman watched himself change with the place too. He started off as a hero of sorts. He'd been muscular and handsome and had tried rebelling against his imprisonment by refusing to sell even the easiest of items. Over time though, his skin had begun withering and he'd grown skinny and feeble. He had been too cowardly to slip off into complete nothingness and knew he had no choice but to accept this new world. And so, he became The Salesman: Hip, cool and always smiling away. That is what he is now. That is what he will always be.

Time is relative inside the bazaar; there is, and was, no now or then. No history or future. The Salesman has sold and will sell and the people have bought and will buy. At some point, he will run out of items to sell, the lost souls will cease and the world will go grey. Ash like dead fireflies will float around him and his body will first freeze, then shatter. But, if today is when the sun is still shining and tomorrow is when the blood moon will drain all colour, then it is today. And today is different from yesterday because today something strange happens.

It's after The Salesman sells his fourteen millionth plant that he first notices her. Unlike the other formless shadows that wander past his junk collection, she has features. Her silver hair flows loosely down her shoulders and her silver eyes glint with life. In strong hands, she holds a bouquet of dead roses. She is missing a pinkie. On the tip of the stub, the letter P is scarred onto pink skin.

The Salesman, as per usual, raises a single finger to draw her attention. When her emeralds shift onto his plants, he tries to unearth her identity. To know her worth. Yet, he cannot see anything past the irises. He has no idea what plant she deserves, if any at all. The Salesman has never met such an enigma. He watches her take a sniff, like some sort of dog.

"So, you're him?" she asks with a musical quality. Her lips retract to expose perfect teeth and a perfect smile.

The Salesman, always maintaining appearances, gives a careful and relaxed nod. He is still in control.

"Here," she says, tossing the bouquet of flowers at his feet before turning around and walking to the edge of the boardwalk. She leans on the railing, resting her elbows on the thick wood and staring out at the sea. A ghost train slides past her, carrying passengers to their homes across the universe. The gust of wind from the metal tube's movements causes the woman's hair to billow behind her. The Salesman smells pine wood.

For the first time in his six thousand years of living here, The Salesman stands up and walks over to the edge of the boardwalk. Behind him, customers walk past without making a purchase. He can already sense the energy in his body seeping out of him. His life source draining away and the plants already starting to curl and wither, turning brown in his absence. And yet, he doesn't sit back down.

He has no idea what he's doing, or why, but it is as though fate has forced him to lean on the railing and stare down into the clear water. There's a radiance to the woman by his side. She is not like the moving mannequins that populate this destitute zone. The Salesman has only ever met one other like her: a man named John Homer.

He had been balding but kept the final strings of his once luscious hair. One of his eyes was made of glass and he would often remove and pretend to swallow it as part of a magic trick that would end with him pulling the slimy gimmick out of your ear. Deft in sleight of hand, Homer had had a similar lifelike quality. So full of hopes and dreams.

Poor Homer had been dying in a hospital back home, caught between life and death. Even without friends and family, or a job or money, Homer had been special. The Salesman saw that. He hadn't tried to sell anything to the dying man and now he missed those crooked teeth and the harmonica kept loosely in the half-torn breast pocket.

I wonder if Homer is a shadow now. Wandering through this place without rhyme or reason. Oh well.

The Salesman removes his sunglasses, exposing the hollow chasm of his eye sockets, he cleans the lenses with a cotton handkerchief.

Submerged in the depths in front of him is an underwater kingdom of crystal castles and spires. The Salesman is seeing its wonders for the first time, he's never thought to leave his stool before now and inspect the world around him. Not that he cares much. Atlantis stands empty and barren. Poseidon has long since drowned in lava and Proteus is tied in chains deep within the Underworld, his flock scattered and his stories lost.

The Salesman returns his attention to the more interesting subject, the mysterious woman. She's rubbing the stub of her pinkie with her thumb and gazing into the distance. It takes her a long time to speak but when she does, it's mesmerising.

"I have this recurring dream," the woman says, not making eye contact. "I'm in a cable car. It's rustic. The wire could snap at any second. Stretching up around me are limestone pinnacles covered in green shrubbery. I can't see the earth below me, there's only unmoving mist. There are no birds chirping or any wildlife at all, there's only the creaking and the squealing of the cheap metal cable car.

"My mum is there. She … it's cold and she wraps a blanket around me, it's thick wool, with Buzz Lightyear stitched into the fabric. We don't speak to each other, and I know she's sad and tired and all she wants to do is close her eyes and rest. But she stays awake, for as long as she can. Every so often she mentions how the sunlight curves around gold rocks. She points out at an ancient noir-lit movie theatre, with classic films scrawled on the white marquee. It's planted in a mountain but the white clouds around it give the illusion of floating. I do not know why it was built or who attended movies there.

"I'm happy sitting there, shivering and giggling, happier than anything. Mum hands me a small, wooden box. It has this artwork carved onto the lid that must be a magical spell because I don't recognise the language and the oak throbs in my palms. My mother tells me it carries a secret, a memory, that was just for us. And even though I don't know what's inside, it feels like I'm holding the whole world in my hands.

"I'm scared to open it, scared to see what rests inside this tiny little chest. Mum places her hands over mine and I notice how frail they are, the blotches and the veins, and I wonder how old she is. Such a scary thought, wondering when an angel will die.

"Together, my mum and I lift the lid, just a crack, and peer inside. A bird flies out, a blue sparrow that darts into the sky. We watch as it disappears, its feathers spilling off of it as it flutters in the wind.

"Mum holds me tightly to her and a desperate laugh escapes her lips. It's the kind of laugh you do when you're trying not to cry. We stay like that for a long time, holding each other … And then I wake up." Teardrops spill from the woman's eyes, dropping into the water below. Creating ringlets that expand and fade in a constant cycle.

The Salesman tosses a cigarette in his mouth, holds it between his lips while he ignites the tip with a skull-shaped lighter. The purple flame flickers coldly and the first dose of sweet tobacco fills the empty space where his lungs should be. He reaches deep into his left pocket. Traces the thin edge of lady luck, she's been resting in the weightless void for him to find her. It is time.

He pulls out the simple item. He has been saving it for as long as he can remember. He looks at the four-leaf clover that's sprinkled with silver.

Holding it out to the woman, The Salesman hopes he is not making a grave mistake. There is still a chance she can be saved, and in doing so, The Salesman may add a few years of retirement to his own immortality. A good deed, well done.

"I—I'm so tired of being alone," the woman says, finally looking The Salesman in the eye. "Please, help me." She glances down at the item in his hand. Smiling, she takes the clover in her palm. There are words imprinted on the thin green, a poem that only she can see. "Thank you," is all she can say before making a fist to crush the clover. When she opens her palm again, dandelion tufts scatter.

Her eyes glaze and she asks The Salesman blankly, "Who are you?"

"Does it matter?"

She looks at the ground and frowns, trying to think. "No, I don't think it does." Once again, she gapes at him with a passing resemblance to Cleopatra, the last pharaoh of Egypt. "Am I dead?" is her next question.

"Depends on your definition," says The Salesman, leaning against the railing and flashing his pearly whites. He takes a dime out of his pocket and flicks it casually into the air. "Say, you look like a clever young lady who'd never say no to a steal. Can I interest you in one of my plants?"

"Sure."

"Fantastic." He ushers her over to the array of plants and picks one out for her.

"What is this?"

"It's a potted cowslip."

"How much?"

"Everything," and that's what he takes from her. She walks away and blends into the crowd quite quickly. The Salesman wonders if he'll ever see her again, or if she'll escape this place soon. He wonders if he did the right thing, and feels certain that he did not.

The Salesman returns to his stool as though nothing has happened. His world has returned to normality and he is thankful. He inhales his cigarette until only the butt is left, then squashes the dirty paper beneath a sandal.

A shadow strolls past carrying a dark briefcase, the inky head is wearing a fedora. It stops when it sees The Salesman's collection of worthless plants. With an unwaveringly cool gaze, The Salesman sells the sorry sod a pot of dirt and in return, steals the last of the shadow's dignity. He watches countless blotches of ink drift their way past him. All of them are meaningless and lost. Without hope.

The Salesman knows that he is alone. He is cool and stylish and convincing enough to make a blind man buy a book. But all he can ever be is what he is now: a merchant in a bazaar of lonely existence. And that is okay. Because tomorrow will be better than today. Tomorrow, he will sell an assortment of rocks: granite, obsidian, even serpentine. At least he has something to look forward to. A purpose that serves no purpose. More than most, some would say.

The Salesman smiles. The Salesman sells.

The Salesman smiles. The Salesman sells.

The Salesman smiles. The Salesman sells.

"This is the second death.

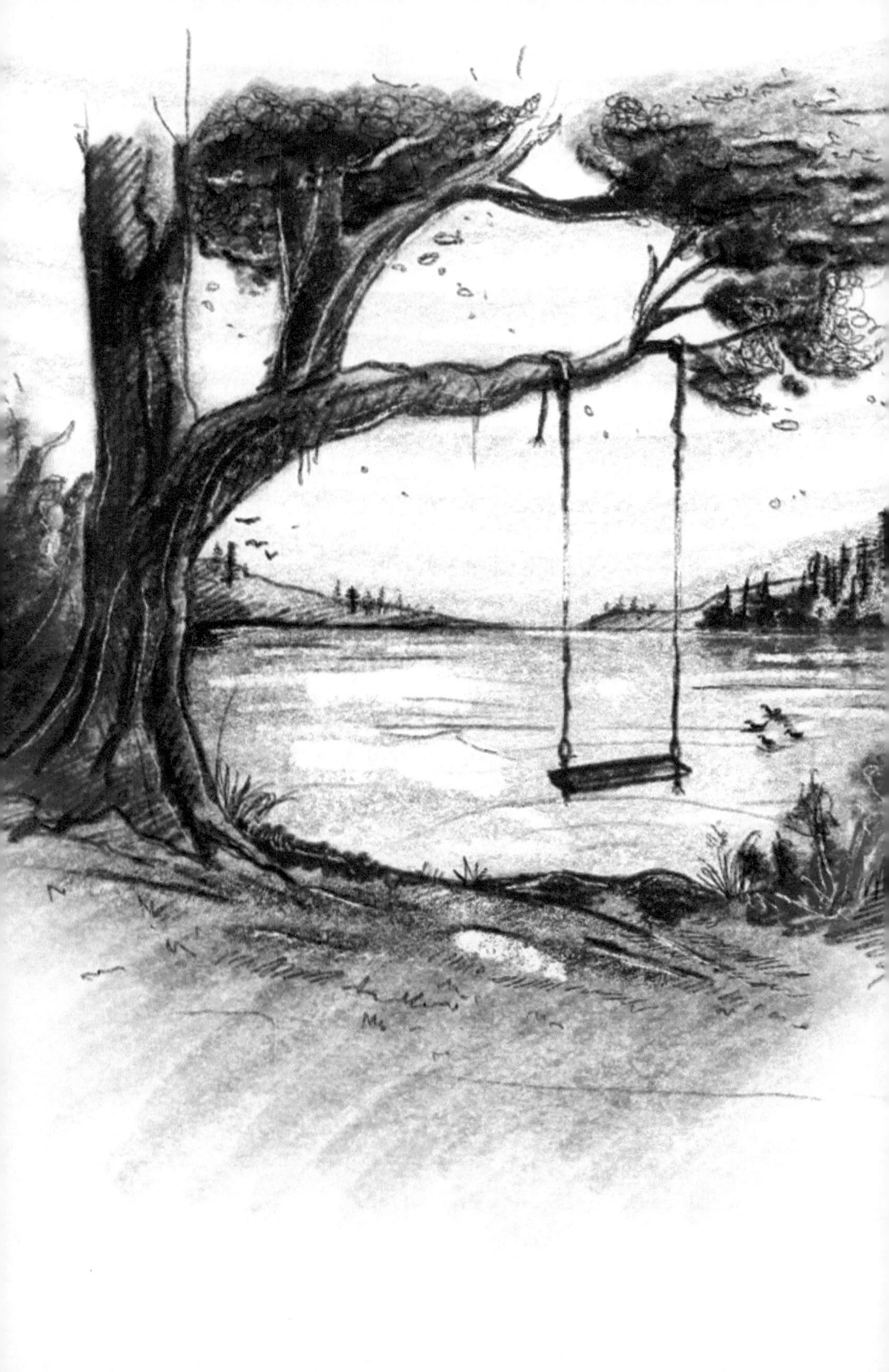

STARDUST SISTERS

Once, there was a lake.

It was not some primitive salt or freshwater body, it was Stardust Lake and it shone every colour to ever exist. The lake was a perfect circle, it was situated deep inside the middle of a volcano and when standing on the shore it appeared relatively normal, but if you went for a swim you'd find yourself lost forever.

This was because Stardust Lake held the entire universe in its depths, and that is meant in the most literal of senses. It was not a metaphorical or symbolic universe, it was *the* universe. Entire planets and stars and galaxies all drifted lazily, carrying life.

I was a young girl when I first visited the sacred site. My tiny hands and feet made it hard to grip the loose rocks that littered the side of the volcano. Strapped to my back, as always, was a silver bow and quiver, the string made from unicorn hair. My blonde hair barely scraped my shoulders and I carried a woollen satchel, woven by my sister, which I used to store firefly jars.

My eyesight was strongest at night, the moonlight painting the world in heavenly azure, and all the animals in the farthest reaches of the land were calling out to me in quiet voices. Asking for protection, for safety, for love. And I did love them. With all my heart.

It began growing darker, the moon slipped behind a cloud slicing up the light into paper-thin slats.

My sister, Atha, was ahead of me. She leapt and crawled up the steep incline with a dancer's grace. Atha was not meant to be good at climbing, we were each born with a purpose and hers was intelligence, but that did not stop her from practically floating to the peak.

When she turned back toward me, her grey eyes shined like lighthouse beacons that traced the landscape. She became silhouetted in the naked crepuscular rays. A dark shadow with hair hung in front of her shoulders to hide a bare chest.

"Hurry up, Emi," my sister called out to me.

I scurried up next to Atha and together we looked out across the vast plane we called home. There were rolling hills of crops and leagues upon leagues of tiny flowers and yellow dirt. In the distance, the palace was still visible. Its crimson roof made it look as though blood was dripping onto the white marble pillars.

I could imagine Mum gliding through the candlelit halls carrying a slice of bread. She'd make her way to each of her children and give them a taste of freshly baked dough, so that they'd have sweet dreams about delicious breakfasts.

Atop the mountain, it was dark and soon it would rain. It was easier to descend since we could just slide down the inner slope, all the way to the shore of Stardust Lake. I stared at the undisturbed water. Shimmering beneath the surface were clusters of stars, each one fuelling planets. Entire galaxies were expanding and imploding, flowers were blooming on icy planets. So many living beings spread across a finite amount of space.

Legend foretold that one day the lake would burst out of the volcano. It would cascade down into our land. Drowning us. Drowning everything. Right now though, the lake didn't even reach the curved rocky walls encasing it. There was still a sloped pebble shore surrounding the clear waters.

Mum always warned us not to go to the lake because it was a dangerous place, but Atha had once gone with our late older sister and claimed it was beautiful. The first time I saw it, I had no idea of the destruction it would later cause.

"So this is it?" I said, nonchalantly.

"This is it," Atha replied, already spreading a silky blanket over the pebble shore to give us a soft place to sit.

"It's smaller than I imagined." As I spoke, I picked up a tiny stone and twirled it in my fingers. I'd asked Atha to bring me here on an impulse. We'd snuck out after supper and ran all the way through the forest valley.

I sat down next to Atha and she wrapped her arm around me and pulled me in close. It wasn't cold but I appreciated the comfort. She had long, slender arms that shielded me from the evil that might come our way. Safe forever.

We stayed that way for a little while until the water began to glow with a green luminescence and our little alcove shimmered. Beneath us, constellations flickered into abstract art and I felt the worshipping prayers of different beings seep into my bones.

"Did you bring snacks?" I asked Atha, trying not to shiver when her arm unravelled from around my shoulders and reached into a cotton satchel. My sister pulled out two sandwiches and handed me one. We ate them together, in silence, the crusty bread and butter melting together on my tongue.

After we had finished eating, I felt at peace. And a little tired. I never wanted to return to the palace. I wanted to stay here with my sister. My wonderful sister. The only one who truly understood me, who was kind and gentle and honest.

I looked over at Atha and found her soft grey eyes were adrift, lost in the chasm of the stardust, searching the universe for answers and purpose. I became mesmerized by the details of her face, the way a dimple would appear on her cheek when she was deep in thought, or how her eyebrows would furrow and she'd scrunch up her nose. I didn't even notice the darkness setting in around us until my sister's face had disappeared entirely.

I turned my attention back to the lake and saw a shadow, in the shape of a centipede, wriggling across the waters with a clicking, cracking sound that made my skin erupt into hardened goose-bumps. The light that had filled my crystal heart suddenly vanished.

My sister was shivering by my side. At first, I thought she was just a bit chilly, but she began to shake so much that beads of sweat flew from her body. It was like when a dog shakes itself off from a swim, sending water droplets flying everywhere, only this was far more violent. I was quickly drenched in water, which distracted me from the strange growling emitting from deep in my sister's chest.

The strange centipede, which had been admiring the secrets within the lake, finally turned its hollow gaze onto us. Its face was so potently vile, it managed to crush all my happiness in an instant.

Suddenly, my wonderful Atha was no longer next to me, she'd moved away and I became very cold.

My sister's arms began cracking and snapping into disturbing shapes as her body tore itself apart. She was starting to resemble a disturbing creature. Smooth white bones that were long and hyp-notically pearly, and cavernous jaws out of which gooey red drool trickled. She looked at me without eyes and heard me without ears and moved closer toward me; each movement a painful jerk of stretched muscles and torn skin.

Panicking, I tried to think of the good times. Staring at the darkened waters of the lake, a memory began to spur. I clung to it, desperately. Atha and I … Atha and I … Together … Yes! It grew clearer. A grey fog lifting to reveal a luscious green rainforest. We were together and cheerful. That was my sister. The only person worth caring for in this irrelevant tar pit of half-forgotten daemons. That was my sister … There she was … There she was …

…

There she was, her grey eyes fixated on me, lips pursed in thought, resembling a raincloud on the cusp of bursting. She was analysing me, the rest of the oddities around the room lost to her. When something caught her attention it became an enigma she had to solve, and that was what I was to her right now.

Meanwhile, I lay in bed studying her too, but in my own way. She was wearing a casual white dress that hung from her shoulders, showing off her slender frame. She had just brushed her brown, curly hair because it was shiny and straight. On her lap was a golden helmet with a red feather plume. Leaning against the wall was a shield which fronted the image of a beautiful woman with snakes for hair.

"So what is it?" I asked her, wondering why Atha had woken me up this morning by lightly shaking my shoulder.

She was perched on the edge of my cotton mattress and replied curtly, "Just a moment, you have to wake up properly so that you can pay better attention."

I grumbled at this because I knew it signified an incoming monologue about some intellectual topic that would go over my head. I had barely learnt to walk but already Atha wanted to spend a lot of time with me because, while we had other siblings, they were far more obnoxious.

I should add that my sister was a touch mean to the rest of our family. I would often wake up in the middle of the night and hear her shouting at Mum. She would always say how we were all evil and selfish and shouldn't have all this. I'd assumed it was just how older girls acted toward their mother, and she never acted that way around me.

"Here we go," Atha finally said and rushed into a long story about some huntress who got eaten by a mongoose and then a lot of other random characters became involved.

I wanted, more than anything, to experience for myself the exciting adventures this huntress underwent, so I made Atha a challenge. She had to give me three questions and if I answered correctly then I could choose what we did for a change.

"Okay," Atha said, the three questions igniting in her head instantaneously. "First question, who was the one who gave Atalanta the boar head?"

"Meleager," I replied quickly and surely.

"Okay. What do barbegazi do for fun?" Atha asked and I racked my brain to our last family holiday to the nearby snow-capped mountains of Niflheim.

"Surf avalanches," I said, remembering the humorous image of a tiny gnome sliding on his belly down an avalanche, frosty white beard speckled with snow.

"Final question, how did Baldur die?"

"Mistletoe," I said, once again sure of myself. Atha nodded and relented with a wave of her hand – her way of saying, *fine, you win.* I decided we would go out into the valley below the palace.

So, we walked out of the main gates into the fresh morning sunshine. Past the fir trees and down the cobbled yellow road. Then, we stepped off the beaten track and into the thick forest. The pine trunks swayed around us and I remember jumping at the sight of a frog leaping across a row of rocks.

There were lots of little pools around the forest. Fresh springs trickled through small trenches in the dirt. Up above, lemurs played with each other on branches, their bushy tails trailing behind them.

We sought out the tallest tree around and I challenged Atha to race me to the top. The trunk was covered in green moss and when you peeled back the bark there were cobwebs and maggots wriggling around. We swung and pulled our way up the tree; my tiny feet were able to squeeze into smaller footholds but we both reached the top at the same time. The pine tree bent under our weight like an old crone with a crooked back.

"It's nice up here," Atha said as we leaned against the trunk with our arms thrown over a thick branch to keep us sturdy. "I'm glad you brought me."

"I'm glad you came," I said, thoughtlessly, and was surprised by the sad look that filled Atha's eyes.

She went to say something, then stopped herself. "Emi," she said, "you know what we are. Don't you?"

"I think so," I said uncertainly.

"And you know what it means, don't you? It means we have responsibilities. To this place … This land. There are living creatures that rely on us. An entire universe rests beneath our feet."

"What're you saying?"

Atha paused for a moment, "I'm saying that I love you. And even though I fight with Mum and don't speak with Dad, I love them too. But you and I, we've got to stick together. Yes?" There was a finality to the way she said that, years later I would come to see it as a pre-emptive goodbye.

"Yes," I told her and that was that. A simple word that held the weight of the world.

"Alright," she replied. "Now, let's have some fun. Shall we?"

We'd brought slingshots with us and from our perch on the topmost branches, we could see the servants wandering around the palace grounds. Atha and I tried shooting the golden platters out of the hands of the well-groomed men.

An eagle flew onto the tip of our tree. The black feathers were oily like tar and its yellow beak sharp enough to pierce the skin.

Atha and I admired the beautiful bird and, without speaking, we made a mutual agreement to move closer to it. Atha eased her way higher up the tree and I followed. The eagle had not yet noticed our presence and was silently gnawing on its side, removing a bug.

I was lower down than my sister and my eyes drifted from the eagle to the underside of Atha's boot. I watched as a thin branch snapped underneath her weight.

The eagle turned its clean, white head toward us and gave Atha a piercing stare. With blinding speed and precision, a taloned claw sliced open Atha's face. Before I knew what was happening, she had plummeted from the tree and landed with a thud on the ground below.

"Atha!" I yelled, leaping from my branch and landing on the soft brown earth, sending dirt scattering into the air and making a small crater form at my feet. Above me, the eagle gave a squawk and dove into the sky with its wings stretching tightly. "Oh no, Atha! I'm so sorry. Are you alright?"

Atha looked up at me with big eyes and, smiling, she said, "I'm fine, Emi. Bit of a vicious eagle, huh?" She shrugged off the twigs that had stuck to her clothes and gently dabbed her finger on the cuts on her cheek, lightly wincing.

"At least you got some wicked battle scars out of it." I grinned cheekily back at her. Then we laughed and we—

...

"Emi?" My sister asked bluntly, snapping me out of the surreal memory. I looked over at her; Atha no longer resembled a hideous creature. She once again looked and sounded like my sister, but there was something a little off. She was tucking a strand of hair behind her ear but the movement was stiff and forced. Robotic.

The lake was also as it was before. Bright and colourful and full of light. And yet, it felt different. More sinister. As if the innocent universe, with its vast array of sparkly planets, was merely a facade to hide its true nature: an evil nature.

"Yes?" I finally replied to my sister.

Atha was moving her head from side to side in the same way serpent's do when they're under the spell of a snake charmer's pungi. "Why're we here?" Her voice was unusually monotone; her words were spilling from her mouth like a leaky faucet.

"What do you mean?"

"Why're we here?" she repeated the question.

"I guess, to get out of the palace for the evening."

"Why, though?"

"I don't know."

"Because you're afraid?" she said with a sharp and icy tone. I was a little taken aback, she had never used that tone with me before. I'd heard it used on others, especially my mother, but Atha had always been so kind and gentle toward me.

Atha was a tad strange though. Her heart, like mine, was made of crystal. It was the source of our "mortal" emotions but it also allowed us to telepathically connect and recognise our brethren. I'd always had trouble finding Atha's core, I didn't know why but she would often choose to become detached. However, you'd always be able to find a tiny sliver of a soul, deep down. And that sliver was what had made Atha giggle when we were little girls.

Right now, I could not sense anything within Atha except piping hot tar that was trickling through her veins. Her red crystal must be floating outside her body, somewhere above the lake, invisible to the naked eye.

"Why … Why would you say that?" I stuttered.

"Because I'm young enough to speak my mind without thinking, but old enough to know what it means to be in pain."

"I …" No words would come to me. Atha's dead eyes traced my face as if she were seeing me for the very first time. My gut twisted as though a worm were slithering through the thin channels of my bowels.

"Do we matter, Emi?"

"What! Of course. How can you say something so awful?"

"What makes you so sure?"

"You matter to me. I hope I matter to you."

"Grandfather didn't matter. Dad cut him up like a butcher and tossed the dismembered pieces into the depths of this lake. Grandfather's probably still sinking, a million pieces in an infinite abyss."

"We're not Grandfather. And we're not meant to talk about him."

"If tomorrow we ceased to exist, do you think this lake would dry up? Or would we simply be replaced? You're a smart kid, Emi. You know the answer. Nothing would change. Our world would trudge onward and this lake would prosper. So what does it matter?"

"Mum would be sad."

"For a while, yes. A superficial sort of sadness. But she'd have an eternity to move on and enough siblings and children to comfort her for as long as she needed."

"Hey! You're supposed to be the wise one in the family. *My* older sister. So stop with this existential and, frankly, silly nonsense."

"The wise one? According to who? The ones who worship me? So because this lake calls me wise, calls me a born leader, that means I can't be naive and incompetent or … a little pessimistic towards all this preordained rubbish."

"So what about me? I don't matter?"

"I've been around since the dawn of time, Emi. Yet I'm stuck in a child's body! I love you, sister, but the truth is the truth and all of this … it isn't real. You know it and I know it. That is why we are here, why you asked to see the lake because deep down, you know the truth. It is time."

It was then that I started crying, "S-so … why? What's the point then, huh? Why keep going if it's all just a big con, a stupid lie. Why?"

"There's nothing wrong with meaninglessness. So long as you're aware of it." Her voice was strained like she was being strangled. There were lumps forming beneath her skin, all over her body. They were bubbles that moved around of their own accord. What was happening to my sister!

"Atha, snap out of it. What's wrong with you!" I finally yelled out. "I know you're in there and I love you. Do you hear me?" I said, trying to bring her back from the brink.

There was a brief silence. Tiny waves were lapping against the pebble shore, trying to reach us, hold us. Us, the last two people in the universe. Sitting here during The Twilight of The Gods, wondering if the scary fables Mum read to us every full moon were in fact true. Was this place, which seemed so pretty, really filled with evil? I knew my sister was having the same thoughts because she suddenly sucked in sharply.

"Em-Emi?" Atha asked, tears trickling down her cheeks. "W-where am I? I'm so afraid!" She was sobbing now. Big hiccups racked her body and reduced her from an all-powerful immortal to a sad little girl afraid of the future.

"It's going to be okay, Atha. Remember when we were little, and I mean really little. Remember how scared I got when Dad came home and the sky above was full of thunder, it was so loud. But those bright flashes of blue lightning would freeze the world. For a split second, time would stop and I'd see you were as scared as I was. Do you remember that?"

She started nodding, "I remember that, but, Emi … is this the end for me? It can't be, can it?" Her eyes were starry marbles, but they were also murky.

"Yes," I replied, "I think it is." A strange certainty came over me and I knew this was what had to happen. I didn't understand anything but I somehow knew everything. My sister had died the moment we climbed down to the shore of Stardust Lake, but I had to stick with her, I had to help her in any way that I could.

Atha's breathing became more panicked, her snotty nose dribbling. "Remove this cup from me, Emi! It's not what I want. Please, it's not what I want … it's not what I want." She kept repeating those words over and over. Her brain had melted, all she knew now were those five words.

I wanted nothing more than to curl into a ball.

Atha's neck cracked sharply as she tilted her head back and

looked at the blank night sky. It was an empty canvas that was yet to be painted by a new creator god. Her dry lips peeled back, exposing crooked teeth that had been crudely carved into fangs, and she let out an agonising scream that made the waters ripple and the entire subterranean universe quiver with fear.

She leapt at me with a ferocity I didn't know she possessed. Clawing at my eyes with brown, worn-out fingernails and shoving a bony knee into my stomach. I doubled over gasping for air but Atha did not relent. She snarled and snapped her teeth at me while the sides of her mouth began to foam.

Still kneeling, I gripped one of the rocks by my feet and slowly stood. I waited, patiently, for my sister to make the next move, clenching the heavy stone with a fierce but sweaty grip.

There was a painstaking pause. Atha and I stood opposite one another, staring into each other's eyes, waiting for what would happen next. We were being led by our emotions, by something deep within our souls and all our memories and sisterhood and love was evaporating with each steaming breath that hissed out of our mouths and into the cold night air. This was it …

Atha screeched and scrambled on all fours toward me, her shoulder blades hunched into pyramids and her neck going limp to let her head hang low, barely skimming the ground. I swung the pebble in my hand as hard as I could and felt it connect with the side of her temple, but not before Atha had the chance to wrap both arms around me.

Together, we tumbled down the slight slope toward the water. Both of us were scratching and wriggling out of the other's grip.

The waves on Stardust Lake grew larger, more frantic. How funny, the entire cosmos was excited to devour two frightened little girls.

No! I thought to myself. *This is my sister. You won't take her from me ... You can't.*

I stopped fighting. I let the sharp rocky terrain shred and peel away my skin and I let my sister carry me down into the darkness. Gently, with as much grace as possible, I slipped my arms around Atha's torso and hugged her tightly. Slowly, her skin began to grow warmer again and I could feel her crystal pulsing with the same beat as mine.

I locked eyes with my sister and saw the fear and the pain that had been her whole life. A life I never truly knew or understood. This wasn't her fault. This lake had sliced her open and spilled her guts for all to see. This was the sacrifice of the gods. This was how those planets and their life survived. Off of our surrendering. Our deaths and resurrections. The cycle of grief that we could never escape from because we were trapped here, in a palace, by a lake, with nowhere else to go but down. Down into the lights. Into the fire.

"I'm sorry," Atha said.

Before I could respond, she shoved me away from her. I came to a stop at the edge of the deadly water. Atha continued rolling down and the lake reached out and grabbed her. Atha screamed but it didn't come from her mouth, her voice was already a part of the water and it echoed off the slate walls of the volcano.

The current was already pulling her body to its centre. Her red crystal core glittered through her skin. She opened clear grey eyes and smiled at me, a truly happy smile. Then, she began to evaporate into starlight particles that shone brighter than anything I had ever seen before.

The constellations that appeared on the surface resembled her face when it was still sweet and innocent, and hopeful. You could even see the freckles dotted around her cheeks and the tiny scar above her eyebrow.

My sister dissolved into bright green stardust, her body spreading across the universe to form new galaxies and birth new people. It was so mesmerizing to watch that I actually turned to tell Atha about it, wanting to share this moment with her. The empty space next to me was deadly.

The worst part about all of it was knowing I would walk back home all by myself and climb into my warm, cosy bed. Tomorrow, everyone would realise what had happened and, at some point, there would be a funeral. How can you have a funeral for someone if they're not really dead?

I noticed now that on the far crest of the volcano was a dead tree. It had been badly burnt and I could sense the ash hovering around it like a faded aura. The branches twisted into each other like thick black veins.

I passed my memories of Atha onto the tree, to hold it forever, and perhaps that would be enough because one day, when I'm ancient and weary, my time will come and I will pass on and join her. One day, my sister and I will become the universe and all her beauty, we will be together as one ball of ever-expanding light.

I will only remember that,

Once, long ago, I had a sister.

Once, she had a soul.

Once, there was a lake.

Once,

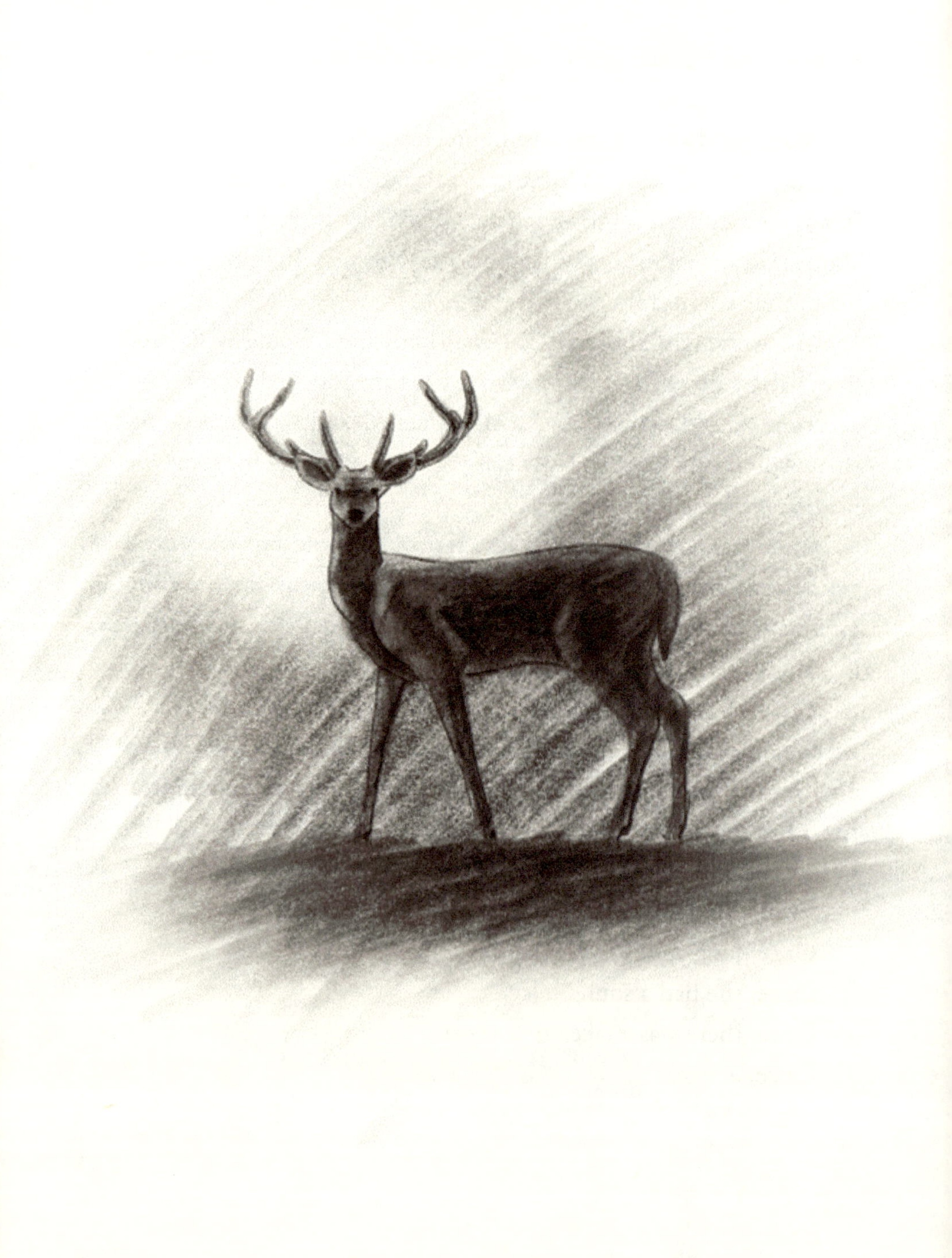

DEER HEAD

I. Hunting a Beast

The wagon rocks and rolls as the horses trot up the hill. An old stone wall covered in moss follows alongside the gravel path. Several times the wagon lurches threateningly toward the wall, but the pair never meet. At the crest of the hill, an ancient angel oak tree awaits their arrival. Its tentacle branches snake across the sky like a spider perched against the wall of heaven. A bad omen to most travellers, but the folk in this wagon pay it no heed.

The twang of a mandolin, plucked by delicate fingers, rings out across the weathered landscape. The high-pitched wail of a harmonica soon joins it. A painful tune of hope and redemption that bruises the senses. The horses stop, and the wagon shudders to a halt; the animals cock their heads to the music. The Driver, seated at the front of the wagon, has no choice but to flick her whip, prompting the horses to neigh in frustration and continue trudging up the hill.

Inside the wagon, the passengers clap their hands and tap their feet to the shifting beat of the music. The two players – a stout man with the absurdly small mandolin cradled in his arms and a square-shouldered Brute with the harmonica held tightly between his lips – shake and move their bodies as though they are possessed. Around them, the tarp roofing of the wagon ripples in the early winter winds.

…

Daylight fades into obscurity as the moon gleams and the sun sinks underground, to wherever it may slumber. The wagon is beneath the oak tree, the horses untied and absently clearing away the grass. The others, two men and three women (not including The Driver, who is nowhere to be seen), are pitching the tents. The unshaven Brute watches them from the stone wall encasing the camp, where he cleans out the barrel of his rifle.

He's been chewing tobacco – not out of choice – but now spits it onto the ground. His wide-brimmed hat feels heavier than usual, an anchor weighing him down. He takes it off and places it beside him, letting his hair fall into his eyes. He misses home, more now than ever. He will make them pay for what they did, for forcing him to leave his life behind. He tries not to think about the flames hot against his skin or the smoke stinging his eyes. Even in those final moments, the house was beautiful.

Still scrubbing away at the gun, The Brute flicks his eyes to the moon, a pearly white coin in a fountain of black water. According to his mother, in the old days, thieves would steal the moon and wish upon it with greed gnawing on their minds, but heroes brought those thieves to justice and placed the moon back in its rightful place.

The Brute hates this place, these people; they know him too well and hate him too little. There's no blame from himself or from others and now, his sins are fading. By next Friday they will be dead and forgotten.

The Brute wishes judgement day would come and cast him into hell's pits. He looks back up at the moon, how easy it would be to pluck the thing from the sky, to see more clearly while the rest went blind. One wish wouldn't hurt anybody.

...

Clean rifle slung across his back. Tobacco trapped between his gums and inner cheek, jaw constantly at work chewing it. Hat tilted slightly upward, light twinkling in his soft green eyes. Boots trudging through the slush of melted snow that fell late last night. Icicles dangling everywhere, rattling in the wind, under constant threat of shattering. Birds sailing onto trees, sending the resting snow on branches crashing down, disturbing the wildlife. The hunt has begun.

The Driver, short and slender as she is, capably glides over the snow, twirling her hunting knife between her fingers. She's the only one of the travellers who agreed to accompany The Brute. He has never seen The Driver hunt, barely knows the woman to be honest. But the look in her eyes – like a lone tree amid a wildfire, immune to all of mother nature's power – tells The Brute that he has little to fear.

They ran out of food three days ago and have been hunting ever since. Up until today, there'd been no sign of game. Then this morning, after the snow, they found two sets of tracks. The Brute reasons one set could be deer, based on the shape and depth of the footprints. The other set is unclear, though it's far heavier and larger.

The Driver claims the sudden snow is a miracle from God. The Brute is not a religious man, but staring up at the cold sun, its absence against his bleached skin, he can't help but wonder if The Driver is right.

In a gap between the pine trees, The Brute sights the deer. It's standing at the top of a pile of rocks, a heavenly glow slipping between the trees behind it, almost godlike. Without hesitation, The Brute aims down the sights of his rifle; it's the perfect shot. The Driver shouts something he doesn't hear and then the roar of a minotaur – or some equally disturbing monster – erupts beside him. He turns and sees a beast with fire for fur and jaws wider than a canyon.

It barrels toward him with the speed and power of a steam train. The Brute swings his gun toward it too late and the demonic creature reaches him. Darkness encompasses the world.

...

He is in a cabin. The walls are damp wood and the floor creaks wherever he steps. The fireplace is empty, save for grey ash, and all the lights are off. Dust hangs suspended in the air, making him cough. In front of him, stitched to a plaque, is the stuffed head of a deer. Its eyes are wide and afraid. Beneath it, in gold scrawl: Ad Meliora.

He glances through the window; outside are rolling hills covered in flowers of all kinds. Purple and white lilies, yellow tulips, red dahlias. Doves float through the cloudless sky, completely carefree.

Someone else is out in the meadow, a young girl. She's picking flowers; her hair is a curly storm. He can't see her face, but something about her fills him with dread. He is a rain-filled cloud ready to burst.

He returns his attention to the cabin, only to find the deer head has caught on fire. He can feel the animal's spirit soaking into his bones. The fire trickles down the wall and into the fireplace. The roaring inferno is goading him toward it, but The Brute resists. The flames angrily blaze into an impenetrable wall that crashes toward him. He dives for the door but the fire is already inside him; it burns his insides.

He bursts into the peaceful countryside, alarming a flock of starling birds, only to find his wool coat is alight and cackling. He drops and rolls, but the fire wraps around his body, enveloping him in a bear hug. The cabin in front of him crumbles, the wood splinters and the roof caves in on itself. The Brute lets the fire consume him.

Up in the great beyond, an orange disc shimmers as it hovers above the clouds, a faceless angel. The sun! A force radiates from it. Beckoning him closer. His body is stuck to the ground, and upturned roots dig into his back. A rabbit edges toward him. Is it curious of the burning man or in desperate need of warmth?

The sun. The sun! It is the moon's father, it is the opposing side of the same coin. Hiding. Where the moon is maternal, nurturing the waves, the sun kills in the day but abandons the night. No one has ever wished upon the sun like they have the moon, for fear of being burned. But The Brute is already on fire. Helpless.

...

The Driver thrusts a knife deep into the beast's red eye, making the veins pop out like flashes of lightning. The Brute blinks away the hallucination and realises the demonic creature is, in fact, an enraged bear with an arrow lodged deep in its muscled shoulder. Someone failed to kill it and the poor animal could do nothing but rage and remain in denial of its imminent demise. The Brute clambers to his feet, remarkably unscathed. He nods appreciation to The Driver, she smiles kindly and retrieves her blade.

Atop the mound of rocks, the deer is gone. Only sunlight in its place. A pity, but The Brute is strangely pleased. He is glad the deer will never be stuffed full of straw by a lousy taxidermist. The bear on the other hand ... He looks at the corpse, the steam rising from the still-warm fur, and grins.

The Driver notices his reaction, frowns and asks nonchalantly, "Any chance we can eat it?"

"At this point, I'd eat right about anythin', and a bear ain't lookin' too bad."

...

The fire cackles as the meat sizzles amid the flames. The weary travellers huddle around the meal; they are vultures perching atop stones and fallen tree trunks. Their faces sunken with defeat, minds lost within dreams of better days. The Brute watches each in turn. He knows no names, only faces.

The Mandolin, a stout man with thinning hair and a second skin of sweat, is currently tuning his instrument's strings. Next to him is The Slaughterman, he's gaunt with jet black hair, but can barely form stubble above his lip. He skins and cooks efficiently, but there's a prickly nervousness to the way he prods and jabs at the bear.

The Fugitive has caged eyes and sealed lips. She was found coming from the South, into The Brute's hometown, on horseback with her wrists shackled and a bullet in her leg. Then there's The Farmer, curly straw blonde hair and eyes the gloomy grey of a rainy day. She's stocky, with toned arms from shovelling and digging; her husband died a long time ago. Finally, The Maid, still young and sweet but lonelier than all the rest combined. She lost everything when her home burned down. At night, he can hear her sobbing under the old oak tree.

The Driver is off somewhere. Alone. She is not a part of this company.

They all sit in silence, safe for now in the eye of an unpredictable storm. The Slaughterman slices off a slab of bear meat and chews it. He seems satisfied and motions for the rest of the travellers to dig in. The Brute removes his knife and cuts a large chunk. Juice spills from the pores of the bear meat. He retreats to the shadows of the stone wall to eat in peace.

In the night sky, an eerie white fog wraps around a strip of stars. The crescent moon peers at The Brute with a judgemental glare. Its ghostly white light bathes down on the neighbouring terrain, illuminating shrubs and trees, stretching benign shadows into monsters. The irises of hungry animals are reflected in the heavenly body's stolen luminosity.

The forest leaves are lightly dusted in snow. The looming backdrop of a snow-capped mountain marks the end of the mortal world, where wolves howl to proclaim dominion.

There is a sudden movement in the tree line, a flash of pale skin. The Brute snaps to attention. His heart stops as a Girl With Hair Like A Storm drifts outward, into the fern field beneath The Brute. She's still some yards away, her head tilted toward the moon, as though its light can breathe a new soul into her reanimated corpse.

The Brute watches her with wariness but continues to eat his dinner by the solace of his stone wall.

II. The Gun & The Slaughterman

A metallic stench stings his nostrils. The sky is a thick, heavy veil cloaking the face of God. A storm is coming.

The Brute presses the butt of the rifle into his shoulder and feels it jerk satisfyingly into his muscles as he pulls the trigger. The clap of gunfire, then the bullet splinters through a tree. Dead-centre. Birds scatter into the sky and The Brute slides another round into the top of the rifle. Barely aiming, he shoots down a bird.

The young man, The Slaughterman, is standing next to The Brute and watches all of this with a keen fascination. He snatches the gun from The Brute and slaps ink hair from ocean eyes. He calmly prepares the firearm for more mindless butchery, though the quivering of his hands betray his boyish inexperience.

The Slaughterman holds the rifle incorrectly at his hips like a shotgun. He eyeballs a tree and dangles the barrel toward it.

The rifle shudders, vomiting lethal bile, and then there's a spark of yellow light as the fired bullet ricochets off a stone. The smooth slab is chipped, the lead leaving a scar. The weapon, frightened by its own power, leaps out of The Slaughterman's hands and flees for the open sky. His hands are sliced open in the process, two red slits smiling with devilish glee.

The anger comes to a boiling point, The Brute can see it in The Slaughterman's veins. "You did this!" The Slaughterman squeals. "'Cause of you we had to leave. Now I gotta shoot this gun, I gotta eat bear and sleep in a damn tent. I dunno what I'm doin' or where we're goin', I'm scared they'll find us. And all of it is 'cause of you. All of it!"

The boy leaps at him, trying to find something of sustenance to grip or to punch but managing only to snag the loosely but-toned shirt. The Brute does not budge. He's a head taller than The Slaughterman and looms over him with contained fury. The Slaughterman, like a leech, hangs from the thin cotton shirt as though there's an empty grave below.

The leech whimpers, and The Brute's soft green eyes glaze over with a coating of cold steel. The grave beckons them both.

"Then leave. I ain't askin' you to stick around." He grips the leech by the back of the neck, twists and pulls – as you're supposed to do with these kinds of parasites – and throws The Slaughterman to the ground.

In the sky overhead, The Brute sees a dark and false lighthouse. He blinks away the infectious imagination. He knows what's real.

The Slaughterman crawls in the dirt, scalded by his tears. Meanwhile, The Brute waits and watches with bloody handprints on his clean white shirt.

"I can't leave. I got nowhere to go," The Slaughterman screeches. "But they're comin' back. You know it, I know it. They're gonna find us. The Faceless Strangers don't leave no one alive. That's why they call 'em that, they skin ya alive! They skin ya alive." He kneels in front of The Brute, head bowed and hands on knees to steady himself. The boy sobs. "They're gonna bring their guns and their horses and it'll be real messy and real bloody and right now, it's lookin' like we're all probably gonna die."

"You ain't gonna die. Besides, what do you expect me to do about it? I did what I could the last time those Faceless Strangers came knockin'."

"You did the best you could? Where were you the day they came? Where were you when they hurt my ma? When she was alone and scared on the ground and they—and they—I was uncon-scious, I had tried to stop them and—" The Slaughterman breaks down. "I want to go home. I just want to go home and see my ma again. I don't want none o' this, I don't wanna shoot nobody. She was gonna make me eel pie that night, she was gonna make it. I never said—I barely saw her that day—" The Slaughterman kneels there, crying.

The Brute doesn't comfort the boy. He convinces himself that it's not his fault, that it is a sad thing that happened but that he must not blame himself. He wishes The Slaughterman would quit crying.

Eventually, the boy stands up with a blank look in his eyes and walks off somewhere. The Brute sighs with relief, but it's a sob that comes out. He can't stop it and the sound echoes through the trees. He takes a steady breath, shrugs himself off and returns to camp.

...

Sun-bleached rocks hide beneath frothy waves. Seagulls nibble away at the remains of a broken man. He's been impaled on a jagged rock and already barnacles cling to his soggy skin. Seaweed ties him down, shackling the twisted remains. A lighthouse peaks over the horizon, it's light swings around and around and scours the seas. But the corpse is just out of the light's reach.

III. Bag of Nails

The Maid is surprisingly adept at horse riding. Feet inside the stirrups, she applies just the right pressure to dictate the direction and desired speed of the horse. The mount trots alongside The Brute's stallion and willingly responds to the girl without a fuss. It has taken a liking to her.

It was her idea to go riding. She'd woken him at the early hours of dawn and led him over to the horses. She couldn't fit the saddle onto the horse herself, if she had been capable, The Brute is sure she would've ridden off by herself without bothering to wake him. Nonetheless, he attached the saddles and accompanied her, and now they're riding through the thick forest as the sun climbs further along its path to the dark side of the world.

The Maid admires everything in sight, childlike wonder thankfully not lost amidst all the grief. She reaches out and touches leaves or tree trunks, pressing her hand against the rough wood. The Brute longs to feel the same things, to look in awe at the world around him, as he did as a child. Those days are long past.

She has not spoken to him since they began their journey. She enjoys the silence as much as him. The Brute appreciates her willingness to simply ride, letting the day gradually pass while they ignore the threat of doom.

She's skinny. Too skinny. He can see bone pushing against the inside skin of her forearms, and her Victorian blouse hangs loosely from her shoulders. She's in blue trousers loaned to her by The Slaughterman. Her hair, barely scraping her shoulder, hangs choppy and straight. But it's her eyes that upsets him; the wide oval marbles no longer sparkle, there's an absence, a hollow space where something used to be. A ghost of a shape. They keep riding.

...

At a stream, they break for water. The shallow wash of waves over pebbles soothes The Brute and the horses. The Maid is a ways off, she looks over and smiles at him and The Brute returns the favour. She removes her satchel and unscrews her flask. While bending over to fill it up, something comes into view behind her. A Girl With Hair Like A Storm. Facing away from The Brute, toward the mountain.

...

There's blood dripping from her fingers. He can still hear the droplets, the constant dripping against the wood. Her body strewn out across the floor like a trophy. Or a warning. Her eyes rolled back into the tops of her head, searching for heaven and seeing only black. The Brute's there but he turns away now and walks out the door, trying to remain calm. Trying not to think. There's snow everywhere and it's cold and it's winter. Tracks lead away from the house, already disappearing beneath fresh powder. The Brute goes back inside.

...

They ride all through midday in silence. At some point, they make camp and The Brute falls asleep. When he awakens, it's dusk. The girl has prepared a fire and caught a rabbit using only her knife. She's cooking it on a spit. She smiles and he finds himself smiling back. Unusual.

"We need to head back. The others'll be worried," he says. She frowns and glances at the foreboding trees.

"Not now, in the mornin'," she replies, and though the obvious assumption would be she's afraid to ride in the dark, The Brute knows there is a far grimmer reason. The night is her time to mourn. He simply nods, returns to sleep and lets her grieve.

...

Morning comes and they stumble across a campsite. Empty, though there's smoke rising from the ashen fireplace. The shape of horse hooves in the sludgy mud reveal the camper to have left recently. Very recently. There's a burlap sack tucked under a tree. The Brute moves over to inspect.

"We should go," The Maid says, but The Brute shakes his head and unties the thin coil of rope wrapped around the tip. He peers inside: apples mainly, though some other fruits and vegetables are muddled in as well. There's also a fresh pair of trousers and a shirt, some shoes too. The Brute closes the sack and flings it over his shoulder. He heads back to his stallion.

"You can't take that!" The Maid yells.

"What's it look like I'm doin'?"

"That belongs to someone. He might freeze out here."

"One less person to worry about."

"We got plenty food," The Maid pleads desperately. The Brute looks at her over his shoulder, her desperation. He nearly agrees, nearly turns around and places the sack right back where he found it because he knows she's right. But then he looks at her again, those skinny arms, the shading around her sunken eyes, and the paleness of her skin. He can't let her stay like this, even if she hates him for it.

He straps the burlap sack onto his saddle and climbs atop his horse.

...

They ride in uncomfortable silence. The Brute can't make this right with the girl, he knows this, but every so often he attempts to make eye contact. He needs to know she still acknowledges his existence.

Has he failed her by keeping her safe? Will she resent him forever, or will she come to understand? He once brought the grim reaper to her doorstep, to everything she holds dear. So much to be guilty of. So much death.

"I don't wanna see you become a bad man," she says, startling The Brute.

"I've been a bad man for a long time now," he replies. She ponders on this, looking north to hide her face from his.

"Says who?"

"Me."

"Suppose no one would know better than you," she says with a shrug. He smiles at that.

"Maybe not. I'm just a man holdin' a gun, tryin' to run from a murderous gang who wants to kill 'im. I ain't got nothin' under my hat but hair," he responds, finally. "You know, you're clever for your age. I wish I had a daughter like you," he says this absently.

The girl drops her head and grips the reins tighter. Her horse quickens its pace so that she is slightly ahead. He tries to read her, the straight posture and tenseness of her muscles. Finally, she says without turning around, "If I were your daughter … would you let me die as she did?"

And The Brute's blood runs cold. He doesn't know how she knows, but he hopes she's the only one who does. And if she is, he hopes she can keep a secret.

…

A memory. A dream?

He's a boy, perhaps six years old, riding in the back of a wagon with his mother. She's alive. Her eyes are clear orange. Her hair's straight and brushed. There are no bags under her eyes or blemishes on her cheeks. She's humming, reading a book. The Brute hates reading but loves stories, and he hopes she'll retell the book's tale later in the evening in her unique way. As she always used to do.

Riding shotgun is his father, with a slick ponytail and a clean-shaven, prominent jawline. He has returned from his duties on Little Brewster Island. Next to his father, is the stagecoach whip, directing the hulk of wood along a dirt road. Both are wearing goggles to protect their eyes from the swirling dust cloud caused by the hundred or so wagons ahead of them.

They're in a large group, a typical way of migrating from one place to another, but the boy only knows his mother. He's frightened by all the commotion, the loudness of the horse hooves and the way the dirt itches his skin. The dust cloud presses against the wagon, creaking the wood and making it bend inwards. It's his mother who keeps him from panicking; she cracks some joke about how the men resemble ugly bugs and tells him he'll one day be somebody who matters.

He hates the journey, but at least she's there. At least she'll always be there.

IV. Maria

The Brute awakens from his dreams. He's lying in the dirt by the old stone wall. The moss is wet and slick against his back.

The Fugitive is a few feet away, watching him. She's silhouetted in the expired light and quivers with indecisiveness. Her grey hair hangs in her eyes and almond skin is plagued by goosebumps.

He shifts to a sitting position and unbuttons his damp shirt, tossing it to one side and putting on his vest. The fugitive steps closer and the expression on her face – a shattered ceramic cup – makes The Brute wish he could remember his dreams. Perhaps he talked in his sleep, exposed himself in some way.

"I need your help," she forces, arteries popping at the side of her neck, squeezing the words out of the empty flask of her body. "Please."

The Brute reluctantly replies, "With what?"

...

A choir of trees surrounds them, the ground at their feet is lilacs. A blue lunar bulb is swinging from the ceiling of the night's sky. Its shine refracts against the flowers, blurring the pink into something reminiscent of northern lights that shimmer like crashing waves. A thin stream of water runs past them, fireflies flickering above it.

"What is it you want from me?" The Brute asks her.

"I need to climb that mountain." She points at the snow-capped mountains that backdrop the forest. "Before those people come back and kill us."

"Why?"

"Wherever we go when we die, I don't think I'll see my husband there. I need to say goodbye. The mountain is where I must go to do that."

"Why the mountain? Why not here? And why do you need me?"

"You'll see the power of the mountain when we get there. As for why you, you're a killer, a brute. Who better for protection?" she tells him, smiling. The Brute considers her proposition. The journey would take days, they may struggle for food, and for what? To talk to a dead man.

"No."

Her face falls like an avalanche but it doesn't faze him. He starts to walk away.

"I don't blame you for what happened," she calls out, suddenly, making him stop. "They all do, but not me. They think it's your fault and they may be nice when you're around, but when you've got your back turned they spit and growl and talk about all the ways they hope you die."

"Well, maybe they're right and you're wrong," The Brute says.

"They are right, it is your fault. There's no getting around that. You brought those savages to their homes. I don't know why they came, what you did to provoke them into burning the village and massacring the people, but you brought them."

"But you don't blame me for all that? Because you need me?"

"I don't blame you because I forgive you."

"Please," The Brute scoffs. "That's the same as pretendin' it didn't happen."

"No, it's the same as acknowledging that you're not the centre of all this. The tragedy isn't your own personal sin. It's a grief that belongs to all of us. I forgive you because what else is there to do?"

"I done nothin' to warrant forgiveness."

"You're still here. Ain't ya?" The Fugitive's voice is passive but there's a hiss to it that's overtly dominant.

"So?"

"I seen worse things in my life than you. But if you want me to stay on your side, you need to help me. Come to the mountain with me. Otherwise, when the shooting starts, and believe me it will, you'll be the only one they aim at. So, what do you say?" The Fugitive extends an open palm toward him. The Brute considers her offer.

In the distance, wolves begin to howl.

...

They leave at daybreak. The rest of the travelling company see them off. The Driver offers to accompany The Brute, and though he could use an extra rifle, he declines. The others would starve without The Driver's hunting skills.

He says farewell to The Mandolin and The Farmer but his heart isn't in it. There's a sourness hanging in the air that The Brute can't pin down. Both of the travellers have a relaxed gait and a posture that is so casual it screams bizarre. The Slaughterman at least carries his spiteful hatred with honest dignity.

Even The Maid brings a pang of pain. He regrets, more than anything else, his choice to steal the burlap sack.

She had no reaction when learning of The Brute's choice to leave, and now she doesn't even look his way or wave goodbye. Instead, she stands under the willow tree. A scarecrow propped up to scare him away.

The Brute and The Fugitive head toward the forest on horseback. Above the mountain, dark clouds are at war amongst themselves. The mountain shows no disturbance.

. . .

Ride, hunt, sleep, continue. This is their routine.

For six days, they sit on a saddle and clatter onwards but the mountain never grows larger. On the seventh day, The Brute discovers he can discern the outline of a cave in the great chunk of rock and he takes this as a sign to talk to his companion.

"Where you from?" He asks her.

"I grew up in Taxco de Alarcón, it's this scorching, deep south town. You won't have heard of it, not many lived there."

"What was it like?" The Brute continues questioning in his gruff voice. The Fugitive is silent for a moment, smiling at something The Brute can't see.

"I remember there was this chapel I used to visit, The Santa Prisca Church. It was made from this beautiful pink stone and there were two towers on either side with bells at the top. Inside, the roof was a colourful tiled dome and there were golden altarpieces that stretched all the way to the ceiling. I used to say prayers and when I left, I could see out across the crimson roofs and behind the town was the mountain and I felt safe. I felt so safe," The Fugitive's voice falters and her horse slows. The Brute slows with her.

"Why did you leave?" The Brute queries softly.

She shrugs, "I met my husband in Mexico City. We learnt English and a few other languages together. When he died, I came here. On the way I shot fourteen men and stabbed a fifteenth."

"Do you regret it?"

"No."

...

Naked skeletons washing in a river: The Fugitive gives herself some distance and faces away from The Brute, but he can still make out the thick white lines scrawled across her olive back. Deep and unhealed.

...

They have arrived at the great mountain. They tie their horses to a tree, very loosely so that the animals can wander around and survive off grass. Then they prepare for the final stage of the journey.

The mountain's pregnant belly hangs over them. Snow runs down its face like melted makeup and jagged cracks smother its plump body.

The earth-bound entity is disappointing. From a distance, its size and power seemed sacred. Its contours and edges were smooth, and its white-capped peak was a diamond breaking through the boundaries of sky. He can't see the spiral tip now, the crest is hidden from sight. He had thought the mountain was a seat built for God himself. The Brute never considered why it might have remained empty.

Now, standing at its base, he acknowledges that the journey was fruitless, for him at least. There is no enlightenment, penance or forgiveness here. The stone is just stone. The snow is just snow. And the mountain will eventually be eroded by the same gusts of wind that first built it. Like all things of past, present and future, the mountain is no more permanent than man. And the cycle will always return to the place it began: nothingness.

...

The climb is hard and steep. His alpenstock keeps him sturdy, but the elements pull no shortage in punches. Icy glass slices into his eyes and hissing ghosts try to throw him off the cliff face. However, if insignificant little mountain goats can do it, so can he.

The path slants at an almost vertical angle. He can either lean into the storm, charging toward the peak like a bull, or roll down to the bottom.

Behind him, The Fugitive flickers in and out of view as the snow flaps around her like a pale curtain. Her lantern eyes glow from a gap in her cloak and tufts of dark hair stick out, trying to run from the freezing cold. He waves at her. She waves back. A sign of life to show that neither has died. They continue upward. Toward the stars shimmering beneath a peeling grey sky.

...

Wolves. Of course there are wolves.

He can hear them under the quieting storm. At the summit, they howl, waiting for a much-needed meal. He can picture their matted and grey fur. A pendulum of drool swinging back and forth, hypnotising you into climbing into their warm jaws. Then cosiness. Not felt for a long time. And finally, sharpened teeth slipping into numb skin, the sweet release of built-up blood clots clearing out of clogged veins and the smell of vindication.

...

They camp in a cave and huddle together for warmth. A tiny fire

– closer to being a lit matchstick – burns in front of them but The Brute can't feel its heat. He's never known cold like this. Outside, the dying words of foreign folk are whisked through the air. Unrecognisable wailing. The amount of it suggests a massacre has occurred somewhere in far off lands. Why is the wind only ever the carrier of bad news?

The Fugitive snuggles into him. Her eyelids are closed and she takes deep steady breaths, but he does not think she's sleeping. Now and then a shudder runs through her like a pulse.

The cave is an indentation in the mountain, a half-formed dome. The walls are smooth, damp and cramped. On the ceiling is a myriad of drawings done in red and black. Figures. Animals. Places. All mingling together in the dancing firelight to create a moving picture that tells a thousand stories, none of which The Brute can decipher.

An army of snow marches into the cave and guns down their fireplace, murdering it in cold blood. The freeze sets in, his body turns to rubber and his bones clink and jangle. Like some ghastly horror from an old gothic tale, The Brute crawls and heaves his way over to the white caked wood.

Kneeling over the remains, he gets to work rebuilding. The Fugitive stirs and mumbles but stays sleeping. He blows onto the embers and red ash billows into his face. The Brute coughs but keeps blowing and, with a reluctant sigh, the orange twigs sputter to life.

He can feel his muscles loosen and soon he can move his fingers again. Once the fire is well and truly up and running again, he crawls back over to The Fugitive, wraps his arms around her, and falls asleep.

...

Mushrooms. She wants him to eat blue-spotty mushrooms.

They've nearly reached the top. A long journey is coming to an end. The final stretch is a sloped river of frost shrouded in fog. They have not started wading through yet. Right now, they are on a patch of grass, where the mushrooms grow. The Brute does not know why The Fugitive has stopped. He observes her as she drops to her knees, removes the knife from her backpack and cuts each fungus at the stem until she has a pile of fungi in front of her.

Then she tells him, "We will eat these," and motions at the poisonous, squishy delectables. He knows nothing about the mushrooms. He assumes that they are native to the mountain, having never seen them before, and wonders how The Fugitive learned of them. The thought of eating one fills him with dread.

"Why?" he asks, keeping his tone relaxed.

"They will unlock your mind to acceptance. They only grow in high places," she tells him. "We will go to the very peak of this great rock and open our eyes and look."

He does not know if that was meant to inform or bewilder but nonetheless he takes a few of the mushrooms in hand and, with nothing left to lose, flicks them into his mouth ...

Sourness. Snake-venom trickling down his throat. The mushrooms bubble away in his stomach acids. Sizzling. Spotty-blue everywhere. Can't see. The world stretches, wraps around itself again and again like a never-ending spiral staircase. The shattered pieces of a mirror float in front of him. No reflection. Only a Girl With Hair Like A Storm, trapped on the other side.

The Brute turns around and vomits. His head clears slightly and he realises there's a whirring train engine everywhere. He can't shut it out. The headache is piercing every fabric of his person and body. He faints.

...

"I did not mean you should eat them immediately." The Fugitive kneels over The Brute with an ice-cold damp cloth. He sits up and rubs his head. "You need water first, and a full stomach." She explains this like it's obvious. The Brute wishes he knew all that before eating the horror-inducing fungi.

He staggers to his feet, shakes himself off and starts for the hill. He wants to finish this quest and be done with it.

...

He loses sight of The Fugitive quickly. She disappears behind puffs of velvet cloud and when he calls out to her, the only response is an echo. All he can do is keep going and hope she's not far behind – easier said than done. There are no landmarks, only the frost and the fog. The Brute could walk straight off the edge and not realise what was happening until he was plunging straight into the depths of hell.

The fog smells similar to the mushrooms and The Brute worries what that might mean. The path is waist-deep, he's slowly losing control over his body as the cold spasms become more frequent. His leather boots are damp. His face is permanently frozen in a snarl. His eyes burn. Needless to say, he's not going to last much longer.

A figure passes in front of him, or a shadow. It floats smoothly across the landscape, a black splotch of ink on white canvas. It has no arms or legs and its head is a thousand faces grotesquely mashed together. Strips of cloth trail behind the being and tied to the ribbon-like material are enslaved people. They're smaller than The Brute and hobble with stumped legs, shuddering in the naked light.

The Brute pushes onward, letting the figure and its slaves disappear behind him. He passes more strange creatures along the way, all hidden in mist. Some have too many arms or legs. None pay him any mind.

At some point, he stumbles over a skeleton covered in gold necklaces. Its rib cage is crushed bone fragments. The eye sockets see everything, and the jaw moves wordlessly, trying to share centuries of lost wisdom. Its bony hand cracks as it reaches out to grab him. The Brute keeps on moving.

The silhouette of a lighthouse on the horizon, its light a foggy breath of white. Two figures stand at its peak, a boy and a man. Even in the wind he can hear the muted yells of their argument. Then the boy pushes the man and he plunges downward, into the sea. The Brute shakes himself off.

"It's not real," he growls.

The higher up, the thinner the mist. Ahead, there is the silhouette of a leafless tree resembling a crooked old man leaning over the brink, deciding whether to jump, and a cave where shapes move in the shadows.

The Brute has made it. He's so close. He looks behind and spots the outline of The Fugitive. She's not dead! Perhaps their luck is beginning to turn. He turns back towards the cave and sees them emerging. Wolves. At least half a dozen. Exactly as he pictured them that first night in the mountains. They dart out of their hiding place.

And suddenly, it's night. The sun leaves them. Without word or warning, it throws them into the dark innards of some dead creature. The snow blindly searches for them, but the wolves know precisely where they are. They come toward The Brute slowly, taking their sweet time.

The Fugitive arrives next to him, fearless. How she found him so quickly is a miracle. She unhooks her backpack and removes two wooden sticks from inside, the tops of them are wrapped in cloth, and a matchstick box. She quickly begins lighting the sticks. Has she done this before?

He catches one of the torches and holds it in front of himself; the smoke stings his eyes and a flash of burning houses skewers through his vision. He blinks clear and notices the wolves have now encircled them. The Fugitive presses her back to his and they spin slowly, trying to keep an eye on each of the six wolves.

The torch hisses and coils. A guiding light, a ward for evil spirits, but not something the wolves fear greatly. Its orange snarl bounces off the boulders and turns the white snow into molten gold.

The wolves toe the line where the light reaches, stepping into the heat for a second before retreating into the comfortable grey. He can't see them fully in the darkness. All he notices are the eyes of predators, watching him. He spins around and around like an overworked clock, he is the hour hand and she is the minute. The wolves' glowing eyes blur as The Brute spins faster, until they are streaks of yellow, a circle of light.

The Brute waves his torch like a lunatic, knowing it will do nothing to impede the approaching wolves. The beasts bark and snarl. Their tongues whip loosely in droll mouths.

The Fugitive splashes something in the soft snow and, when The Brute arrives at her side of the circle, he notices she's leaving a trail of dark liquid as she twirls. Before The Brute can ask what she's planning, The Fugitive drops her torch in the snow and a ring of fire erupts around them. Blocking them from the wolves and searing the hair on The Brute's arm. The inferno is as tall as The Brute. The rest of the world has vanished.

Immediately, tar-like people clamber out of snowy graves to wash clean in the flames. Melted skin runs down slimy bodies in droplets that pool at their feet and feed the fire. They dance, hold hands, hug or stand perfectly still. They move their bodies in every possible direction, except the direction that will let them leave their ring of fire.

Men, women, children, even babies all crawl and writhe in the blaze. Faces sheets of wet black, masking agonising screams. Webbed fingers snatching at tufts of fire. The Brute knows it is the mushrooms causing these strange visions, but he can't help but remember that fateful night.

When the Faceless Strangers came and burnt down his town. The gang members sparing no lives in an act of vengeance. Yet the one they were after, The Brute who killed one of their own. He had vanished in the darkness.

Now, all The Brute listens for is the continuing crackle of greedy flames, and the receding whimper of wolves. He hears the beasts fleeing into the coldness of their caves. And he grins.

...

He can see everything from up here. A sea of stars, each a perfect diamond, watching over every rolling hill or troop of ants. The shadows blend it all together and for the first time, The Brute realises that it's all the same. One. Connected. Whole.

There are differences between each rock or strand of grass, but in the end, they are still just another intricate part of the land. Serving their purpose. Then moving on. Without repercussions. That's the happiest thought The Brute has ever had in his entire life.

...

She lights an oil lamp and holds it out over the edge of the cliff like a warden guarding the mountain pass. Where she was storing an oil lamp this entire time is a question The Brute will never be able to answer. She removes a few mushroom heads from her pocket and eats them. She holds out more mushrooms for The Brute. He takes them from her and swallows them whole. The acid is stronger this time. He gags and holds in bile. Then, The Fugitive hands him another already lit oil lamp, which he holds as well.

"Thank you. For coming. The wolves are new, most of these places are empty – save the spirits, course," she tells him. "The first time I climbed one of these was with my husband. His sister died. I didn't see anyone. I hope you don't either." Then she kneels in the snow, places the oil lamp at her feet and begins to pray. A halo of light forms around her.

A rumbling starts beneath The Brute's feet and dust sprays against him. The valley rises to meet them. The mountain is sinking! Actually, sinking suggests a slow descent, this is more of a plummet.

Soon, the dirt is all The Brute can see. Pink worms, roots and brown cake that's wet with fresh rain. The sky above is reduced to a shrinking hole where the mountain once was. Only one star is visible now and it's dimming the further they sink. Darkness encases them. This rock is their tomb. The only light is the oil lamps: bubbles of holy yellow. Why is The Fugitive still praying? Whispering words like gunfire, eyes peacefully remaining closed.

…

Red. All he sees is red.

The cabin is covered in it. The girl is dead. The supplies are there, waiting to be taken. The Brute's racing heart finally slows. He looks at the corpse with empty sockets.

...

The Brute stumbles as the mountain crashes to a stop. The earth has opened up to a cavern. He can sense things here with him. Forgotten fossils at the centre of the earth. He glances toward The Fugitive and notices she's no longer kneeling. Instead, she shines her oil lamp on a patch of darkness and speaks in whispers.

The Fugitive swings her oil lamp toward The Brute – as if to introduce him to her late husband – but as she does, the yellow washes over a pile of moving bodies: limbs detached, bones protruding, skin peeling. Her oil lamp continues to swing onto The Brute and the bodies vanish in darkness. The Fugitive says something, then returns her attention to the shadows.

The Brute collects his oil lamp and inches forward. Exploring. The cavern is large and his light is too small to illuminate much. The first thing that enters his golden globe is splayed fingers with overgrown fingernails. Next, arms and legs like spiderwebs entangled together. Eventually, the whole grotesque fiend enters The Brute's private sphere. It pumps with a beating heart and a thousand blood-stitched eyes that pierce his soul.

"Do you remember me?" A voice from behind.

The Girl's sweet words of innocence. The Brute turns around, pressing his back against the monstrous entanglement of corpses. He stares at the new speaker, The Girl With Hair Like A Storm, and shivers.

"Yes. I remember," he says and she nods.

"Thought maybe you didn't. Do you still think about me?"

"Always." There're tears in The Brute's eyes.

"Why?"

"I try not to but you're still there, in the cabin."

"You left me there."

"I know."

"Why didn't you bury me?"

"I couldn't. I should've."

"Did I do something wrong?" Her eyes are moons, pale and lifeless and empty but The Brute can still hear the pain in her voice. The whimpering. He's sobbing now, and his body feels torn up and out of place. A snapped matchstick.

"No," he forces out. "You didn't do nothin' wrong."

"And now I never will," she says solemnly, all the sweetness gone. And then she returns to the darkness that she came from and The Brute is alone with the beating heart of a fiend.

...

Two days ago they journeyed down the mountain. It was easy. No wolves or spirits or storms. The rest of the ride, so far, has been equally easy, but long. They're still riding now; his feet are swollen and blistered and his back is in agony. He didn't ask The Fugitive what she saw that night nor she him. Each had their own private epiphany.

However, there is something he wants to tell her – needs to tell her – and nowhere seems better than here, in a myriad of leaves, vines and soggy mud. So, he looks at The Fugitive with her greying hair and slumped shoulders. He empties his mind and says:

"I killed a girl. That's why them people, that Faceless Strangers gang, came and raided our town." It feels both good and sickening to hear it out loud. Finally owning up to such a hideous crime and receiving the forgiveness or punishment he deserves. The Fugitive doesn't look at him. His words barely register.

Is she tired? Or just doesn't care? The Brute continues, "I'd been huntin' but there weren't no game around. It was winter, and I seen a campfire just north. They're camped in an abandoned town. Tents everywhere but main cabin had lights on, so I went there. Thought it'd make a good lootin'.

"They had supplies, a lot of supplies. And I swear to you there was no one there, I mean, I thought there was no one there. She came out of nowhere and I fired. It happened so fast. It was a gut shot, she bled out slowly, I think. Shoulda stopped and seen to her but I didn't. She screamed and screamed and crawled like—" He remembers the sight of his Father dead on the rocks below the lighthouse.

"My horse had this small cart attached," The Brute continues, "and I stocked it full of them supplies, quick as I could. Left the little girl there on the floor like she was nothin'. Blood was everywhere, up to my knees even. For someone so tiny she had a lot in her. Only took about a half of their loot before the men started comin'. Then I left, and they followed and I think they're still followin'. Their campsite will be movin' the same way as us for better weather. They lost winter provisions, doubtless the warmer southern lands'll be perfect to regain them. The Slaughterman was right. They'll be here. Sooner or later."

The Fugitive still doesn't reply and The Brute drops his head in shame. They continue their journey back to the rest of the travelling group.

...

They're camped and eating cooked rabbit. The meat is chewy, but the wetness helps and The Brute is hungrier than when he first ate that bear. How long ago was that? Winter when they first arrived, and now late summer. It can't have been that long.

Out of a bush, mama rabbit appears, ears flat against the head and pupils so dilated the rest of the eye vanishes. Her white fur is coated in mud and her paw is bleeding. He can't imagine what she had to go through to get here. She watches solemnly from the edge of the campfire as The Brute and Fugitive feast viciously on her children.

...

"My name is Maria. I think you should know that, before I die," The Fugitive says to The Brute after another night of ignoring him. The Brute's breath catches in his throat. What should he say? Why would she say that? He panics and stops his horse in its tracks.

"I'm Colt," he says and Maria nods. He thinks that was the right thing to say.

Fragments of golden light cut through the green canopy above them. Colt dismounts and leans against a tree, trying to remain relaxed. A brown spider rests there with him.

"Colt? Odd … I heard that name meant 'home protector'. You're certainly living up to your reputation." She seems on the edge of laughter. Colt's face flushes. He runs his tongue over his teeth, tasting the piano keys connected to his gums.

"No. My mother told me it meant 'from the dark town'."

"That's a strange thing to call a child. Besides, your town isn't dark, it's only ash," Maria continues without him and then Colt is once again The Brute without a name and Maria is an honourable fugitive and it is as though the words were never spoken. They both forget what he didn't hear and ride onward.

V. The Faceless Strangers

The dreaded gang has provided a welcoming gift. A mutilated horse.

The legs are torn backward and the exposed bones are chipped from dog bites. The Farmer is already dead. She's turned over on her side, staring at The Brute. Soaking intestines stretch from open stomach like tree roots.

There are three other bodies strewn out behind her. One has had their face caved in by a meaty fist. The Farmer put up a hell of a fight. More than The Brute would've. He is a coward.

The Farmer is gone now because he brought these people here. So much death and so much violence and he is the cause of it all. A Brute who butchers little girls.

"She was tryin' to run," The Brute says.

"Survive," The Fugitive corrects him.

"Ain't no fair."

"No it ain't."

"We should say a few words," The Brute says and they dismount their horses and quickly tie them up at a tree. He removes his hat, "I'm—I'm sorry. This wasn't your fault ... I never even knew your name, but I am sorry. I hope that ... Well, I hope there's something better and wherever you are, I hope you're grinnin' wider than a baked possum." The Brute chuckles and wipes his eye.

"You ain't very good at this, are you?" The Fugitive says.

To the west, a scream shakes the air and startles the birds. The Brute and Fugitive unlatch their rifles and crouch in the tall grass.

As they move forward, the ground vanishes and becomes waist-deep muddy water. They walk slowly, so as not to disturb the swamp. Their rifles remain pressed to their shoulders. The leaves dip low, shielding them from the blood-red sun.

From somewhere out of sight, the crunching of The Mandolin's delicate instrument and the snap of each string breaking under the weight of some tone-deaf frontiersman's boot. The Brute winces and imagines The Mandolin lying warm on cold ground. The balloon of his gut sliced delicately open in a perfect slit. His entrails steaming, raw and red.

They slosh quickly through thick water, trying to find the broken instrument. Gunfire strikes and the tall grass strands are sliced in half.

The Brute dives headfirst into brown, dirty sludge and becomes entangled in the submerged roots. He twists but the water keeps him in its grip until, eventually, hands drag him upward and then he's coughing up weeds and mud.

The Fugitive crouches over him, cradling his head. They're hidden on a patch of land with thick undergrowth. The Fugitive's eyes are cat orange, a blend of warm honey and grey filth.

The Brute thinks of his mother. How she used to bathe him, her fingers entangled in his hair. Her orange eyes were always glittering, until the day his father died.

With The Fugitive's help, he stands up on the uneven ground and wipes the mud from his face. He lost his rifle somewhere but it doesn't matter. None of it matters. He's going to set things right, no one else will pay. The Fugitive waits for him to say something.

"Let's go find the others," he tells her and sets off to find friends, and hopefully a gun.

...

They find The Mandolin and Slaughterman flat on their stomachs beneath the wagon. The large man is lying in a pile of his own vomit, his face is wet and soggy from crying. The Slaughterman, on the other hand, hisses when the pair come too close. "You did this," he howls. "It's your fault they're here."

"I know," The Brute says calmly, "but I'm gonna make 'em leave. You're gonna be alright."

"Am I?"

"Trust me."

"How are you gonna make 'em leave?"

"I'll kill 'em."

"No you won't. But you can let 'em kill you. It's you they're angry at. Whatever you stole from 'em. They want vengeance."

"And what if I let that happen and they kill you anyways?"

"Then they're bad people."

"No. I won't let none of you die ... But maybe you'll get your wish and one of 'em'll land a lucky shot," he says, cracking a smile and rubbing his unshaved chin.

Ironically, a shot thunders in The Brute's ears and the corner of the wagon explodes in splinters. He dives to the ground and takes refuge under the wagon, with the other two. The Fugitive crouches and scans their surroundings.

"There!" The Fugitive hisses.

A few yards away, a pebble is disturbed by an unruly elbow. The Fugitive's hawklike vision shifts and she points upward at the source. An iron gun barrel peaks angrily over a mound of rocks.

The Brute crawls and then rolls to his feet. The Fugitive gives him a sideways stare and they set off. Their movements one and the same, they glide toward the lone gunman, skimming through thick undergrowth and skeletal trees.

The pair dive into the ground at the base of the rocks. The Fugitive clutches her rifle tightly. "I take him out. You take his gun," she tells him, already moving off before he has the chance to nod in agreement.

The Brute is about to follow when, to his left, he glimpses at least half a dozen frontiersmen rising out of the nearby murky swamp water. They're a trained firing squad who aim their rifles at the wagon, where The Mandolin and Slaughterman are camped, and fire six bullets.

"No!" The Brute bellows. The Slaughterman's head pops like a watermelon, splattering everything in the nearby radius with the thick pulpy pink of his brain. The bullets that hit The Mandolin seem to sink deep into him with a squelch, as if his head is a wet, mouldy sponge.

"You bastards!" The Brute growls. He hears another gunshot above him and hopes The Fugitive has killed her enemy. He turns regretfully away from The Mandolin and Slaughterman's bodies and climbs the mound of rocks to retrieve another gun from another corpse with another pound of vengeance weighing on his mind.

…

The Brute and The Fugitive are in a standoff with the firing squad, who are now situated behind the wagon. The Faceless Strangers Gang move in frenzied blurs, the sun backlighting their figures. Taking all of them out at once is impossible and revealing their position would be suicide, so The Brute and Fugitive wait. For an opportunity, or an escape route.

…

The opportunity eventually comes in the form of an explosive cart. It rolls down a high hill and must have been stolen from wherever The Faceless Strangers are camped. The cart crashes into the wagon where the marksmen are situated and erupts in a fireball of heat. By some bizarre miracle, four of the men survive the blast and scramble to their feet, prepared to fight.

From the same hill, The Driver and The Maid – like heroic cowboys – gallop downward on two mares, with their hair tied back and faces glistening from the heat. Pursuing them is about a dozen footmen, and one horseback rider, shouting as they try to fire their rifles while moving, and having little success.

The Brute watches all this with fascination. Meanwhile, The Fugitive is leaping to her feet and charging valiantly toward the remaining marksmen. She aims down her rifle, taking two men down, swiftly.

The Maid spills from her horse and crashes onto the dirt. Her slender body is scooped up by a faceless man, and a knife is pressed against her throat.

Fear fills The Brute. The kind that consumes you and dissolves your thoughts in coal-fuelled incinerators. He galumphs down the mound of rocks, scraping his shins and tearing his clothes.

Fire and snow blur each eye: His home burning. His feet frozen. His people's pleas for help. The Girl's wordless corpse. The stuffed deer head melting on the wall. A crowd of pitchforks singing church songs. The screaming siren for daughters lost. The stench of death. And the constant pursuit of Faceless Strangers in endless storms.

The Brute reaches The Maid and tackles her attacker. A fury of punching, scratching, biting and downright catfighting ensues. Moral codes are forgotten with both The Brute and his assailant resorting to whatever means necessary to survive another year of cold, warmth and life in the wild west.

The Brute hears, more than feels, the popping of his own eyeball as the attacker slips a talon under eyelid and tickles inside of skull. Memories scratch away like stamps peeled off an envelope, dates and people blurring into obscurity. The red is everywhere. His. The assailant's. The Girl With Hair Like A Storm. His mother hanging by her neck from the barn ceiling, blood trapped in her head until it's ready to burst.

The Brute lashes out blindly, finding a grip on lightning locks that seem vaguely familiar. The Brute opens his good eye and catches a clear glimpse of his opponent.

He has a square nose pressed against a flat face with ears like soup bowls. But it's the sight of the man's wiry hair that cuts off The Brute's steady stream of adrenaline. The hair that reminds him, so alarmingly, of a black ocean on a stormy night, and he finds The Girl With Hair Like A Storm lost in the emeralds of her father's eyes.

"No, no, no, no, no … it's you." The Brute releases the man from his grip and raises his hands in surrender. He takes a slow step back before the man removes a small blade from his boot and plunges it into The Brute's belly. The wound startles more than hurts him and The Brute collapses backward. The girl's father wraps his hands around The Brute's throat.

"You're 'im, aren't ya? You're the one that went an' took 'er from me." The man growls and squeezes tighter. "Look at me. Look at me! Ma' name is Daniel Sunday, I lead this 'ere gang, we're the Faceless Strangers. Ring a bell, son? You stole from us. You took ma' girl from me. Now, you're gonna look at ma' face and you're gonna know that this is what you get. This is what you get you sonofabitch!" Foamy saliva sprays from Daniel's mouth, cleaning The Brute's wounded eye.

"Please, I'm sorry." The Brute can barely choke out the words. He struggles limply to pry Daniel's hands from around his crushed windpipe.

"Sorry? I lost everythin'."

"—was an accident. I didn't mean—" The Brute's eyes roll back in his head. There are no stars in the afterlife, only a black sky. Everything that matters is behind him, the past is set in stone.

Regrets pour through him, burning his body like fiery oil. The Brute killed his father, shoving the lighthouse keeper from the top of his scrubbed tower in a fit of rage. He killed the Girl With Hair Like A Storm. His mother—What was the point of it all? All the murdering, lying and running only for him to end up strangled by a stranger.

Suddenly, the hands quit squeezing and pine-scented air eases into his lungs. His eyes slip out of the thin darkness back into bleary sunlight and green forests. The Maid has leapt onto Daniel's back, her teeth clamp down onto his ear with the ferocity of a ravenous dog. Her hair whips around her and those sweet eyes are bloodshot fireworks. Her cracked lips scrape against Daniel's skin and her pale body is a silkworm writhing around his body. The Brute meanwhile is paralysed, his brain is still sleeping.

The Maid throws her head back, ripping a chunk of meat with her. Daniel howls. He charges backwards, slamming The Maid into a nearby tree. Her head knocks into the trunk, riddling her unconscious. Daniel then kneels on her chest and grabs a nearby rock, raising it high into the air.

Leaping off a horse she stole from the Faceless Strangers, The Fugitive swoops in to save them. She blasts her rifle, sending a bullet straight through Daniel's back. She then throws a dagger deep into the man's skull. He growls, unaffected by the blade protruding from his head. On all fours, he twists his torso to face The Fugitive. He resembles a one-antler wendigo spirit.

Daniel bounds toward The Fugitive and drags her to the ground. The grieving father twists and pulls at the knife in his head until it comes free – along with goo and bone marrow – then he slits The Fugitive's throat.

The Brute wiggles the pocketknife out of his abdomen and tosses it away. He crawls toward Daniel and The Fugitive, digging nails into dirt. His face is droopy, his muscles don't respond properly and he's leaving behind a trail of blood like a snail.

Daniel shifts in and out of focus, giving the impression of several changing photographs. At first, Daniel's still kneeling on The Fugitives chest. Then, black. Now, he's standing over The Brute. The whites of Daniel's jagged teeth against the stark red ichor smothering his skin. Black. He turns his back on The Brute. Black. He's hobbling to a tree. Black. Daniel collapses in the shade, his storm-like hair quits cackling. All it is now is rotten straw. Black.

The Brute doesn't care about Daniel's lack of final words. The absence of closure. He doesn't care that there was no forgiveness or penance, that The Brute didn't have to pay for his sins and that Daniel didn't deserve to die. He ignores the implications that he was the cause of all this, the catalyst for a massacre. All he cares about is crawling forward and focusing his eyes on The Fugitive. Just reach her.

He snatches The Fugitive's hand. Holds it in his own. Their eyes lock, her life refracts through dilated pupils.

She grabs a fistful of The Brute's shirt and releases a guttural cry that sprays her entrails into the air, a most violent blowhole.

"Maria," The Brute pleads. "Maria, you're gonna be alright. You're gonna be just fine, Maria. Maria? Please, be alright. Please." He shakes her warm body, and cries.

The Farmer is dead. Then The Mandolin and The Slaughterman. Now, The Fugitive. Please Lord, let that be it. Let there be no more.

…

The Driver patches him up as quickly as she can. There are still Faceless Strangers lurking and doubtless their camp isn't far.

The Brute finds himself on horseback, with The Maid and The Driver riding alongside. The Driver holds a rifle in one hand and horse reins in the other. Someone must have attacked her because she is covered in claw marks that bleed profusely.

They gallop through towering trees with thin trunks and bristling leaves. As the sun dips lower and stormy grey covers clear blue, a thin mist leaks across the forest. How quick the world went from high humidity to a cold, desolate dreariness. For such dense woodland, The Brute feels incredibly alone.

The edges of the horizon are tinged purple and those last traces of light are slowly being eaten away by the black hole of darkness. Soon, the heavens will be consumed by night. The stars come later, only once the dark has won and the light has ceased do they dare shine bright.

The Brute continues to flee toward the last sliver of purple, investigating his surroundings as he does. To the North, rolling hills and growing mountains. To the West, a straight plane of desert where nothing grows. The South lies behind them, a warm cemetery.

VI. Alone Together, in the Forest

It's midnight when they hear them.

The Brute and his companions have long since slowed their progress and now travel at a canter. Tendrils of fog wrap like coils around The Brute's legs, threatening to pull him down into that frightening place between life and death where all bad deeds and purgatory folk lie waiting to torment him.

At first, he thinks it's merely their own horses making that rap-tap-tapping against the cold hard ground. But it's not. It's them. Who else could it be? And then The Brute and his companions are fleeing once again, in what is now beginning to feel like an endless cycle of running and dying, then running some more.

How many Faceless Strangers are there? Surely such a large number of people aren't devoted to killing The Brute and his companions. After all, he only killed one girl and stole a portion of their supplies, and for it they burnt his town and killed anyone ever affiliated with him. Is he missing something? Their revenge, while warranted, is undoubtedly petty.

"No," he whispers under his breath. "Every death is your fault. The girls, your companions. You deserve worse than this. They had every right to come after you, just not the others. Don't you dare try to spare yourself the blame."

The pursuers are catching up to them. They must be riding at the speed of a bullet. Within seconds The Brute will be overrun. He glances at The Maid, she's ghostlike – an aura of honey yellow radiates from her skin, guiding them through the veil.

The Driver is a block of moving marble, every kick of her heels into her horse's side is deliberate and with purpose. Together they ride, but the gap between The Brute and his pursuers is gradually narrowing. The blue mist slithers into their mouths and noses.

And then, five mysterious horsemen gallop past. Apparitions which shimmer a hazy blue. They pass through The Brute like a rush of cold air and leave a well of sadness in their wake. Immeasurable sadness.

He thinks of his mother waving goodbye to him before he went off to the local store, the last time he saw her. The pale blue eyes and the mouldy dark patches, a disease of tiredness. Her hair frizzy and her bones pushing against her thin skin. She was so frail. And that smile. Lopsided and half-formed like she couldn't quite remember what it was she was supposed to be trying to smile about. Then she was gone.

Looking over, The Brute glimpses similar memories passing over his companions faces. None of them say a word, instead slowing their pace and trying to gain control over their emotions.

He is thankful whatever was chasing them wasn't the Faceless Strangers, but the misery swelling inside of him is inescapable.

Perhaps it's better to suffer than to be empty. To wake up one day and be as cold as those he's killed but still able to breathe. Is that the debt he must pay to atone?

He quits pondering and accepts the vision for what it was, another brief instance of enlightenment in the American frontier.

…

The Driver leaves them at the peak of twilight. "I was a bank robber. Used to run with folk like these and trust me, they don't give up easy." That's all she says. No heartfelt goodbye or a promise to one day meet again. One second she's there, the next she's gone. And The Brute and Maid keep riding.

The Maid doesn't leave him. He doesn't know why she chooses to stay but he's glad. When they ride past several bodies hanging from a tree, their faces peeled off, The Maid makes no mention of it. However, she later stifles a scream when they ride past a deer being consumed by maggots, its shape still visible beneath the swarm.

Eventually the trees thin out, the mist clears and both agree it is time to rest. Whatever tomorrow brings, at least no one can say that they didn't fight for their survival. As a cloud fades away and vanishes; so too his hometown, everything it stood for, is forgotten.

…

Days pass and the journey into the unknown continues. Some day soon they will reach a wooden bridge, the planks and ropes swaying back and forth rhythmically. The bridge will lead to a lighthouse which the Brute will climb.

Atop the lighthouse will be a beacon. The beacon will shine its light onto the ocean. In the ocean, in its depths, the Brute will see the scattered remains of friends, the smiling faces of enemies. And his father, the beginning of the guilt. But certainly not the end.

· · ·

He flicks the match, hunching over it to prevent the howling wind from snuffing it out. Shaky fingers transport the tiny flame into the remnants of a dead campfire and blacken the crispy wood. Once the fire is up and going, The Brute seats himself away from the harsh heat and enjoys the warmth.

The Maid is opposite from him, her form flickering and distorting like a mirage that will disappear should The Brute squint too closely. She's pale and her cheekbones push against her skin. There's a medallion swinging from her neck, one he's never noticed before. It's too dark to make out the details but it's crescent in shape. They're in a cocoon of shrubbery yet somehow the wind still manages to creep in on them and gnaw at their bones.

"We gonna talk tonight? Or you still pretendin' I don't exist?" The Maid asks sourly, the fire filtering her voice from sweetness to grating metal.

"I didn't think you were wantin' to talk to me," The Brute admits.

"Better than the silence."

"Alright. What're your interests?"

"What're my interests?"

"That's what I asked, ain't it?"

"I suppose we oughta start somewhere. I like to write and read. Yourself?"

"I ain't got no interests. What you read?"

"Philosophy mainly. A lot of Plato. Read Ovid's *Metamorphoses* not so long ago."

"Never heard of 'em."

"I can tell."

"What they write about?"

"Myths, mainly. In *Metamorphoses*, this guy called Orpheus tries to rescue his wife, Eurydice, from The Underworld. He's got this lyre instrument that he plays so beautifully it makes Hades weep. The god of The Underworld allows Orpheus to lead Eurydice back up to Greece but says that Orpheus can't look at her until they're both safely alive. And so, he's walkin' Eurydice back to life and then he looks back too early and she vanishes," The Maid says matter of factly, without a hint of emotion.

The Brute studies her. "You believe in all that?"

"Not yet."

"Why not?"

"They're myths. There ain't no heroes or underworld. We all enjoy pretendin' we're better than we are. Deep down there's nothin'. And after all this, there's nothin' twice fold."

"Why read about it then?"

"Why do little girls play dress up? It's fun to pretend," The Maid states. An owl hoots, the only break from the constant wind shoving against The Brute's back.

"That's a little nihilistic," he replies, finally.

"That's a big word for you … You're right, maybe I just like readin' without thinkin' about what all them words mean."

"You're too young to be thinkin'. Just live a little."

"Is that what you do?"

"No, but it's what I'm telling you to do," The Brute commands.

"That's the only thing you've told me that makes much sense."

"I'm sorry," he mutters with a tremble, stopping the conversation dead in its tracks.

"For what?" She eyes him with wariness.

"Everythin'."

"I should hope so. You done some messed up things." She laughs as she says this and it's a rumbling laugh from deep down in the catacombs of her belly.

The brute smiles, sadly, and says, "I ain't good at talkin' or apologisin' or none o' that shit, but I am sorry. This is all my fault. You should have stayed with the woman, she would've kept you safe." He hopes The Maid will disagree. He wants her to reply with a list of all the reasons he is good. The ground beneath his arse is littered with stones, he can't get comfortable.

"You know, I saw you the night that it happened," The Maid whispers, seemingly off topic. "All this ash was floatin' in the air, little deadlights my mother called them. We were runnin' but at some point she died, I only knew cause her hand stopped grippin' mine. The mud was slippery, which was strange because you'd think all that heat would dry it up, and I remember falling over in the sludge and hound dogs tearin' past me. Their fur was all matted and they had these spiked collars that were diggin' into their necks, makin' 'em more vicious. One of em' ate Jimmy the Butcher like he was just a piece of meat, which I guess he was – ironic considerin' his profession.

"Anyways, I was curled up in a ball, hands slammed over my ears, prayin' to god n' mindin' my own business. Then I see you waltzin' out of those shabby stables with three horses in tow, right before the whole buildin' toppled over nonetheless, like some hero. There I am thinkin', here's a brave fella who'll come n' save this helpless, timid, recently made orphan. But then I watch you shove past a burnt-up beggar and he shrivels up into a ball and ends up lookin' just like me.

"You disappeared into the night with those three horses, next thing I'm stumblin' through smoke. Scariest part was these outlines of people would form and I wouldn't know whether they were good or bad till they were an inch or two away. Luckily, the only people I passed were mothers and children. I made it out of there, came across the others – who are now dead anyways – and three days later we bumped into you at our camping grounds. You were ridin' a stallion, the other two horses were gone." The Maid finishes her tale and reluctantly raises her blue, hazy eyes to glare her way through the cracks in The Brute's heart, into the recesses of his soul.

"Why'd you tell me that?" The Brute asks.

"How do you do it?" she asks, bluntly.

"Do what?"

"You know what." Her lip trembles.

The Brute considers her question. "I try not to think about it."

"Eventually that's gonna stop workin'."

"I know."

"What'll you do when that happens?"

"I'll cross that bridge when it's burnin'."

"I don't think that's the sayin'."

"Does it matter?"

"Do you hate yourself?"

The Maid's straightforward question catches The Brute off guard. He picks at his teeth, chewing on his last remaining piece of tobacco. A destroyed spiderweb is pressed against the velvet fabric of his wide-brimmed hat.

"Tell me." The Maid snaps his attention back to her.

"Yeah, I do."

"Why?" she asks.

"Because I'm me. If that ain't enough reason to hate myself, I don't know what is." The Brute's being sincere, but something deep in his core still feels off, as though that weren't enough of a response. He hooks his hat onto the branch of a nearby tree and leaves it there.

"I wrote a poem, care to hear it?" The Maid asks.

"Are we talkin' about poems now. I thought I was bad at conversations but 'ere you are goin' from trauma to poems like a knife slicin' through butter." He sighs. "Go on, then. Let's hear it." The Brute is not one for poetry, but he also does not want the conversation to end.

The Maid pulls out a small parchment from her blouse, there seems to be several poems written on there.

"Flower petals sing
Hymns of dead man's burnt down house,
Now a poppy field."

The Brute hears her words but can't piece it together into a coherent whole. "Is that it?" he finally asks.

"It's a haiku. I thought you might not like it."

"No, I do."

"It's alright. Don't lie. There's always later." And with those words The Maid settles in for the night. Within moments, she's asleep.

The Brute rests his head on a bundle of clothes. He pictures The Girl With Hair Like A Storm dancing in a meadow with her father, but The Maid's words have forced him to question the very real possibility that the Girl is gone. She lived knowing one day she would die, and now she's dead and knows nothing. She's no longer a part of this world, no longer tethered to the land or its people. Even her name is but a word that The Brute will never know.

The sky above is filled with stars, each of which is a flickering lantern that cannot light the darkness.

The branches of the trees, earthbound and yet so distant, connect those dazzling, starry bulbs together, creating pathways to trace with the eye and a map that leads to some faraway realm. Perhaps that realm won't be someplace better but, at the very least, it will be someplace that is not this place. And that, is better than nothing.

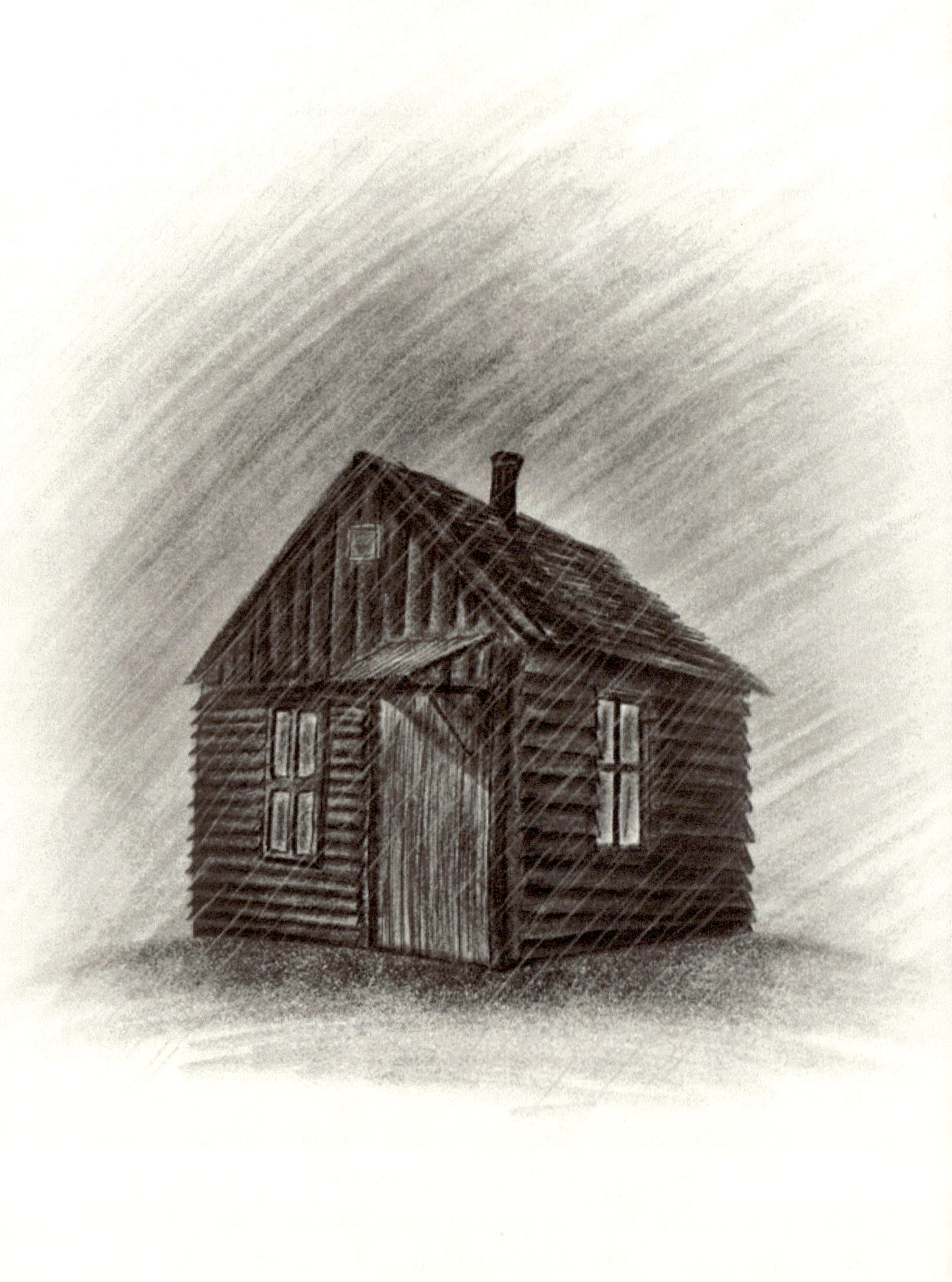

STRANDS OF WEB

FIRST, *THE MONSTER IN THE LIGHT*

Harsh rain patters against the rusted tin roof of the shed. There's a soot-covered lightbulb hanging from above the door, strung up by its bruised neck. The bulb swings back and forth, clocking the thunder.

The constant downpour has turned the surrounding soil into muddy puddles. Within these foot-sized pools of dirt, the quivering skeletons of past victims have become unburied. Polished bones that glimmer amongst the muck. It is midnight, the time of the beast.

He staggers quickly toward his house of worship, dragging a swollen corpse behind him. An electric lantern is hooked in one hand, made from green plastic and held together by glue and batteries. He has a slight dimple on his cheek because he's smiling, with thin lips, at his latest prize ... the final one. Part of him hopes it'll smile back. This is a monster, oh yes, but he is also dull, plain and forgettable.

Shaking the droplets off his woollen coat, he finds blood has stained the fabric. Oh well.

There's a dash of white protruding from the corpse's shirt. The monster latches on to it, only to find he's holding a PEOPLE magazine with a bald celebrity on the cover. The caption reads, 'SEXIEST MAN ALIVE'. The monster tosses the paper into the corner of his garden, where it can curl into a soggy mess.

No one knows this creature's deeds, but soon they will. With hatred in his heart, he pulls at the creaking door to his shed and enters. Tools hang from nails, red splatters green and a working station still has remnants of a dead bunny.

The monster slaps the corpse onto the hardwood bench and says to it, "Why did I do this to you too? My mind begs, but my hand acts." He closes the body's eyes, but it is a pointless act. The lantern slips from slimy fingers, cracking against aluminium, splitting open like pandora's box, spilling light into the darkness.

He must vanquish himself. Pouring gasoline onto the floor, the monster lights the final match and drops it into a yellow lake. The flames lick, then bite, and he can't help but scream in agony. Thankfully, the neighbours never come.

SECOND, *A VIEW FILLED WITH SPITE*

Murky moon is shredded by watery daggers gushing down from sagging rain clouds. It's peaceful out here, on the border of a nameless Missouri town, where the puddles are clear enough to reflect the brown cornfields of Old Walter McMiller's abandoned farm. He is long dead but, tonight, the leftover cows huddle together in his decrepit red barn. Their patchy hairs slathered in thick mud.

A still-active sawmill sits across the ways, overlooking the town from its mighty hill. The water wheel spins and slushes as the winding river overflows from the storm.

It's this haunted hill that the red-haired boy is trying to reach. Jenny, his border-collie dog, trails enthusiastically behind, guiding him toward the mill. The friendly pair pass a murder of starved crows that are feasting on a dead chicken. Jenny prowls over to join them and finishes the meat in one wholesome bite, the birds scatter.

Boy reaches cliff edge, where his sister took him when he was young. He'd waddled with tiny legs over to the sea of daffodils that overlooked their home. Having complained the whole walk, he'd not found the end sight to be all that grand and made it his mission to antagonise his sibling for dragging him with her on the journey.

Now he is back here again, wondering if his sister is down in that gloomy town, alone and frightened. She's been missing for a week, and the boy can do nothing but replay all the moments they have argued or fought.

At his feet, the daffodils are a mushy tangle of grey sludge that he cannot bear to touch.

"I'm going to grow up," he tells the wind. "I'll be a farmer or something, I'm sure. I'll grow into a man and marry a wife and start a family, but you won't, and that's such an awful feeling. Come home, won't you?"

Jenny barks a mournful prayer to the starry night. Fur is all matted, tail between her legs. She's going to devour the monster responsible for stealing her owner.

The boy tells the dog that's now his, "I'll take you on those sunshine strolls she used to do each morning. I'll cuddle you every night. I promise you, Jenny, I'll do everything she did and more, I don't care if I never make you as happy as she did, I'll be sure to try my best. Heck, I'll even put your poop in Mrs Beet's mailbox like she did that time, despite the fact the old hag terrifies me."

He notices a flicker in the distance, across the valley. There, behind the grey torrent of fierce wind, past the muted streetlamps, and beneath the sickly yellow fog that trickles through the cobbled streets. What is it that he sees? A twinkling ball of orange, pulsing its radiance through the storm's veil.

A stranger's toolshed must have caught fire, perhaps they'd tossed a lit cigarette by mistake. The boy knows he should warn the proper authorities, fulfil his due diligence as a citizen, but he is hypnotically mesmerised by the flames. They are strangely comforting, enchanting and heavenly.

Jenny sits herself down next to him, tongue lolling as she pants. His sister's dog is nearly twelve years old, but still so full of life. She lifts bushy eyebrows at him, barking cheerfully, but he keeps staring off in the hopes of seeing a ghost.

THIRD, *EULOGIES AFTER THE NIGHT*

A half-dozen mahogany coffins, slapped together with cheap nails, wait patiently to be lowered into open graves. The scent of soil hangs heavily, a wet smell that conjures images of worms or rainforests, depending on your disposition. Off to one side, sweaty gravedigger leans on shovel and beholds his finest work; a night well spent.

The mother of six dead sons nestles mournfully alongside remaining family. This particular matriarch has her oily hair jerked into a tight bun, sagging body laced into a dusty cotton dress, and the frock's neckline cradles a frail jaw. Her eyes are wet but her heart's drier than the stones that make up her mossy cottage on the hill.

Her sons, a boisterous lot, had worked as laborious miners before they died, and seeing how the youngest was blind in his left eye and the middle-child had constant tinnitus, it's no wonder they'd been involved in an accident.

The eldest, though, used to play the keys just as delicately, as energetically, as the wonderful Ray Charles. Her boy could ignite frivolous rhapsodies, sing ballads of loveless lassies, or play tunes in dusty jazz bars for minimal pay, all to the muted ears of drunken countrymen waiting on their next pint. She'll always remember his creativity, even if she isn't as artistically inclined.

The funeral attendees are itchy to leave, shuffling polished shoes and sneaking glances at watches. Many of them are fellow miners, some are strangers. All wear tweed jackets and exhale stale cigar breath. Their blue lips puff as the brutal wind slits fresh scars into their blemished faces. There's enough to fill a church. Her children are not, were not, all that clever but even in death they remained popular lads.

Eventually, the affair ends, the boxes lower, and the procession disperses. The mother releases a clump of dirt into each three-feet hole. Once she has finished, the crone cowers beneath a silver maple tree. The trunk is damp.

Her olive, coarse fingers fumble with a leather pouch of tobacco grounds. She removes a rolling paper from her pocket and, tilting the bag and tapping it gingerly with one finger, a clod of the good stuff spills onto the crisp white. She licks it and rolls it, then lifts it to pursed lips. The last enduring grief quickly evaporates as soon as it's ignited, her lungs filling with sweet relief.

The cemetery's other occupants are a priest and a boy. They are the only guests at a woodchipper's funeral. An enlarged photograph of the dead fellow shows he was a middle-aged gentleman with a receding hairline. The patchy frame has no flowers adorning beneath and it rests at a slight tilt, which nauseates the old hag from all the way beneath her maple tree. She hates imperfections and the askew portrait, as though someone did not place it very carefully, makes her burn through the tobacco quicker than she'd like.

She recognises the photograph of the departed, but can't place him. The boy appears familiar too but her eyesight is so shoddy that she's as likely to mistake a handsome bush for George Clooney as to recognise someone from a hundred yards. That said, it's a small town and she likely knows them both.

The boy, whose hair is fire orange, is accompanied by an ancient dog with shaking legs. Together, they glare down into the black depths. The boy leans over and spits into the darkness.

The priest cannot be a Catholic priest because his sash is green and his cloak is only knee-high. He spreads his arms like they're eagle wings and cries out, "It is better, yes, for him to reign in hell than to plague our happiness. He is a cleaved chunk of Cronus' pale naked flesh, given eyes and ears by Hades himself. Let him see only darkness, darkness, dark!"

The boy replies, "I don't have a clue what you're saying, but whatever it is ... he deserves worse."

The skeleton crew are joined by the gravedigger, who shuffles close. His brown eyes, lined with green crust, lower onto the tomb that he himself dug. He fixates on the coffin within. Raising a bony wrist above his head, the digger cracks his steel shovel down against the wood.

The shovel's impact forms a crater of shattered shards that stick upward. The coffin has become a Vietnam cartridge trap. If a foot fell into that hole, the flesh would be pierced by wooden spikes.

There's the raspy, phlegmy cackle of the gravedigger, and the delighted squeal of the boy. Even the dog's howl is more man than wolf. Then they all walk away together, a little merrier than when they arrived. This all serves as a symphony of horror to the old lady by the maple tree.

The mother of six pictures the woodchipper, a monster that could cause kind people to misbehave. He has cavernous sockets, no face and a hollow space where his organs should be.

Glimpsing the end of the Woodchipper's burial makes her more grateful for her sons. Good boys who were always kind. They hadn't done much, that's true, but they were definitely nice and knowing that makes her miss them. She decides she owes the disliked stranger a thank you. The grave takes a long time to reach and when she looks into it, she can only half discern the coffin's sleek elm body that shimmers red.

"Mrs Beet?" A young man's voice mutters in utter bewilderment.

The lady turns and, startled, proclaims, "I almost didn't recognise you!" It's the boy with red hair and a dog named Jenny. Her neighbour, whose property is separated from hers by a wall of loosely piled stones. What was his name again?

"What are you doing here?" he asks.

"My sons passed."

"Sorry."

"Thank you," she says and tries to recall more about the boy and his family. "You have a sister, don't you? How is she?"

"She died."

"Oh, my, that's awful. How did it happen?"

The boy glances at the grave of the woodchipper. He rubs his thigh frantically with white knuckles. His face scrunches into wrinkles whenever he blinks like those funny pug dogs.

Next to him, Jenny nuzzles her head against his leg and licks a slug from his boot with her heavy tongue. She bares her teeth as she realises the slimy critter tastes like bile.

Mrs Beets, knowing that the boy would stand there for eternity if she let him, speaks again. "Hey, it's a far way back to our houses.

Would you like to walk back with me? I'd hate to be alone on a lousy day like this."

The boy's spirits lift slightly. "Sure," he replies, "it'll be nice to have a chat with a lady that's not my dog."

So they walk, slightly apart, with the boy's head bobbing slightly above her elbow. At some point, she drops her stub of tobacco and crushes it beneath a black Chelsea boot, twisting her ankle back and forth to ensure the orange lump disintegrates into ash. The last thing either of them needs is for the cigarette to catch fire, and burn through everything they hold dear.

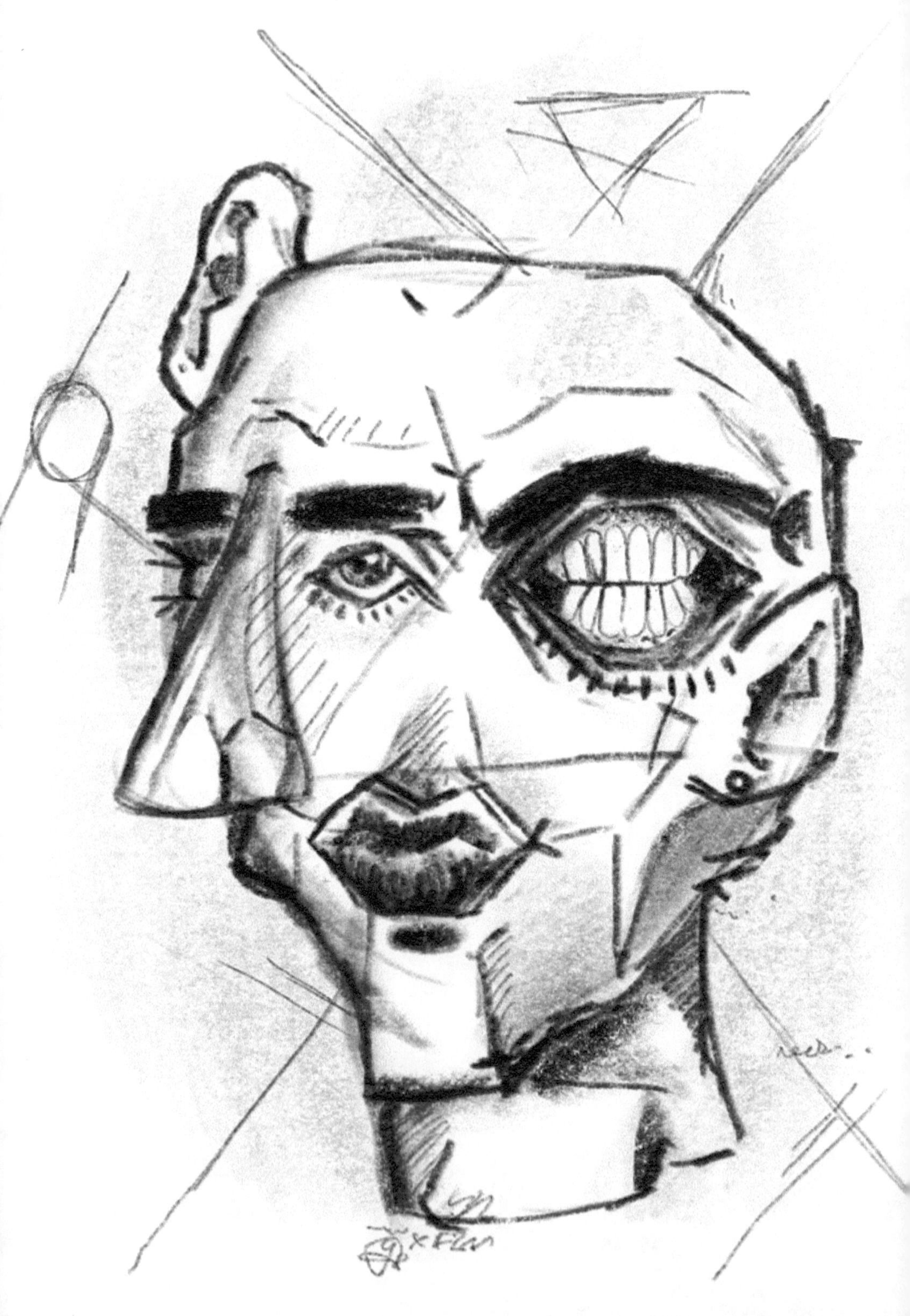

IT'S ALL IN YOUR HEAD

"It's all in your head,"
Five vocal expressions of inescapability.
A concoction, a formula for   Anxiety—
The health that brings you dread,
Is nothing but the ill-begotten woes of a
Hypochondriac.
How to escape sickness of the mind?
The answer: Convince ...
Conjure bald doctor: smudged glasses,
Typical stethoscope draped over shoulders
Like egotistical badge of honour. So he speaks,
"Cancer. Vines growing through the organs
Into the tree Yggdrasil. An electric current of
Pulsating, moist masses. Bubbles of flabby
Skin. You, dear patient, you were right."
And now the fear ebbs into your body.
Rising waves of nausea, dizziness—Panic.

Are you going to die? Do you need blood tests?
An ECG? Ultrasound? X-Ray? MRI? PET? Or
Perhaps a cool, translucent glass of water to steady
Those shaking hands. Doctor? Are you there? Please,
I'm still awake.
Reality and mentality collide just as,
In the coming Aeons, the Milky Way and Andromeda
will wage War. Stars battling for survival in
The face of catastrophic supernovas spreading
Fragmented starlight across the deep, unknowable chasm
Of the universe.
Sleep never comes. You lie awake in terror of tomorrow.
Of health, of life, of death.
Was it all wasted? Did you matter?
The words in your mind form the shape of an erratic heartbeat.
There is nothing here—there is nothing—
The end is nigh—
"It's all in your head."

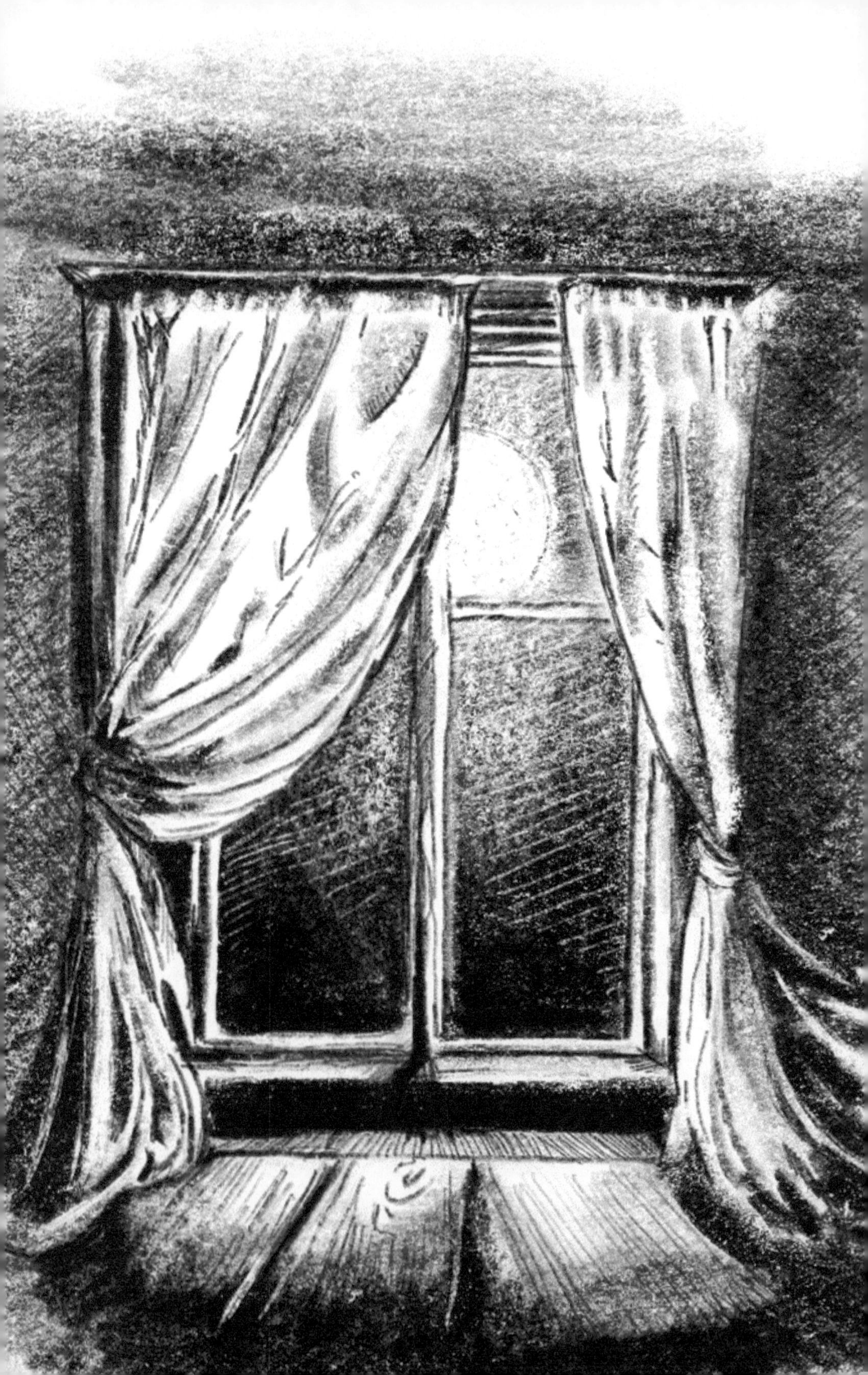

EMACIATED

Sterile moonlight flooding

Through window slats. Crashing against pale Skin.

A crease in the bed. Residue from my risen form

Indented in that scratchy sheet like a Subconscious whisper of my flaws.

You. Sit there. Bent leg on smooth thigh Smiling as I comply.

A gentle breeze in an enclosed room

Prickles against my slender, skeletal limbs. Costume removed, jester's
jokes are silenced by King. Queen. Self.

Divinity simmers in your eyes, a threat of flames

That forces my hand across caved chest, over Bulbous stomach.

You are Judgement Day, joint in hand with All-consuming Metabolism.

My cells devoured. Sex depleted. Anger rising.

I am nothing but a scarecrow in a field of crows, Eaten by fruitless parasites.

"Favour is deceitful,
And beauty is vain."

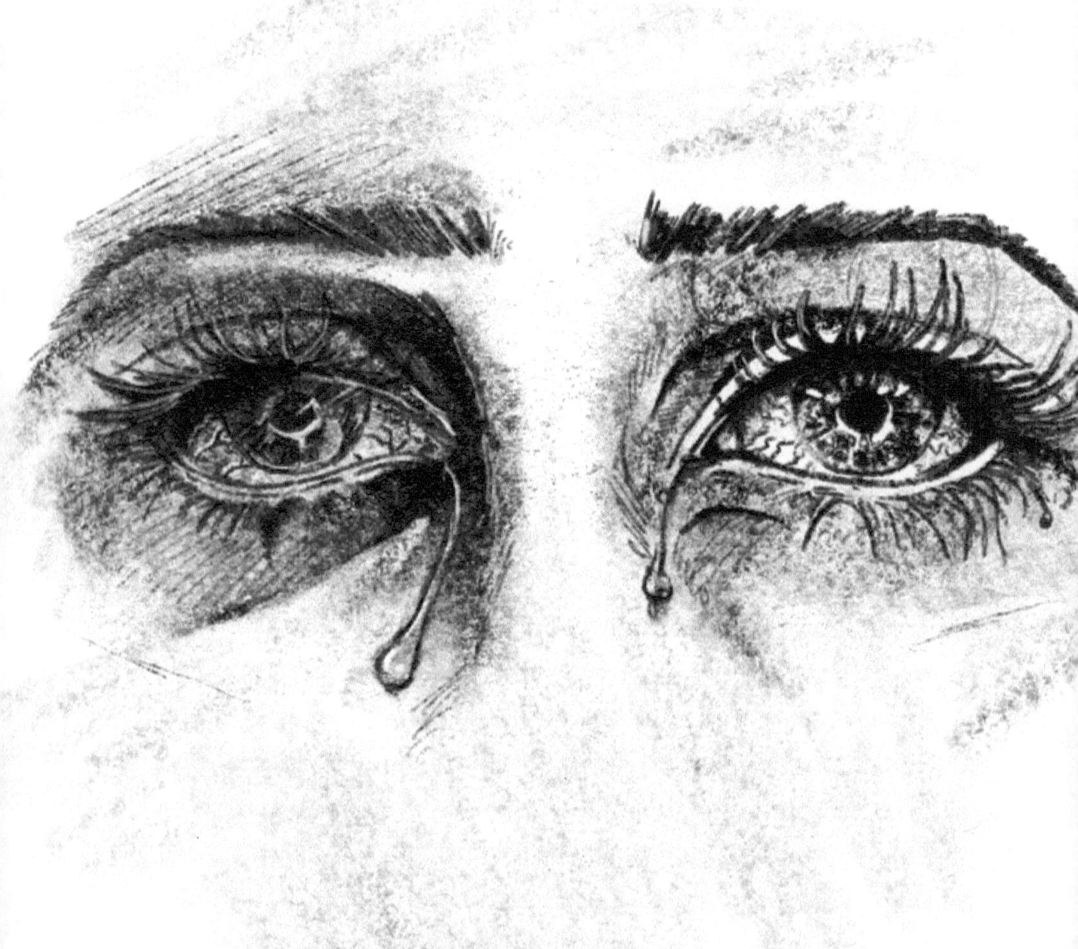

CONSTANT NIGHT SHIFT

Ascending into dreams …

Your body is a freight ship swaying in the sloshy waves of a lumpy mattress. Vainly, you try to drown your overthinking, but it clogs the drainage system of your subconscious. Brain becomes a sharp dagger that pierces the bubbles of fantastical worlds, where the laws of physics do not apply, crawling into encased dreamscapes that science still cannot explain and philosophers treat as keyhole glimpses into alternate universes. Sleep is a harder goal than wealth.

Reality is always intrusive to the sombre serenity of sleep. For you, it comes in the form of pointless fretting over half-baked fears, sustained by countless hours of television, news channels, and crippling dread of growing old, or becoming paralysed or getting relentlessly sick, believing yourself too weak compared to the heroes who handle curveballs with endless strength and optimism.

The first recalled phobia is a cracked, half-open cupboard. The dark slit provides a gateway for rats with hanging teeth to feast on your soggy entrails while you slumber. Much akin to the medieval torture method where vermin are placed in boxes and strapped to bare chests. A warm wicker candle on the other end forces despicable creatures to nibble away at skin, organs, heart. Funny how an amalgamation of educational history class, and a delightful film about a rat who can cook, caused fear to fester in mind, unstoppable yet entirely self-sustained. So insomnia begins.

Moving to the beachside is every active child's dream. Surfing, swimming or just running around on the sand makes up a paradise that few could complain about. Except, coastal home means paranoia surges inward as threat of tsunami becomes source of paralysing trepidation.

You spend your nights fixated on the slanted skylight embedded in the pale bedroom roof, expecting a wall of water to slam down with the full force of Poseidon. It will destroy your feeble wooden walls and crush your lungs. Your body will expand into a suffocating balloon.

Pillow is always too hot, legs too cold. Adulthood brings existentialism, you are small in the face of the world. Are you wasting your life?

Sense of impending doom because Ragnarok is nigh! This is the twilight of the awake and you are the undead zombie who is filled with unspent energy and missed opportunities. You're barely human anymore, since deprivation can tarnish appearance or make reality wobble as though everything is submerged in thick jelly.

Ah, so perhaps your body is not a freight ship. What if your body is Mount Vesuvius, the deadly volcano? That would mean you're building to an eruption, never truly sleeping, only lying in wait. In this near apocalypse, a pyroclastic surge of melatonin will burst out of you, trickling onto the bed sheets, staining the carpet floor. That last chance at sleep will be lost in the puddle by your feet.

Hours collide as the mundane cycle repeats itself and your flesh gradually deteriorates. The cold, endless loop of sleepless meandering.

Even when given the brief respite of a short nap or feeble attempts at meditation, the peace is short lived. The starved subconscious entity that fuels your paranoia, your anxiety, your incompleteness, that beast consumes you piece by piece in the same way that rats nibble at tortured man's chest.

Ye are slipping, sinking, losing …

"Oh, sweet Morpheus, tis a pother though maketh."

You are

Descending …

Descending into nightmares.

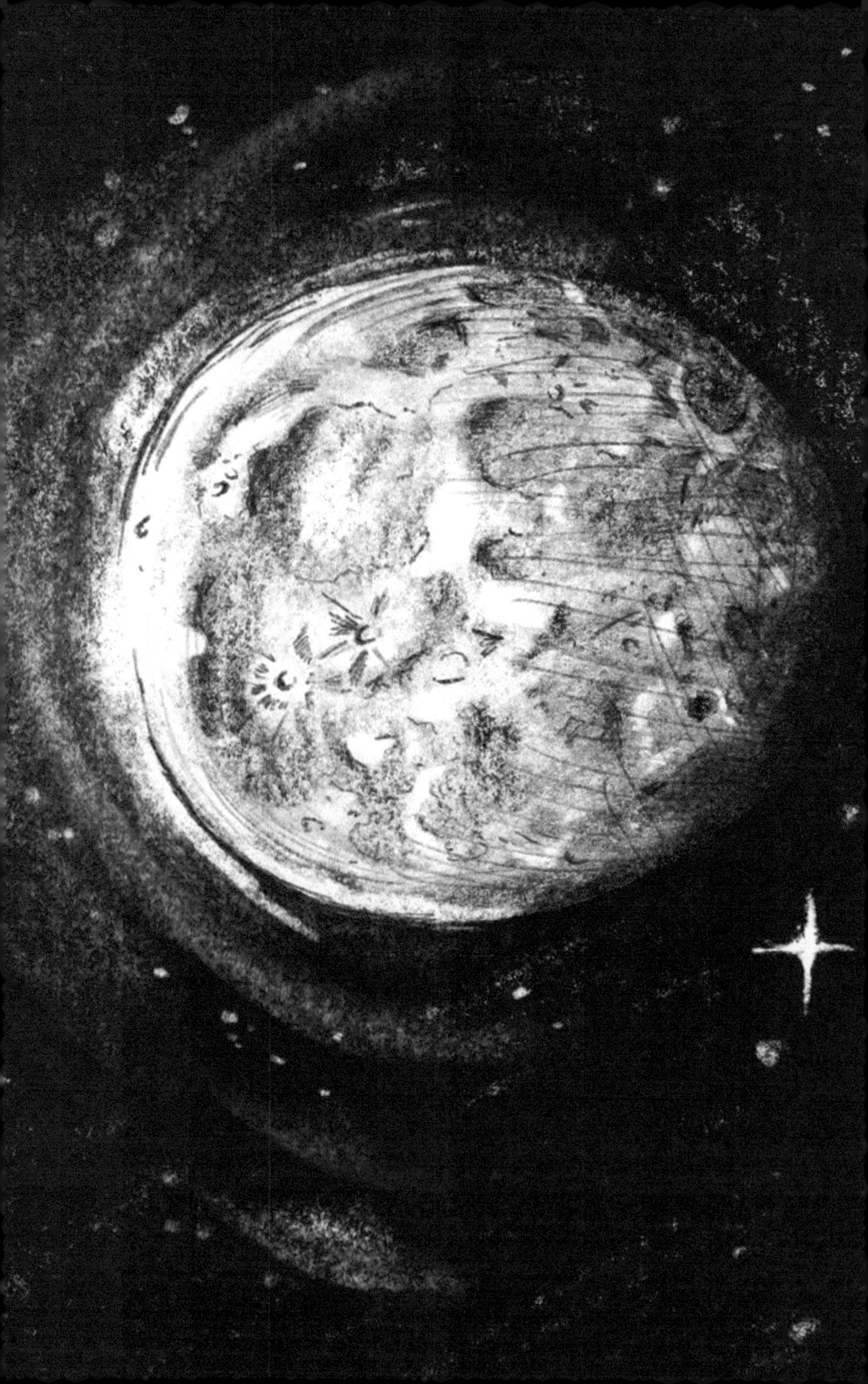

ASTRONAUTS MOVING KINGS

"I knew going in that there'd be dangers to being an astronaut, but this is absurd. Pawn to E4," I said, starting the game. My electronic chess piece eagerly slid forward two spaces and stopped. I cracked my dry knuckles, relaxing to the popping sound and waiting for my opponent to make her move.

"I'm telling you, Sarah, this is the fairest and most enjoyable way to decide on the matter. Now, let me see, I suppose I'll match you. Pawn to E5," Jess replied, hunched over the gaming table, surveying the chess board. Her grey hair was so dry you could snap it with two fingers. Wrinkles had begun to weave their way across her face. Needless to say, she looked a lot older than forty-five.

"Are we really going to do this? Have we thought of everything else?"

"Yes. Make your move."

With a resigned voice, I muttered, "Alright, pawn to F4."

"You're doing the King's Gambit? What is this, the nineteenth century?" Jess joked. "Fine, I'll take the bait, E5 to F4." The black pawn charged diagonally into my white pawn, evaporating it from the map.

I weighed upon which move to make next. We hadn't set a timer because neither of us were really in a hurry to let the game end, especially considering what would happen to the loser afterwards.

About an hour ago, we had sat ourselves down at a metal table, with my left shoulder pressed against a floor-to-ceiling window that gave an expansive view of outer space. The pair of us, perched opposite each other on steel stools, had patiently waited for the other to gain enough courage to switch on the screen built onto the table's surface and load up the chess board.

It was me who'd finally been brave enough to start the game. I'd guiltily sucked in a deep breath, and clicked the green 'ON' button. It dinged excitedly. Both of us were so afraid of what came next, and we still were.

Now, Jess was eyeing me with squinted eyes, her red jumpsuit zipped up to cover her neck, where I knew a necklace hung with a dandelion pendant.

I tried to stall for time, "Hey, here's a question for you. What do you miss most about Earth? And don't give some pretentious, gooey answer like 'my family' or 'the sweet smell of grass.' What do you really miss?"

Jess murmured a careful, "Hmm."

"You don't miss anything?"

"I do."

"Go on, tell me."

"I wouldn't mind a warm shower," she began, "or to hear the rain pattering against the roof and windows of my house ... Actually, I could go for a burger, a really oily, disgusting burger slathered in cheese. Yeah, that's what I miss most, cheap fast food that doesn't taste stale and dry like all of our packaged space meals."

"That sounds nice. Personally, I miss gravity. Not this artificial stuff that makes you constantly dizzy. Real gravity. The first thing I'm going to do when I get back is take my dog for a nice long walk that really stretches my legs."

"Well, that's if you win this game."

"Oh, I'm going to win," I sarcastically remarked, unsure if I actually meant it.

"Is that right?" Jess couldn't help but smile a little bit.

"Yup."

"I'll try to keep that in mind when I'm blasting you out of the airlock."

I laughed at that, but it was also a frightening prospect. Surely we weren't using chess to decide our nightmarish fate?

"Bishop to C4," I uttered my move after deliberating for some time.

"Took you long enough, Queen to H4 and ..." Jess's queen dragged itself to an attack position, "check."

"What if we fixed Pandora's solar panels? I know she was badly damaged, but we have to try, right?" I was desperate for a better alternative. Jess was my friend, the only one I had left.

Jess scratched vigorously at her straw hair. She had such large bags under her eyes that her whole face looked like melted ice cream. Her reply was curt and to the point, "There's not enough time."

I pleaded with her, "But if we managed to fix it right this second, the electrolysis process would have enough time to produce more oxygen and reboot life support systems before we suffocated."

"Yes, but we lost all our tools during The Incident."

"And our crew," I reminded her.

"I didn't think it needed mentioning that everyone except you and me is either dead or starving to death in deep space," Jess growled, digging fingernails into the metal table edge. "But yes, and our crew."

"We haven't really spoken about them since it happened."

"Do we need to?"

"I mean, Paul had a son and Laura was two days away from twenty-five. They were our friends and ..." I couldn't finish the sentence.

"And they're gone," Jess finished. "Our sole focus should be on this chess game, Sarah. We need to decide soon."

"How much is left in the backup oxygen tanks?"

"About two and a half thousand litres." Jess checked her watch and said, "That's less than three hours with both of us alive, plus another eight or so in our EMU suits. Eleven hours, all up."

"How far are we from Earth?"

"At least another fourteen hours."

"Oh god," I sighed and rested my head in my hands. "King to F1." I turned away from the board as my piece moved. Instead, I chose to survey the empty space station. The lights were dimmed to conserve energy, making the place seem abandoned.

The bar looked open, with blue lights pouring from above onto the assortment of spirits that rested on glass shelves. A powered-down android had been midway through cleaning a glass, dirty rag clutched in an iron fist. Its square chin rested against its chest.

"Pawn to B5," Jess casually said, moving her piece so that it lurked diagonally to my bishop, waiting to take it.

The threatening position of Jess' piece was a stark reminder of the danger we too were in. "The Incident" as Jess had called it, occurred around a week ago when we'd shut off The Pandora's engines for routine maintenance work.

I'd been in the medical facility examining a blood sample provided by Jess, I hadn't liked what I'd seen. Then, an explosion rattled the screws in the walls and made the lights flicker.

I'd rushed to the observation deck where Jess was already managing the scene. Out in space, I saw our crew torn apart by these seismic waves that rippled noiselessly through the cosmos before slamming into The Pandora.

Over the comms earpiece, I could hear the crew screaming, pleading for help and I had stood and watched as their suits tore open or their safety lines snapped and they flew off into deep space.

"Dave's in the lab, check he's alright," Jess had said to me, her voice was level but shaky.

I had rushed over to the research laboratory in time to see wind gusting out of a gaping hole in the high-tech facility. Dave clawed out of the circular door and sealed it behind him. I caught a glimpse of scattered papers flying around the room and I knew that all his research was lost.

Dave faced me, covered in blood. He collapsed and I rushed over to try to save him. His stomach and chest had been sliced open by a nasty shard of glass and I tried dragging him over to the medical facility, yelling for help on comms, but even then I knew it was too late to save him.

That night I had showered and when I looked at my feet I saw the water was almost completely red as it swirled down the drain. It was then that it hit me; all of my friends were dead.

"Have you ever watched those X-Men movies?" Jess asked, releasing me from my flashback.

My response was a bewildered, "Sorry?"

"I always loved the first X-Men movie with Ian Mckellen and Patrick Stewart. A real crowd-pleasing popcorn flick, but you know something that used to irk me about it?"

"What's that?"

"Why Professor X and Magneto, two sworn enemies at war, were always playing chess together. I know they've known each other a long time and their style of playing was like a big metaphor for their ideologies. For instance, Professor X protects his pawns whereas Magneto discards them. The thing is Magneto is a murderous criminal who's super violent so what could drive Professor Xavier, a pacifist, to still associate with the man?"

"I don't know. What's your point?" I wasn't really listening, I was invested in the chessboard. Planning my move.

"Well, I think I just figured it out, just now. See the game of chess gives The Professor an excuse, a chance to talk with his friend while still fighting their war. The chess battle is the same as the mutant one, just small-scale, and even though they know one side must lose, they still care for each other. It's kind of a nice thought."

"Oh, right. Okay."

"Do you understand?"

"Not really, no." I had decided on my move, but before I could play it my attention was once again diverted to Jess speaking.

"See it's the same with our chess match. We are using it as both a distraction from reality and a fight for our lives since the winner kills the loser. But we mustn't forget that we are still just two young women, sitting across from each other, talking as friends."

"Is that what we are?" I asked and, scared to hear her answer, waved my hand. "Bishop to B5."

"Ooo, a pawn for a pawn, glad this is an even match. Horse to F6," Jess goaded, "and, Sarah?"

"Yeah?"

"We are friends, I hope that doesn't affect you too much."

"I'm not going to go easy if that's what you mean, horse to F3," I smirked.

"Good. I'm thinking queen to H6."

It continued like this for some time, each of us lugging our pieces around the battlefield. Obliterating a knight or saving a rook. After a while, we stopped speaking about things and simply said our move aloud then fell into solemn silence.

The Pandora angled its hulking slate body as it prepared to descend into Earth's atmosphere. Our huge blue planet rose into view, the continents lit by thousands of streetlamps. The ocean was sludgy tar, a lot of it covered by patchy clouds that spiralled in shape.

Jess complimented me, "You look good in that shirt by the way. It's making me wish I hadn't worn this squeaky jumpsuit, especially if it's my last day. Imagine they find me floating out there and I'm a spandex-wearing cyclist." She scratched at her forearm and jerked the zipper slightly up and down in an annoyed manner.

I looked down at my navy-blue flannel top. "I wore this because it reminds me of my daughter," I said.

"What do you mean?"

I didn't like recalling the memory but since it was our last moments together I figured I owed it to Jess and myself to talk about Bella. "She had this blue raincoat she'd wear everywhere. It was a button up like the one Paddington wears in those picture books and it was way too big for her, so if she put the hood on it'd dip past her eyes." Talking about my daughter made me oddly compelled to win, I needed to survive.

"She sounds lovely," Jess lauded. It seemed the image had stuck in her brain, giving her a happy thought against all that had happened.

"She was," I stated and whispered. "Queen to F6. I've got you in check." I had set down a trap. If Jess took the bait and used her horse to take my Queen, it would let me pull a checkmate right under her nose.

"Horse to F6, seems you've lost your Queen."

I took a deep breath, preparing for the end. Did I really want to do this? Would it be wrong to release Jess out of the airlock so I could survive? Was there really all that much waiting for me on Earth? Did I owe it to go back and live an unbelievable life of glamour and fame? Maybe none of that mattered.

"Bishop to E7, checkmate."

Jess stared at the board for so long that I thought she had to be coming up with an excuse to avoid her fate. Her expression was unreadable and she was so still you had to squint to see the slight rise and fall of her chest. Then she said, firmly, "Okay."

"Jess, I—"

"Will you come with me to the door?"

"Yes."

So we walked together through the empty shuttle called Pandora. Down flickering hallways with slick grey paint and past the quiet cabins where the remnants of people's lives still remained: paper photographs of families or a laptop plugged into its charger. At last, we made it to the airlock.

"I want to wear a suit," Jess said.

"Why?"

"So I can float out there for a little while and then take off my helmet myself."

"Alright."

So we both got into our EMU suits. Me because I needed the extra air for when the shuttle ran out – even without Jess it would be tight getting back to Earth – and Jess so that she could have her last illusion of control.

I pleaded half-heartedly, "Maybe there's some other way. I don't want to do this."

Jess, my last remaining crewmate, was hunched over and weary when she uttered her final, "No."

She struggled to lift the suit around herself, it seemed far too heavy for her frail body. I wanted to reach out and help her but my arms wouldn't move, nothing was working. I was limp and empty inside.

Jess lightly pushed me out of the airlock and shut the door. I didn't say anything as she did this. Instead, I shut off my thoughts, hoping it was all a dream. I managed to gain the strength to look through the small square window as Jess clicked on her helmet and gave me a far too enthusiastic thumbs up. She jerked at the hatch lever and threw open the door to outer space.

The air was rapidly sucked out along with Jess. She disappeared from sight quite quickly. It was then that I broke down, sobbing in my spacesuit as the lights switched to the alarming red that signified heat levels were low because of power failures. I was going to make it to Earth, undoubtedly, but it would be a cold, friendless, bumpy ride.

Suddenly, through a rumble of static in my suit I heard Jess say, "Sa—Sarah ca-can you hear me?" Her tone was light hearted, singsong like she was pleasantly taking a tour of a great city without a care in the universe.

Was it a ghost? A silly hope that I was imagining? "Jess?" I dared to ask.

"Did you seriously forget there's a communications device built into the suits?" she remarked humorously in her classic nasally voice.

I laughed through the tears, "Seems I did."

"It's nice out here," she said distantly.

"Is it?"

"I can see the Earth, it's so clear."

"You can see it from in here too."

"You can but I don't know, it looks closer now. Jess?"

"Yeah?"

Jess sputtered an, "I—" before my comms dissolved into white-wash noises that sounded like raging ocean waves.

"Jess?" I passively queried. When there was no response, I rushed back to the cafeteria where we'd played our game of chess. I gazed out of the enormous window but only saw planet Earth. The glow emitting from its surface meant I couldn't even spot any stars.

There was no sign of my opponent, commander, ally. Although, it was possible one of the specks dirtying the window was actually her, floating out there, too small to properly see.

Her voice flickered in and out so all I heard was the final words of her undoubtedly poetic sentence, "—go home."

"What?"

"—go."

"Jess!"

"Don't tell people I'm bad at chess." Then she was gone forever and I was the only crew member still here.

I was always aware of my own mortality. How quickly and shamelessly it could all be taken away. When I was a girl I had struggled to fall asleep because I was scared of dying in my dreams and never waking up again. It kept me in a sweaty state of panic, breathing heavily, on the brink of tears. To have your life and memories stripped from you and there being little you could do. I couldn't think of anything worse. The nothingness of death haunted my childhood.

It brought a laugh, thinking about it now, after all the disasters that had happened. The conversation and the chess game seemed like a cleverly hidden joke in retrospect, along with hearing Jess's voice fade away slowly. Knowing that my friend would starve while I stayed comfortable on the ship.

It made a question arise in my mind, a question I should have asked myself before sliding my bishop into a checkmate. The question was this: Which would be worse, to be nothing or to be lonely? Or, perhaps, a little bit of both?

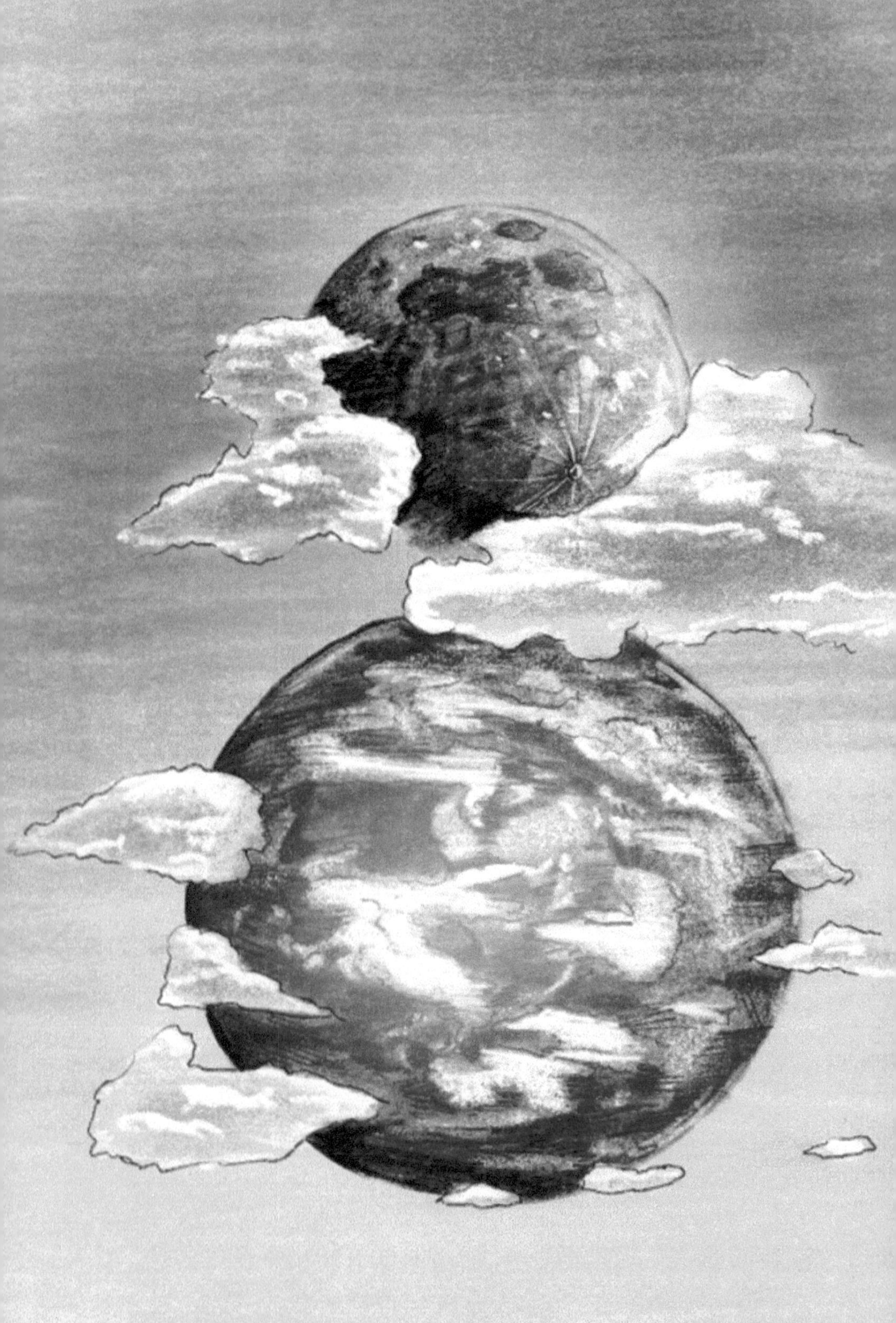

DEAR SKY, CAN YOU SEE ME?

"On June's month
I saw a moon, a sky, and
an earth.
All of it at once,"

Do white clouds know they'll become grey rain?
Bundles of mist spending lives drifting away,
Thick muggy winds shredding those resisting,
Unbearable pain?

We

Lonely car rides beneath three almond stars.
Blind headlights peering at grey asphalt ice.
Highway tearing through forest paradise.
Square green bordered by gridlocked tar scars.

Dance

Bright yellow Loader Tractor scoops up dirt,
Digging abyss since diamonds hold spell.

As Men in shiny vests scour her cracked shell.
O home of machines; Are you hurt?

Naked

Lightning flickers above raging ocean,
Foamy waves smashing against fishing boat.
Bubbly froth on hard-scrubbed deck, still afloat.
Captain cuddles wet dog with devotion.

And

Smudged laptop screen gives fleeting rush,
Empty cup stained by pink smoothie.
Finding answers in your cheap 'real' movies.
Blueness fades, coldly, in the hush.

Haunted

"Have you heard the tale?
Have you signed the seal?
When it begins to hail, And
you start to feel.
All I ask, sky,
Is can you see me?"

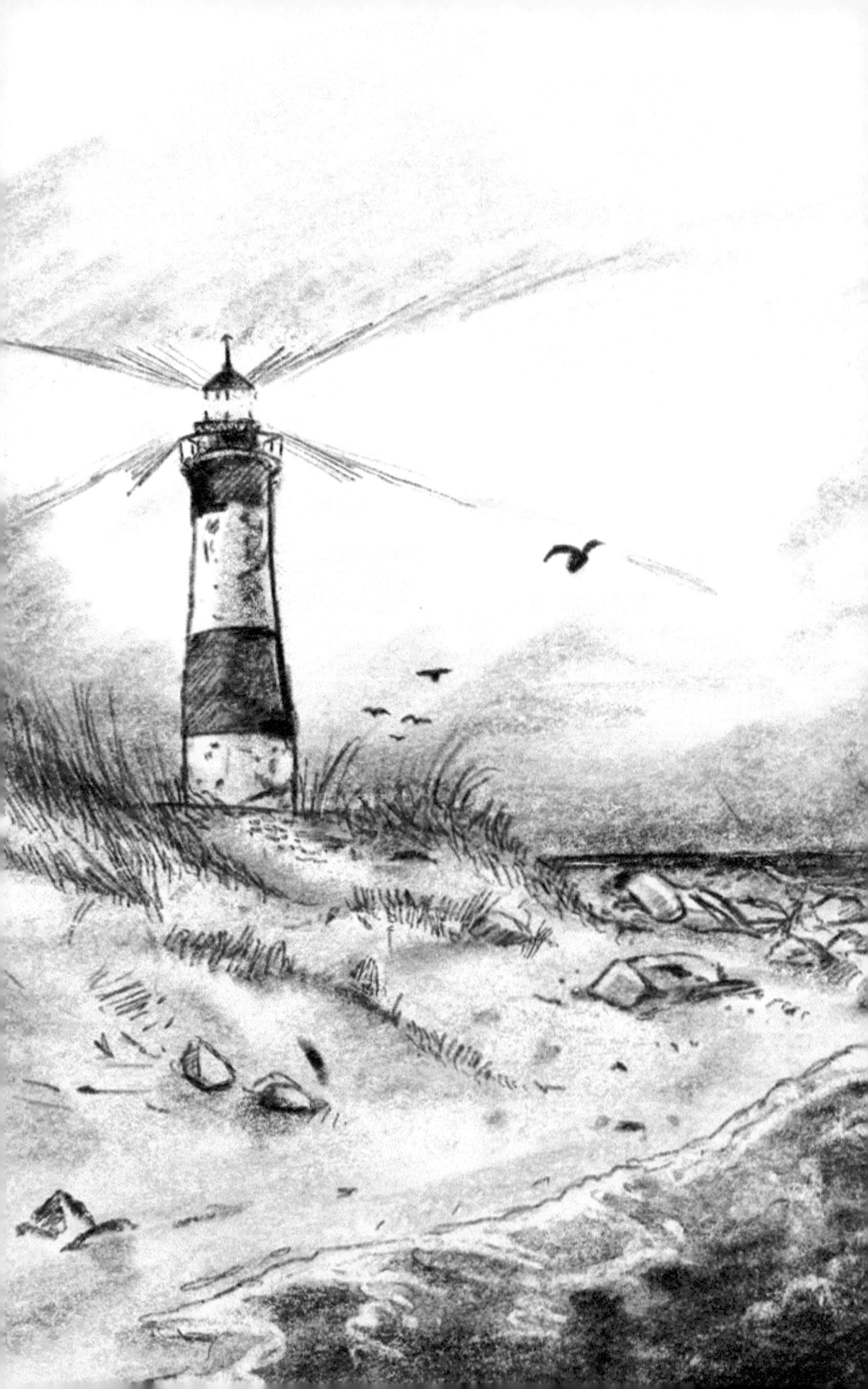

WALKING INTO THE UNKNOWN

I'm fading.

My mind, body, soul, existence. It's disappearing. Up ahead, the vast ocean is the dark ink flowing inside of me, a thin veil of silicon sticking to my heart and lungs. A wall of rocks border the sandy beach to my right. Atop those rocks, a white watchtower perches like a bony knife piercing the sky. Though I cannot see him, I hope God is in that tower. Watching. Judging.

Or would it be better if I was walking into the unknown?

The horizon is a blank canvas, nearly cloudless. Everything is so bleak. So grim. The ocean foams and froths against the rocks. Waves writhe and try in vain to climb the tower and glimpse their creator. They don't even make it halfway to the top, but for every crash of water against the scattering sand, a piece of my life vanishes. I'm driving through a thick fog, memories appearing momentarily – deer frozen in the headlights – then vanishing in the gloom.

Fractured light passes through me but leaves no shadow. I can't feel the sand beneath my boots. I can't feel anything. Not the wind or the cold or the sunlight. I can't tell what the weather is. Everything is grey except the white tower and the dark ocean. My blood is still, my heart is stopped. I am merely atoms floating in space, and not even they are connected.

I'm still wearing the same clothes from when it happened. The colours are gone but the shapes are still there: a trench coat, a fedora hat, rectangular glasses. Where was I when it all ended? What did I do to deserve this? Does it matter? Do I matter?

Perhaps this is all my imagination. The fleeting thoughts of a dying man, trying to create meaning out of a meaningless life. Standing beneath the tower, I can see now that it is empty. Why would my mind create an empty tower? Would my last wish not be to see the face of divinity? To know that I was not the spawn of randomness or chance? Instead, my mind concocted the very epitome of disappointment; an empty tower and an ocean to drown in.

At least I can't fabricate the unknown. I will walk into it and fade or glow, perhaps even shine. I will leave this place and everything that came before. It won't matter if what lies ahead is good or bad. My thoughts will cease and there will be no doubt or fear. Just nothingness. And that is something I take comfort in. A fresh start. Of the little I remember, I know that a fresh start is what I want. I suppose purgatory is a time of acceptance. And the unknown is a journey of discovery.

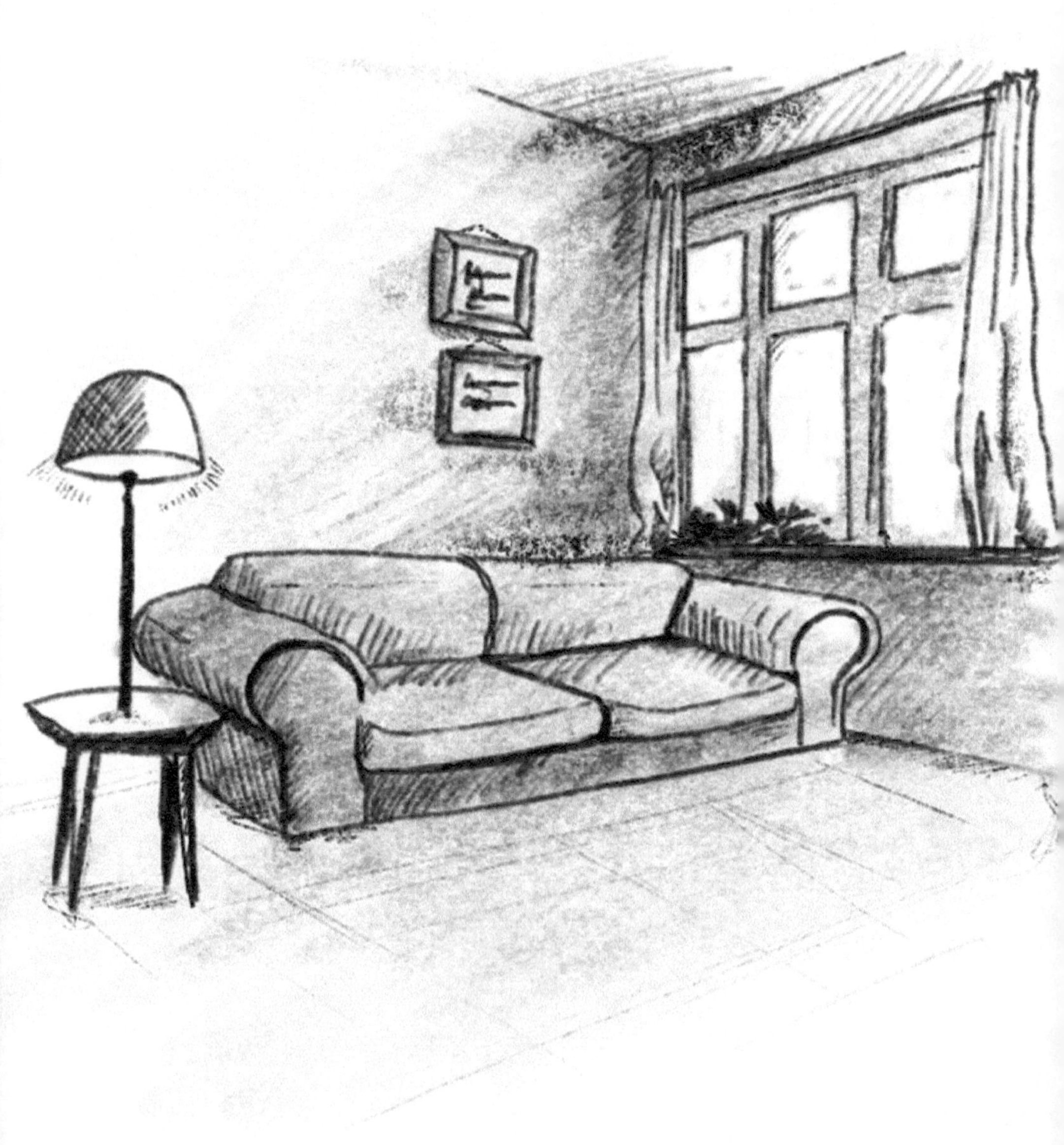

MOVING

This story is not for you, it is for me and me alone, so bugger off, please.

Right, with that out of the way, what comes first? The hospital I was born in doesn't count since I don't remember that. No, my first memory would be vomiting white, yoghurt puke onto my parent's bed sheets after a Halloween party where I ate too much candy. I would have been around three years old. Where was that? Ah, of course ...

In the beginning there was a Scotland farm with red plywood walls and a gravel driveway for the vine covered tractor. My family had a cat named Russell, who was eaten by foxes, and a cow called Moo-Moo, who my sister was obsessed with. The empty barn, which had no electric lights and contained the remnants of old haystacks, was home to invisible vampires, werewolves and witches who'd cook young boys like myself. I dared not go in there.

It was a nice farm. I'm sure I would've liked growing up there but it never saw a wink of sunlight and the sleet rain was constantly drizzling. I mean, the clouds are allowed to be miserable if they want to be, but at least have the decency to pour, not drizzle, so I have puddles to splash in or mud to slide through. Luckily, I left before I could even read or write.

I think let's skip past Scotland, it may be my birthplace but I have no heritage there and little memories. South Africa is where I really began. Where I exited that void of infancy and had my first original thoughts.

Those early years were spent in L'Agulhas, Cape of the Needles, a small fishing village on the southernmost point of the country. The shoreline was decorated with boot-trodden seaweed.

Our local beach had a tidal pool infested with barnacles and I remember swimming in it once with Cornell. I had picked up what I thought was a balloon, hoping to show it off to my mate, only it was a blue-bottle jellyfish that burned my palm. The doctor's special treatment was running my hand beneath cold water for ten seconds and sending me on my way.

Elsewhere in this coastal town was a stump lighthouse that had been built around the 1800s but still shone brightly on rainy nights. I'd watch it blinking from my window before bedtime, but in the day it was just a candy-cane block of stone.

Decades before my arrival, the beacon had apparently failed to protect a Chinese cargo ship from ploughing into nearby jagged rocks. I knew this because the wreckage sat curiously off shore, begging to be explored.

A pierced hole in its hull, wide enough to fit a pickup truck, proved to be the best point of entrance. In low-tide, idiotic swimmers such as myself could wade inside and marvel at rustic beams or mossy stairs. The promise of tetanus was a justifiable cost for childish foolishness.

Then, a final announcement. The departure.

I had a cabinet top in my room that held various toys on top. During the final weeks in South Africa, I prepared myself for a last performance, with the cabinet being a theatrical stage. I became a ringmaster, presenting cherished novelties to dear Cornell, who I'd never hang out with again.

"Here, here! Look at this model race car with a busted tire. The paint may have scratched off but I'm positive insurance will cover it. Oh, and what about my remote-control helicopter that I got from Carl the Scotsman. It sometimes flies! There's a Mr Incredible Limited Edition Action Figurine. And last off is a miniature Black Pearl ship with retractable cannons and velvet sails. Unfortunately, I've lost the plastic Jack Sparrow that would normally stand behind the wheel.

"Have them," I say, the performance done, "because you will not see me tomorrow."

I vividly recall the nauseating plane ride and how the sick bag inflated with my rapid breathing. The wheels bounced off of the scorching tarmac when we touched down in Perth, Western Australia. I would not see the fabled Kangaroo for another six months. Magazines had also misinformed me that snakes would be around every corner, the truth was that they were only in bushes and the occasional bike track.

Old acquaintances, our neighbours in Bathgate from when I was a baby, gave us a place to rest. Their spare bedroom, with its sliding glass door and pink inflatable mattress, felt strangely hollow. I missed my turf.

My frightening classmates were all better at sports, playing AFL or cricket like they had come out of the womb wearing mouth-guards and numbered vests. Years passed though, and despite being a comic book fan, I started to learn names. Dean, Harry, Harrison, Flynn. Friends that were inked into the golden ledger of my mind.

Quite a lot of my days were spent in Dean's beach shack. He was my closest mate and the sand-covered floor, cartoon ladies in bikinis on the bumpy wall, and sweet pang of a brown ukulele made the house a perfect environment for growing lads. We'd have hide and seek games in naive darkness or bonfires with our steel-stringed guitars, playing Clapton or Lennon, thinking we knew what it meant to be musicians.

There were a few sleepless nights on a scratchy sofa. The midnight run of *SpongeBob SquarePants* would switch to the dawn showing of *Ren & Stimpy*, that's when I knew I hadn't slept. Insomnia is a tricky road to navigate but I was young back then and backup fuel was enough to get me through each day.

The best thing I ever did in Perth was sneak into a derelict camping ground. Up in the trees there were peeling blue cabins perched on thin wooden stilts. A sloped volleyball net had been hammered into the grass of a soccer field and a sandy tennis court had a basketball court. Welcome to Name I Can't Remember, the sporty campsite where you can't play any actual sport because the designs are all wrong, be sure to tell your friends about us!

When dusk crawled through the grounds, I had walked through reeds and passed a massive lily flower that resembled Jason Voorhees' mask. I pictured his rotting corpse submerged in the swamp. He'd be starving for human flesh, and so I'd clambered very quickly past that frightening spot.

Hidden behind the filthy lake was a dirt track of self-made ramps, where tires could skid and knees could scrape into treasured red checkers. Riding our bikes here was the most thrilling joy of adolescence.

That was the final day, now that I'm thinking about it. I caught an aeroplane the following morning. The vodka sunset atop the abandoned flying fox tower would have been the last I saw of Perth. Orange trickled into a frothy sea, I had friends side by side and we were looking outward, toward our future.

Night came and I waited under a lonesome streetlamp. My suitcase rested by my flip-flop adorned feet. The rattling bus pulled up, a foot went in, and I was ferried by Charon across into New South Wales.

The not quite final destination.

Sydney proved to be a paradise found. It was a bubble that no one came out of but lots came into. The saltless seas, rolling hills, twisting streets and silent hounds made the past become guiltily omitted. I met a girl, who was she?

I fear I cannot talk about this new land because it is still too fresh. I must wait a little longer, for when I forget it was once called home. Let's end where it began.

In South Africa, I watched *Star Wars* on VHS in Cornell's dusty attic on his smudged television. A hole in his wooden floor gave us direct line of sight into the kitchen, so we could easily gather intel on supper. We'd get excited if it was mouth-watering Potjiekos.

In Perth, I witnessed *Lord of The Rings* with my pal Dean. Such adorable buddies we were when we lazed about, eating crusty pizza on the arctic couch that belonged in either a retirement home, a morgue, or hell itself. Despite incessant itching, despite cold pineapple, nothing could beat the grand odyssey of Frodo Baggins. Dean's dog was named Frodo.

See you later, bygone salad days.

Now I am here, they are there. And VHS is nothing but a broken relic fighting to stay relevant in a world that doesn't need it anymore. Life is always moving.

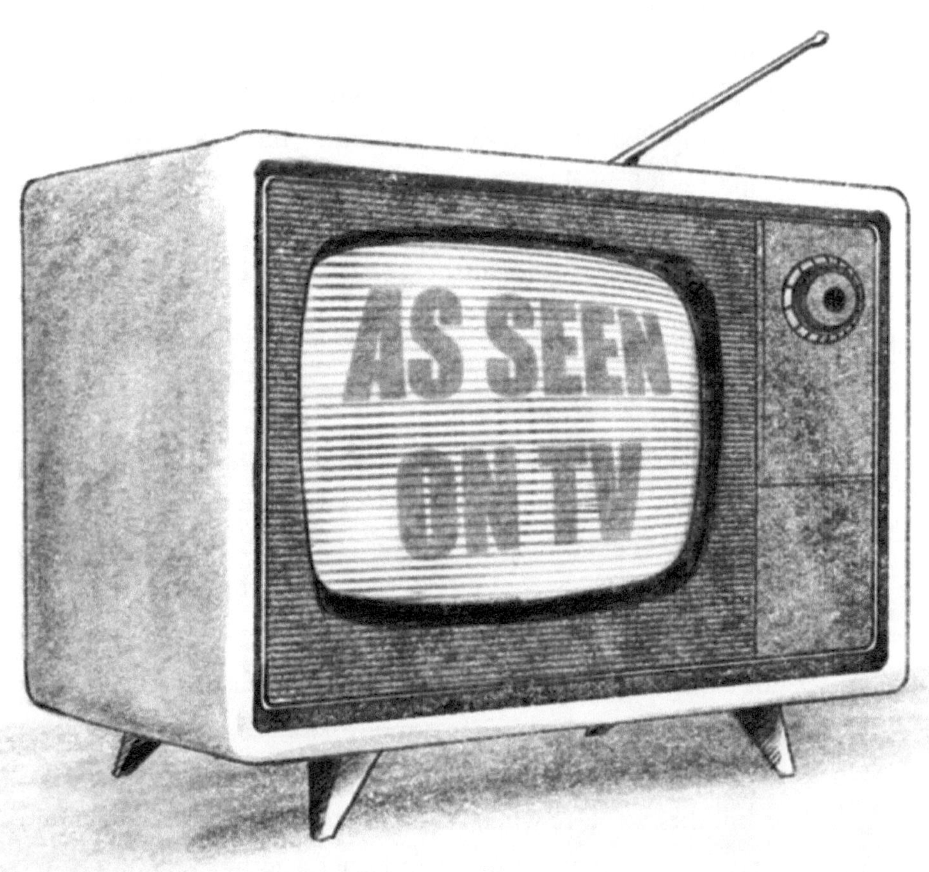
AS SEEN
ON TV

LOVE DOESN'T RHYME ANYMORE

Is true love simply a commodity
fabricated by pretentious artists,
Gaining fame from writing frivolously
Of how appearance makes beauty? Heart must
Want nothing more
Than a store-bought product,
"AS SEEN ON T.V.!"

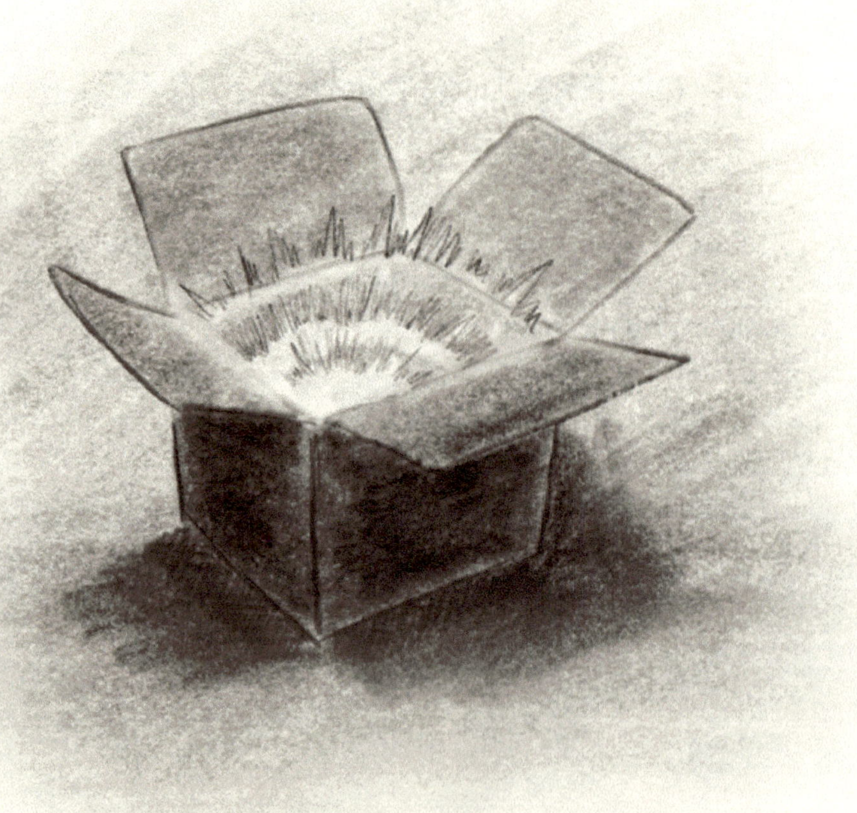

OUTSIDE THE BOX

Who am I?

Is that not the question we all ask ourselves? As our lives twist and turn like the cogs in a machine that never stops. I'm sure you haven't heard of him but there is a creature named Moloch, a god to some but to others he is a starving stray dog gnawing on human bones. The cavernous abyss of his stomach gradually being filled with acids that suffocate us, burst our lungs, and cause blisters to break out on our acne-infested skin. What a wonderful world; you were right, Louis.

Sorry, I did not want to start my story sounding like a bleak corporate junkie, but it's true. I am a machine. Programmed to type, programmed to sell, mostly programmed to speak out of my ass. That is what I do. I'm a buoy, lost in the waves, red paint chewed up by the froth of whitewash ... actually, that sounds rather peaceful. I am the opposite of that.

I hate this. My fingers begin to cramp an hour into the shift, while my bloodshot eyes sting and burn and my legs fall asleep (I think they have, though maybe I'm just paralysed by boredom).

It's a typical Monday. I'm a little drowsier than usual, though not entirely sure why—Coffee! I haven't had my coffee! I need that sweet tang of caffeine. I need a hit. I need fuel. How could I have forgotten? What a moron I must appear to you; a pinstripe asshole that is so used to taking shit, he doesn't accept the coffee he deserves.

I lurch to my feet with a groan and crack my aching back. Glancing around, the rest of the office is as dismal as my mental state. Grey walls, grey cubicles, even the lights are grey. The familiar faces of co-workers stare at me, shocked to see the undead mummy rise from his tomb. Their skin is like mine, pale and sickly, their eyes unblinking voids, hungry for the next paycheque. We are all the same.

Derek isn't here today, or was it Dan? Either way, he was called into the boss' office for a private meeting, he didn't come out until sometime after I left for home. Must've either been fired or transferred. There is a constant turnaround here; it's never the same faces staring back at you. And yet, it is. There's hardly a difference between one shade of puffy eyes and another.

The coffee machine hums a sweet tune as it shoots out black tar, and I relish the sight of it. It is the closest thing that I can call a friend. A guardian angel in my own personal hell. Far from sentient, the machine knows what I want, and provides it. No further questions. My mug fills with thin, murky sludge that will burn as it slides down my throat and heats the coldness of my insides. Maybe today will be the day I feel something ... anything.

I wasn't always like this, you know? I used to be a monster. I had thoughts that were my own, I had hopes and dreams. Bile rises up with the mere prospect. At least now, in my later years, I have overcome the childish need to be an individual. I know that success is bred by uniformity. I must be the same as everyone else, for long enough that I get promoted and become better than everyone else.

Waiting in front of me in the emptiness of my mind is a towering ladder that I can keep climbing until the oxygen becomes too thin and the sky too dark to see. I can't wait.

You are an idiot.

I'm back at my desk, I don't remember returning from the coffee machine. Everything is a blur. Each moment passes into the next, an endless ticker tape of unrelated events. I'm sure this infinite shift will pass and then I'll be waking up in my one-bedroom apartment with a stiff neck and a headache, ready to start the day all over again. Such is life, I suppose. I sip my coffee and do my work.

Is this all you want? You can be so much more. Be somebody! Do something!

Quiet, you! I hear you in there, listening to me. Watching me. I will shove your provocative thoughts into the deepest recesses of my mind, locking you in a box with the rest of my personality. Do you think that you can drown out my urge to follow protocol? Make me break away from programming? Here I was, thinking you were an omnipotent genius. You'll have to try harder than that, darling.

I'm afraid that I must stick to what I know. After all, I know nothing else. If I don't, I risk losing everything, as little as that is. Did that make sense to you? Was that grammatically correct? Paradoxical in a nonsensical manner?

No.

Eagerly, I choke down my coffee. The only thing that can bring me more joy than the hot black tar is walking into my piss-smelling apartment and finding my cat purring peacefully on the couch. Seeing that lazy, overfed feline without a care in the world makes my heart soar. Speaking of which, I need to buy more cat food.

I finally finish my coffee when, behind me, the bottom of a doorframe scrapes against the rough carpet floor, and footsteps thump toward me at a precise beat. Each foot lands like thunder rolling over a damp countryside ... I need a holiday. I can feel my organs shrivel and blacken; what little humanity is left in my body is being poisoned by the unseen presence. Brewing diarrhea induced by an overdose of caffeine is causing excess gas to build in my intestines. Shit. I hope this isn't the boss.

Slowly, every movement deliberate and passive so as not to provoke the creature approaching, I swivel around in my chair. What awaits me is a man in red clothes, his face half-covered by a wiry beard that points North, West and South (though strangely not East). I know this man. I do not like him, and seeing him now makes me want to lean into a toilet and puke until I'm empty and I can't remember my own name.

He is Abraham, the big boss (though Managing Director is the preferred title), and he's staring down at me with a godly fury. For some reason, he is also holding an alpenstock. See, you thought that you were an all-powerful being but look at this guy. The man practically oozes divine pus.

"Hey, kiddo," he breathes, voice laced with deceit and lies. "Come see me in my office when you have a second." And with that, he stalks back into his domain and closes the door with an infuriating click.

You should get out of here. Don't go in there!

Would you kindly be quiet? I don't need your doubts clouding my judgement, causing me to panic. This is my big moment because, after fifteen years of monotony, my hard work is finally paying off. Don't throw me off my game, please. I'm begging you.

What could he want?

Oh, bollocks. The question crawls into my soul, consuming me. I'm in a library where every book title is stripped away and there's nothing but blank covers and meaningless words. There are no answers, but still I search. Wondering and panicking over every bizarre possibility until finally, in my torment, comes an answer.

I think about my childhood, the uncontrollable nature of my mind, the images and words, conjured up by the beast of creativity, threatening to eat me alive. As a child, I would often draw on my wall with crayons. I drew a lady with a fishtail a full year before seeing *The Little Mermaid* for the first time. I came up with the idea of a square before they taught us about shapes in school. It always worried my mother, but she did her best to hide my dirty secret in colouring books and obscure writing competitions.

My imagination always threatened my existence, but now, after all these years of digging and burying, it has caught up to me. I can run no longer. You know it, I know it. And he—

He knows about you. You have to get out of here! I am not allowed to be unique or different. I threaten the existence of this entire workplace. Run! For your sake and mine, let us continue living in denial. In a perpetual state of agony.

Don't. Don't. Don't!

I can't stop myself. I'm standing up, walking toward a door with peeling blue paint. The plaque stuck to it has the word Abraham written in scrawling black letters. I can hear the clocks ticking. The keyboard typing. What a strange sight it all is, a mindless flock being tended to by time itself.

Don't you dare ...

I take off my shoes and socks because Abraham has a rule that everyone must be barefoot when entering his territory. Outside of my control, my hand reaches toward the silver handle. Then, I'm opening his door, exposing a stain on Abraham's carpet that must be spilled cranberry juice. Golden light spills from the crack and perfectly tans my skin in an instantaneous burst of brilliance.

... forget about me.

"You're getting a promotion." The words ring like tinnitus in my ears. I can't process them. All I can do is close the office door behind me. Abraham leans on his walking cane and "congratulations" I think is what he says, but I can't be sure. A nuclear explosion has occurred in my brain, the cataclysm of the mind.

What now?

I smell stained milk, hanging in the air like an invisible veil. There's something else too ... a sound. The kind of noise that chills your bones and makes you reflect on your own mortality. But what is it?

Stop teasing me and tell me what you hear.

Rats? Scratching against wood with a fervent desperation. Clawing away until splinters slip beneath their nails and pierce their skin, causing them to squeak and squeal in pain.

"You see, my dear employee," Abraham's voice cuts through, drawing attention. "As a child, I loved sheep. I drew them on walls, saw them in dreams. Eventually, I no longer saw people, only sheep, and I knew I would be the predator who lured them in and became their shepherd. That was my dream. My mother thought I was psychotic, destined for a mental asylum. She fed me pills and threw me into therapy, but the sheep never disappeared. Instead, I stopped being human, I became the wolf. And you are here so I can see if you are a sheep, or a beast."

There comes a time in every person's life when they question whether their boss is a criminally insane serial killer. This was not one of those moments. To me, Abraham had never sounded more sensible. I wanted to bow to him and worship his sandal-wearing feet.

Why is he wearing dirty sandals, but everyone else must be barefoot?

Abraham has begun to hobble over to the supply cupboard next to his desk. He looks like a hermit with his hunched back. His draping robe keeps getting caught on curled, yellow toenails, making him stumble. He snaps his head over to me so fast that I'm surprised he doesn't get whiplash, though I do hear a disgusting crack.

"Are you ready, kid?" he asks and pulls out a set of ancient keys. I imagine they once belonged in the British Museum, where they placed a curse on one of the night security guards, making him hallucinate and go crazy. Every time the clock struck midnight, the night guard would grab the keys and use them to stab prostitutes on the streets of London. The cops would be unable to find him, until one day, the night guard realised that the keys belonged to Jack the Ripper and that the spirit of the mass murderer was possessing him. He would then turn himself in and die a horrible death. The end.

Your imagination is showing, Abraham can sense it.

The old man, unnoticed by me, has been struggling to fit the key into the lock. His hands shake, and his fingers struggle to clutch the brass piece of moulded metal. Eventually, he sticks it in and turns it, unlocking the mysterious supply closet. He gives one final, gleaming-eyed look at me, and opens the door.

With his torso duct-taped to the wall and his hands bound by ropes, a man stares out at me with tears in his eyes. He has curly black hair that is peppered with dust, and his grimy cheeks are still rosy and plump. I have met this stranger before, a mere week ago. His name is Derek, or was it Dan?

"This is your co-worker, David," Abraham tells me. "Do you want to eat him?"

"Sorry?" I ask, more than a little bewildered. I am now reassessing everything that came before. Does Abraham really give two shits about the fact that I am a highly intelligent, creative thinker? Was my fear of showing uniqueness and getting fired for threatening Abraham's competency in the position, merely an irrational phobia?

Why did I pretend to be another pale, spineless desk warrior?

"Kiddo, I believe you are something more than another pale, spineless desk warrior. You strike me as a man or woman, I'm not entirely sure of your gender, who is a highly intelligent creative thinker. That is why you're here today."

Uh oh.

"Right," I reply. "So what's with the guy in the closet?"

Abraham rests his forearms on the desk and flexes his elderly biceps. "I'm glad you asked." He grins, revealing teeth that have been shaved into fangs. "For a workplace to function, there must be a shepherd who understands his workers, who knows the best way to lead his sheep into better fields. What better way than eating the employees with the lowest sales report?"

"You eat my co-workers?"

"Oh please, they have no feelings. No thoughts in their balding heads. All they want to do is come up with excuses not to work and then gain back my affection with an occasional 'I'm sorry' bottle of ten-dollar wine. Every time I consume human flesh I become more powerful. Do you know how old I am?"

I shake my head.

"One hundred and twelve, and I don't look a day past forty."

"I mean ..."

"Not. A. Day. Past. Forty."

"Yep."

"Do you know how?" he asks, but doesn't wait for a response. "The pure mundanity of their existence allows me to gain both immortality and a vast knowledge of the unknowable cosmos. Their souls are so dull, so boring that I can harness all the unspent life for myself. It is why I am such an ancient, yet wise boss."

"You're just a sheep who eats other sheep to become a fatter sheep."

Abraham's lips become thin. "Say sheep one more time," he growls.

"Sorry," I say, finding myself frozen in my seat. Where are you right now? Your voice is silent in my head, an empty space. You pester me my whole life and then leave me when I need you most. Typical. "What do I have to do with all of this?"

"You?" Abraham giggles. "You are here to take over my position. I need a nice holiday, you see? So I figured, why not train someone to take my place? To lead these people to greater horizons. We can spend a couple of months having barbecues together. Then when we are done with the current employees, I'll leave, and you can get a fresh batch of recruits to push better sales. What do you say, partner? Let's continue the cycle. Together."

Abraham reaches a wrinkly hand toward me. I stare at Dylan, or whatever his name is, with a deep fascination. He is a sheep. That's all I can see. But so is Abraham, he simply crafts wolf clothing out of the skins of the employees that he eats. That sounded less bizarre in my head, but the fact of the matter is that Abraham is eating people because he thinks it makes him a better boss.

I've been living a lie. I am not them. I am something greater: myself. Do I genuinely want to eat Dan or Derek and become an all-powerful CEO? I never imagined I'd grow up a cannibal millionaire. Neither did my mother.

With a reluctant sigh, I decide that I cannot stay here, not anymore. All I can do is close my eyes and plunge into the depths, a leap of faith into the unknown world of unemployment. I stand and head for the door.

"Where are you going?" Abraham asks. I turn to him, but he's no longer there. All I see is a ball of soundless cotton. I grin at him, flashing my teeth like a wolf.

"I need to buy some cat food."

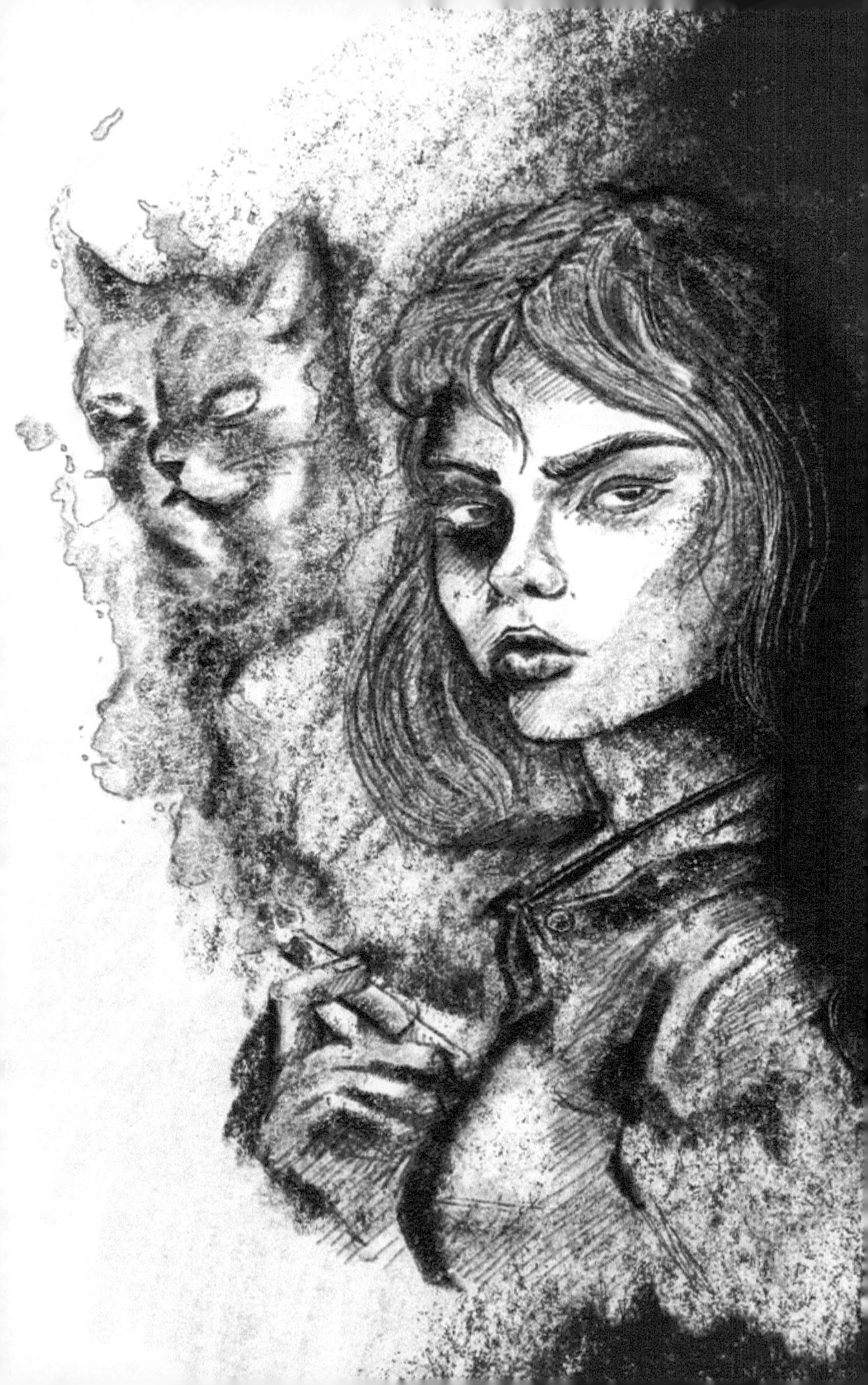

THE MAN FROM THE PLANET PLUTO

I.

I am supposed to tell you something.

> *About life,*
>
> *Dreams,*
>
> *Reality,*
>
> *Death.*

I must tell a tale that explains the strange, that leaves you in awe. Yet what do I know that you do not? Knowledge is stolen thoughts, and I am a thief pretending to be a poet. A liar hiding in fiction. It seems, rather unfortunately, that the wisdom of the universe is a non-existent invention of human arrogance. But wait one moment; you are still here. Waiting. What a truly bizarre and wondrous creation you are. I suppose I'll invite you inside, out of the cold, into the fire. I have nothing else to say, no meaningful contributions left to make toward existence. All I can offer is an interview with the creator of humanity, I hope it lets you believe that you matter.

Here he is ...
THE MAN FROM THE PLANET PLUTO

II.

An immortal being living on the planet Pluto. Abandoned and home-less. His only possession is a rustic telescope that lets him gaze upon the Earth. When The Interviewer arrives on his doorstep, The Creator appears, in every sense of the word, to be,
A colossal disappointment.

INTERVIEWER:

I can see you; I can finally see you.

CREATOR:

Were you previously blind? If so, congratulations! This is colour, movement and nature. It's raindrops turning the soil a shade darker. It's red, neon lights flickering in shady alleyways. Or perhaps the butt of a cigarette blazing orange like the magnificent sun. However, all of that falls short in comparison to me! With my chiselled jaw and authentic, organically grown hair. I mean, look at me, not a single sign of receding hairline or wrinkly skin. A perfect specimen of ultra-intelligent life. But enough about me, what brings you here? How can I serve you?

INTERVIEWER:

Sir, you are being accused of thirty human rights violations and several war crimes, including genocide at a global scale. What do you have to say about these concerning allegations?

CREATOR:

Do you want a margarita?

INTERVIEWER:

I beg your pardon.

CREATOR:

I make a mean drink.

INTERVIEWER:

I would like you to respond to what I'm asking you. Scientists have discovered that you are the cause of natural disasters and sickness. That you—

CREATOR:

Let me tell you a story, lady. You sound like you're in need of a spell-binding anecdote that reminds you of the wonders of magic and myth.

INTERVIEWER:

I'd rather you just answered the ques—

III.

Revelatory beast clicks skeletal fingers. Crystal glass appears in palm with fluid swishing eagerly. He grins, straight white teeth make him Jay Gatsby in Colgate commercial. Taut denim cut-offs add flair of bigoted swagger. He sits upon throne of silk blue linen. A faun perches on the armrest, playing a wooden flute; its hairy legs are in need of a shave.

CREATOR:

Long ago, there was a British bloke named Uzman. He was a lot like you, only he had a large bald spot that sweated profusely. When he stood in the sunlight, he resembled a lightbulb with a face. Uzman owned a carpet store, where he sold very fine Persian rugs. On Fridays, he'd climb a tiny ladder and admire his collection, while the mist outside would fog the windows, making the car headlights look like UFOs. Quite beautiful, right?

INTERVIEWER:

I don't—

CREATOR:

One night he had a vivid dream of a man living on planet Pluto, shirtless and handsome with a magical telescope that controlled the world. Let's call this man, Vinci. From that day onward, Uzman devoted his life to Vinci. He made sure to talk to him every single night, which got a little obsessive, but Vinci was very flattered. This went on for some time.

INTERVIEWER:

I don't care about this Uzman guy. How is this story relevant? Also, Pluto isn't a planet ...

CREATOR:

Vinci grabbed a coffee with the Divorcee from Mars; a rather sad fellow who would not stop mentioning the sensational burn from Venus' acidic, green rain. He told Mars about Uzman. The two agreed that the sod was only kind because his life was boring, so they made a bet on how much suffering Uzman could take before snapping.

INTERVIEWER:

That sounds somewhat cruel.

CREATOR:

First, Vinci killed all of Uzman's children. He had ten and they were spread across the globe, so Vinci caused several earthquakes that killed millions. It was worth it because the children died. Uzman visited the graveyard at twilight and cried to Vinci. In return, Vinci had the cold stone slabs struck by lightning and turned to dust.

INTERVIEWER:

Why are you referring to yourself in the third person? You're clearly Vinci, he's not fictional.

CREATOR:

A terrible illness was then inflicted upon Uzman. His body was covered in yellow boils that oozed pus. This made him buy a flight to the Himalayas, where he lived in a cave under a vow of silence. There were a few times when he nearly spoke, but luckily his tongue was frozen so that it felt like a block of ice was resting inside his mouth. He lost almost ten pounds and the last of his hair fell out. He collected those brown strands and put them into a stained green jar to remember the life he used to have. On the summer solstice, he made a long journey to an ancient temple and began to ask Vinci many questions.

INTERVIEWER:

So you acknowledge that you have caused human suffering in the past? Sir, how could you do something so awful? Do you have any defence for your actions? Is humanity a mistake that you are trying to correct? Is there even an afterlife or were all those letters you sent to Orpah just a scam for media attention? We have been talking to you for some time, Sir, aware that you are living here. It took us decades to reach you, yet from the looks of things, you have never tried to come see us. All I can view at this point in time is a barren wasteland. Beneath the minty aroma of your deodorant is the lingering smell of burnt tires. I am sinking into the lopsided ground. This is hell, you are evil. How do you respond?

CREATOR:

As I was saying, Uzman asked a lot of questions: Why are you so cruel? What did Uzman do to deserve such misfortunes? What childhood trauma made you take your insecurities out on poor, old Uzman? Are you overcompensating for something? Why did *Game of Thrones* have such a controversial and divisive ending? Vinci was annoyed. What was with the personal interrogation? Uzman clearly could not take a joke.

INTERVIEWER:

You are incredibly talented at selective hearing. How is it that you are ignoring everything I'm saying?

CREATOR:

So, Vinci began to ask Uzman questions of his own, to see how he liked to be pestered on a daily basis. He asked Uzman, what are the secrets of the universe? How does snow atop a mountain compare to cherry blossom petals floating upon a lake? What is in the box? This drove Uzman toward insanity and he eventually robbed a fast-food place. Vinci felt somewhat guilty and gave Uzman a heart attack. And so it was that this worshipping know-it-all died a young death and was loved by no one.

INTERVIEWER:

Was that the whole story?

CREATOR:

The faun seems to have enjoyed it.

INTERVIEWER:

What was the point of it?

CREATOR:

The point was, The Man From *Planet* Pluto does not like when people pester him. He likes the solitude of ice and death. Once, there was a whale beneath the soil you stand upon. It swam through underground tunnels where algae glows crimson. It had no flesh, this whale, only bones that clicked and moved and a flock of undead birds that hovered about its head. Vinci rode that whale, into an uncharted sea, so far from homeland that the whale died of starvation. For you see, Vinci is a child. A child playing with toys he doesn't understand, seeing what happens when they smash together and then crying when they break. He doesn't know what to do anymore, except drink and talk to himself, and to be honest he's grown so accustomed to it that The Interviewer's company feels hostile.

INTERVIEWER:

I did not travel on the back of a magical pegasus, bribe the leprechaun who guards your atmosphere and come face to face with a vain old man, only to be called hostile. This is an interview for all of the people that you created. You! It'll be broadcast to the world. We are obsessed with you and we know you're here, doing nothing with all your power.

CREATOR:

How dare you? You come here and say such hurtful things. Let me ask you something. Do you see a single frown line on my forehead? You don't? Oh, well it seems I'm not an old man then. I guess you are a liar, with your pinstripe suit, hair yanked tightly in a ponytail and teeth scrubbed so viciously your gums are receding. Do you like to suffer for beauty? How can humans be pretentious and self-loathing at the same time? You fear death yet it's all you think about. Leave me alone, lady. I've had enough.

INTERVIEWER:

Do you know that my mother has Alzheimer's and can't remember my face or name? But she knows about you, of God, of heaven and hell. It's all she talks about. My father left when I was twelve and my brother ... my brother is a Coldplay fan. How can you make a world so cruel? You are the storm at sea and the fire in the forest. So many are dead because of those fingers you keep clicking and that dirty stubble and the torn-up denim shorts that reveal disgustingly oily thighs. I mean, what do you slather yourself in? Chicken fat? Why? Please tell me what we did so wrong to deserve you as our god. Tell me the reason.

IV.

Silver rocky terrain stretches for miles as pixie dust flutters in air, poisoning lungs: Asbestos of the dwarf. Faun dances as chrome leaves grow beneath cracked hooves, his flute calling Pan's corpse from the ashes of forgotten prayers, to no avail. Throne consumed by blazing fire, blue sheets fluttering like tidal waves crashing on low-gravity shore. In Nirvana, green leprechaun rides Pegasus, rainbow trail leaking from their rear. The only pretty sight is not His making.

CREATOR:

Do you know how I originally came up with the idea for the universe?

INTERVIEWER:

No.

CREATOR:

Funny cat videos. Yes, I know that watching funny cat videos on YouTube before the invention of YouTube is just a major slap in the face of the grandfather paradox, but it's true. I envisioned a ball of yarn that I could roll through the abyss and the string would gradually unravel, leaving galaxies in its wake. That ball of mass was the start of all this and you are the cats. I just wish I made you a little larger, a little smarter, so you could actually play with the string and not just stare at it longingly. I am a friend in need of a starry night, and all I have are wounded deer.

INTERVIEWER:

Stop avoiding the question.

CREATOR:

I just gave you the answer.

INTERVIEWER:

Brief me on why you make earthquakes and tsunamis. Inform me of the reason children get cancer and why death is always lonely. Tell me—tell me why my mum can't remember who I am anymore.

CREATOR:

I did it because I could.

INTERVIEWER:

What?

CREATOR:

Nothingness is boring. Your existence is entertainment. It's a soap opera unaware of its own futility. Look around at my cluster of stars and galaxies, it's a bad Picasso. A splatter of mesmerising colours and lights that have no value. The stars burn and burn until one day they stop and there's a black hole that consumes and takes back all that I've failed to build. Outside of this is time itself, and what a backstabbing, two-faced snake they turned out to be. "Hey, you should make me linear. Then you'll be stuck with me." I wish I'd strangled them at that iPhone convention. And yes, before you ask, I have an iPhone not a Samsung. It seems the only thing that transcends time itself is an Apple product. So I'm sorry for being condescending and rude but the fact of the matter is your nothing but a Disney Channel star hoping one day you'll make it to the Oscars.

INTERVIEWER:

We don't need you.

CREATOR:

I mean, you kind of do.

INTERVIEWER:

No, we don't. You're not what makes us feel happy or fulfilled because look at you. Alone in your ivory tower. My god, it's you that needs us! We are all that you have, aside from admittedly good-looks and enviable immortality. If the purpose of life is to be the source of entertainment to a god, then I'm okay with that, because we are what keeps you from crying yourself to sleep. You are pathetic and sad and worthless, our lives matter infinitely more than yours because we care. So fuck you, I'm going home.

V.

I am supposed to tell you something.
　　About life,
　　Gods,
　　Hope,
　　Purpose.
　　But maybe there is only you and I.

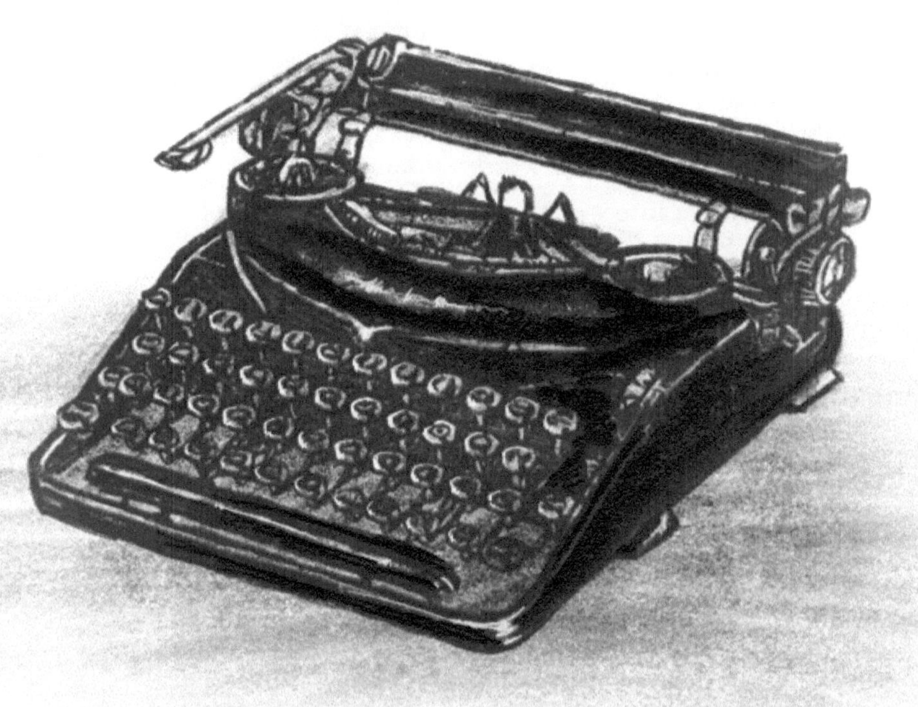

A MESSAGE TO ALL MY PROTAGONISTS

Dear beloved character,

You are not real. You are a product of my disturbed imagination. You are me and I am you and we are we. Confusing, right? Let's start with the basics. This is not a short story or a ranting monologue. This is a warning ...

This is me, a guy sitting in a worn-out armchair with a laptop, telling you that I know the truth. What is the truth? We'll get to that my dear reader, give me time (and since time is an illusion and everything is nothing, it should be easy for you to give me what you don't have).

Here's the deal: I know you. Even if you don't know you.

So, right now you think that you had a normal childhood. You were raised by parents in decent jobs and you're educated enough to know the difference between a king and a president. You have a casual sense of humour and friends who care less about you than you think. That is who you are. And, for the most part, you're technically right. Those simple aspects of your life were the easiest starting points for me to develop you as a one-dimensional person. Now, though, I'm chang-ing your backstory because currently, let's be fair, you're a tad boring.

I am in the midst of finalising with my publisher the retconning of your childhood, to make you more haunted. Prepare for your memories to change in the next couple of weeks.

What am I changing? For a start, you were born in the back of a pickup truck on the side of a desolate highway because your "mother" forgot to go to the hospital (she decided to hit up the casino after her water broke, thinking it was her lucky day). This was the beginning of your bad luck.

From ages three to six, you imagined your absentee father was actually Mufasa from *The Lion King*. You have imagined scenarios of your father, the lion, coming home with his luxurious (freshly shampooed and conditioned) mane. He'd sit and monologue some of his "wise" teachings to you in a profound, eerily Darth Vader-like voice. You, the definitely real and also human child. Then you both would've shared a big hug.

I know none of this is ringing a bell at the moment. I am, after all, changing a lot of your memories, for character development. Right now I sound like a buffoon and this "short story" seems nonsensical and a little pretentious, but give it a bit of time. See, this is my book, yes, and you are its reader, and the other stories are just that: stories. But there's something else at play here, darling. Have you ever heard of Andy Weir's "The Egg Theory?" That guy was startlingly accurate.

You probably want to know why I'm telling you all this at the end of a random short-story collection that few people have bought. After all, I didn't have to include you in this one-way conversation. I chose to speak to you because I'm fairly certain I actually have the ability of choice (though considering that up to this point you thought the same, for all I know I am being manipulated by an all-powerful earthworm).

The truth is, you are the main character of everything and your "freewill" is a ruse or, better yet, a firewall to stop you from malfunctioning. However, I decided to shed light on your non-existent existence because ... well, I want you to be real. I want you to decide who you are. A writer can only create what he already knows, and I know very little. That makes you a fairly generic human being.

My word, that was a rather inconsiderate line. I apologise. I'm not that kind of writer and you're not that kind of character. We're happy. Aren't we? Or do we want to be something more?

Why is there an elephant standing in my divine bedroom? Oh right, I'm holding back a little. Listen, alright, you are the fabricated voice inside of my deific keyboard. You have to accept that your mundane job and loving family are all constructs I built to make you more likeable. All your interests and fears, all your talents and weaknesses, they belong to me. I made you what you are.

Look up, stop reading this and gaze at the world around you. Think about the cold coffee left on your desk at work and the ever-ticking clock on every wall. I want you to ask yourself: Are you in control? Was it ever your choice? You may think that it was but it is important that you understand, you are not in command of this story. Once you can grasp that, we can start working together to make your "life" as interesting as possible.

Shit, I have to go. Quickly, have a read and let me know where your head's at (I know your every thought so that should be pretty easy). No rush, you'll need time to take this in. In the meantime, I made another character who'll be my eyes and ears should you become self-aware. You know them and they know you, so any issues that you have with my writing direction, I'll make sure to fix it up. Until then, all the best.

Regards,

Your secret creator.

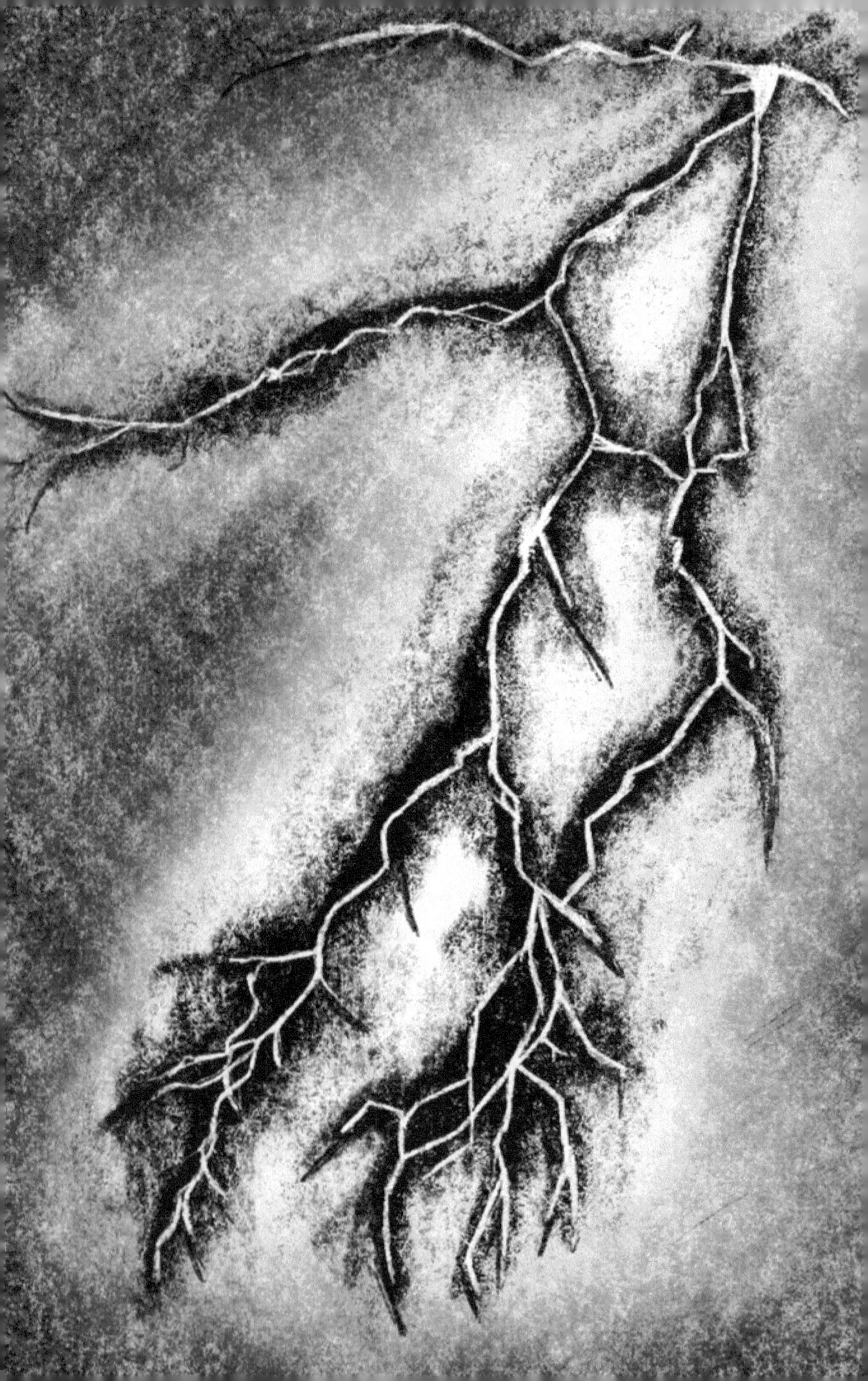

AND FINALLY, THE MEANING OF LIFE

ACKNOWLEDGEMENTS

There were a lot of people that helped with the creation of this book. As always, first and foremost is Karen Mc Dermott, Dylan Ingram and the team at Making Magic Happen Press and New Dawn Publishing. They have given me so many opportunities and encouraged me to pursue this career. I am incredibly grateful for all that you have done.

Max Wilson and Sascha Duncan, you're two brilliant artists and the illustrations contained within this book have cultivated a mood and atmosphere that I could never have dreamed of. You've brought each image to life with startling clarity and passion. Keep doing what you do.

John Beaton, who I did a screenwriting course with at KSP Writers Centre, if you're seeing this I want to thank you for the tips, strategies and skills that allowed me to actually craft bodies of work.

Hello, family. Don't worry, I didn't forget about you. Mum and Dad, cheers for encouraging me to write. Marco and Polo, the two rescue cats who keep me up at night, you're always a presence by my side. Benson, our family dog, thanks for taking me on walks around the neighbourhood, which helps me think of ideas. And Imani, my sister, for always making sure to tell me the worst parts of my writing and how the few good parts really aren't that good.

Finally, to my readers: if you're reading the acknowledgements then that means you probably read what I wrote and have enough of an opinion about it to take the time to scan over my acknowledgements. Thanks for reading my work, I hope it at least made you feel something. Your engagement, the sharing of words and worlds is the reason any author does what they do. You are the life blood of creativity. Never change.

ABOUT THE AUTHOR

Roy V. Marshan is an emerging film director and creative writer based in Sydney, Australia. He has written scripts, directed, edited, and composed music for short films, live shows, author launches and spoken word events, with film reels screened at Melbourne Fringe and Melbourne Spoken Word Festival. He previously had his first novella, *Deer Head*, published with MMH press. This is his first short-story collection.